Certain Freedoms

Certain Freedoms

R. R. Bell

King & Market Press

Published by King & Market Press,
Canada
www.kingandmarketpress.com

Cover design by Virtually Possible Designs. Image of

Madonna and Child painting courtesy of Wikipedia

contributor Sailko. Image of woman holding book

courtesy of Pixabay user Unsplash.

For My Parents

INTRODUCTION

THIS NOVEL is set in Russia during late summer and early autumn of 1993, with the exception of several chapters that occur in earlier periods in the country's history. Most of the events in the story take place in a fictional city, Galinsk, though some chapters are set in places such as Leningrad and Moscow. Though this book is set within specific historical periods, it is, nonetheless, a work of fiction. Any parallel between the novel's characters and real individuals is accidental. Similarly, where necessary, I have changed timelines and the order of certain events. When historical fidelity has been sacrificed, it has been done so for the sake of the story.

Much has been written since 1989 about Russia's vacillating relationship with democracy, and most accounts focus on the events of 1991, in which Boris Yeltsin and others faced down an attempted coup led by leaders of the old Communist regime.

However, in October 1993 there was another standoff at the parliament (then known as the Supreme Soviet) which was far more prescient of the present relationship between the Kremlin and the country's faltering democratic institutions. The events of 'Black October' – in which Yeltsin, who had by then become the nation's President, bombarded the elected deputies inside the Russian parliament – were a kind of 'Rubicon moment' for the country, and arguably became more predictive of the nation as it stands today than any other single event in modern history.

After the fall of the Soviet Union, Russia became overwhelmed by new freedoms and civil liberties, many of which had devastating consequences for average people. David Remnick refers to the "sometimes unbearable present" that characterized life in the country through much of the 1990s, during which many Russians struggled with "essential questions about themselves: What is our country? Who are our heroes? What is our past? What do we believe in? Who are our friends and who are our enemies?" This existential siege of questions confronts the novel's main characters, Russians and Western expatriates alike. Characters use these questions to grasp the new "unbearable present" that confronts them. The answers determine each character's future, just as they do for that of nations.

PROLOGUE

Leningrad, 1941

"EVERY ENDING is also a beginning." This is what his father used to say before the war began.

In June 1941, Ivan was twelve years old. That same month he was sent to the Luga Line – the last perimeter of hope between Leningrad and the invaders from the West. Children from city schools dug trenches and tank traps, ran communication wires, cut down trees for gun placements. Around them worked crews from the universities and institutes, the elderly, office workers, a group of women who specialized in laying mines.

The atmosphere of impending crisis made the children giddy, and they filled their free time with a frenzy of unfinished games and last laughter. They played in the late afternoons, running through abandoned homes, falling asleep on the hay in someone's barn. The children sometimes asked who would need the trenches they dug. Always they were told it was for the retreating soldiers that everyone expected to see.

No soldiers appeared though, and in their place emerged units of the People's Volunteers brought up from the city – factory workers and clerks, architects, bakers, professors, poets and minor bureaucrats, grandfathers and grandsons, convicts from the jails. By July the sound of fighting grew close and those on the Luga Line could hear the distant thud of shelling.

In the evenings the children sat in the tall grass that grew on the hills and watched smoke bleed across the horizon. They stopped their games, instinctively seeking out the company of adults. But the women and men around them could offer little reassurance in these days and only looked at the girls and boys with glances of mute apology. Seeing the fear in their faces, Ivan recalled what his father had told him, and for the first time in his life the boy did not believe in the future.

Then one evening the explosions appeared over the children's heads, and they were caught up in a storm of cries and rushing in the darkness.

Ivan was trapped during the retreat by the enemy's advance. The last artery into the city had haemorrhaged with humanity, bleeding over with refugees – peasants still clinging to a cow or a goat, abandoned equipment and lost soldiers, riderless horses, children searching for parents – until the air itself seemed to clot with smoke and fear. When they were in range, the bombs of Junkers-88s and the strafing of Messerschmitts turned chaos to massacre. As the planes roared low overhead, the succeeding concussions were sometimes so close they knocked people back on themselves. Those who got up found they were entangled by wounded, stumbling over a wounded animal or a head, the snarl of someone's intestines. Ambulances filled with the injured now ran down new casualties. People paused next to buildings, writing messages on the walls to those they had been separated from, or stopped to carve their own names in the birch trees that grew beside the road. For many, these letters were the last utterance they would ever make.

Two miles from the city, the truck carrying Ivan was struck by a shell.

When he gained consciousness the boy found his arm pinned beneath the vehicle. He lay for a moment dazed by the commotion. There were now groups of soldiers among the crowd, and the boy watched as they ran past. Pain in his arm brought him back to himself, though, and he tried to get free. About him lay tools blown from the truck, and his eye settled on an axe half buried in the mud.

There was a wail, and the boy pressed himself against the vehicle. People covered their heads, fell headlong into the ditch, behind bodies.

The shell exploded, lifting a soldier into the air and dropping him back onto the road, his body twisted now and wrong-looking. The man began to cry out for his mother – a parched, shrill sound that seemed to silence other noises.

Without turning from the wounded soldier, Ivan found the axe and drew it out of the earth.

The fighting was close by then.

More people staggered past, and the boy stared through their legs at the pleading face of the soldier. Bullets came in bright, discordant bursts, kicked up dirt, struck people.

His fingers flexed on the handle. Ivan looked at the arm and then closed his eyes and concentrated. Air left his body as the blade came down above the elbow. It was like falling into freezing water, shock making him disoriented, unable to breathe, eyes searching for the surface.

The pain ignited inside him, consuming his resolve until he could only stare desperately at the sky. He began to sob. It was then that a haggard face appeared over him, and Ivan felt the axe being pulled from his hand. A voice yelled to him through the noise of gunfire and engines and the boy's own cries, and Ivan saw the axe appear above his head where for an instant it wavered in the smoke and flame. And then it fell. This time his body suddenly disengaged from the weight of the truck, and he felt himself roll into the road, the hard press of stone on his face. Opening his eyes he saw he was lying next to the soldier who had become silent.

The edges of Ivan's vision darkened. The haggard face reappeared, blocking out the smoke and fire in the sky. The boy felt himself lifted from the ground, the embrace hesitant at first, then gripping him with resolution.

The air filled with shrieking. As he slipped from consciousness Ivan's only thought was that his own cry must be there too, lost in the pandemonium, a tear falling into the ocean.

PART I

What our time of troubles consisted of
and what kind of transition we were
passing through I don't know, and I
think no one does for sure – except for
a few of those visitors of ours.

Dostoyevsky, *The Devils*

ADAM WOKE and felt the dark.

His hand reached out and found the photograph. He let his finger caress the smooth celluloid until his breathing slowed.

Pulling back the curtain, he squinted through the window at a large McDonald's billboard which shone at him through the predawn gloom. Beyond the sign, apartment blocks barricaded the horizon. Fingers of rain tapped at the window.

"What am I doing here?" he whispered.

He shaved in front of the cracked mirror next to the door. When he had dressed Adam put the photograph by the bed into his pocket. He went into the hall, passing beneath laundry hanging like scarecrows from lines strung between each door. Dim, buried sounds stirred behind walls, voices calling from a dream.

As he stepped into the street, he paused to

21

draw up the collar of his coat. Morning dew clung to the heavy leaves of the linden trees along the sidewalk. At the corner, the chimney of a vendor's cart sputtered with blue smoke which drifted into the street. Soon a tram pulled up to the curb, and Adam stepped into the clammy grip of morning commuters.

The vehicle was full, and he had to stand next to the door for most of the ride. Though it was early the sky was still dark, and with nothing else to look at he stared at himself in the window, his reflection resting uneasily on the glass like the shadow of smoke. Bodies and limbs pushed against him, faces coming and going. More people squeezed into the tram. Men removed hats and scarves, women fanned themselves. Adam loosened his tie.

The tram turned onto a busy street where men stood holding the tool of their particular trade – wrenches, welding visors, pneumatic drills – mutely offering themselves to the new businessmen and factory owners who drove by. 'Perestroika's prostitutes,' someone would call these men for whom unemployment was the first of their new freedoms. Above their heads a splendid new banner welcomed the bus tours from the West which took the road into the city.

Welcome to Galinsk

Adam wiped at the window with his sleeve, peering past his reflection at the horizon of concrete and rust, some buildings still bearing the hammer and sickle. This route led into the city's core, passing through the shabby ring of recent construction, tracks of prefabricated apartments with sprawling parks and wide streets. On one corner stood a woman and a small child, who waved to those on the tram. The vehicle swayed heavily as it rounded the corner, and Adam shut his eyes as the child passed across his own reflection in the window.

Next to him a woman stood reading. He squinted for a moment at the book in her hand as if trying to identify it, not its title but the thing itself. This would happen to him more often in the weeks to come, the miscarriage of recognition between him and previously ordinary things. He would be staring at something – a child or a bird, a man's ring – and be struck with the knowledge that these things had different names now, that he no longer knew what to call them.

The tram groaned along the avenue, caught now in a shuddering current of traffic and people. Through the window he spotted the obelisk he had been told to look for. Adam pushed past the other passengers and moved toward the door. It began raining as he stepped off the tram, and without looking back he hurried beneath the war monument and up the hill toward the university. He crossed over a bridge, glancing down at the river which dragged along leaves and other debris. In the coming weeks, Adam would sometimes stand on this bridge to watch the water, with its sunken wreckage, its fleeting silhouettes of almost recognizable things.

The university was housed in a series of grey buildings that faced onto a common square. Into this space jutted the entrances of each faculty building, their reflection of mean grandeur thrown across the puddles in the square. Adam found a statue of Lenin here, and he paused to find his bearing amid the perimeter of grey and nameless buildings.

The rain came harder. A woman ran across the far end of the yard, her arms held up against the sky. Pigeons called as Adam passed beneath the columns and into the gaping vestibule of one of the buildings. He came to the great wooden door, then passed through to a corridor with rows of empty classrooms and the smell of damp. In the stairwell he tripped over an old woman on her knees.

"*Izvenitzia*," he muttered. His only word in this new language. *Excuse me.*

The woman did not look up, but grunted and went back to scrubbing.

At the third floor he followed the hall toward a blade of light peering out from a doorway. As he reached the door, he started at the sudden brightness in the room, pausing with a gasp until his voice returned to him. There was a hushed rustling as he entered the lecture hall, and Adam felt their eyes following him. It was a room of modest size, but full of people, though it was an early class. As he took off his coat, a feeling of cold and trepidation came over him, and for a moment he felt far away from himself. He set his things on a chair hesitantly, reluctant to be empty-handed. Then, he went to the board and wrote *ENGLISH* in large letters, looking to the students for a small sign of confirmation before continuing.

"Yes?"

Heads nodded.

He turned back to the board and wrote his name. Your name, Clare once told him, was an empty room that only you could fill.

"You can just call me Professor," he said.

The faces blanked. Two of the boys in the front row looked at each other, shrugging.

He pointed to the board. "This is me."

One of the students looked up, and Adam caught his eye. "Would you like to try?"

The boy stared, committing to nothing. Adam gave him a pleading smile.

"*Ingleesh*."

Adam looked around. "No," he hesitated, pointing again to the board. "Professor. This is me. Professor."

No response.

Looking up, he saw the class now as if from a great distance. Its treacherous silence.

One of the girls in the back row put up her hand. "*Shto etta?*"

"What's that?" he asked, but her head ducked back behind the rows of faces.

Adam looked again at the board. "Professor," he said, pointing to the word.

A glimmer. Someone by the wall nodded.

"Do you know any English?" he asked, the answer staring back at him.

The girl in the front row: "*English?*"

Adam could feel his face growing red. He turned back to the board. "This is the class for introductory English..."

He continued like this for an hour, stumbling with the students through the first vocabulary lesson. Reciting together those orphaned words. The class was spent, as far as he could tell, in mutual agony.

When Adam got to his second class that morning he was already exhausted. But as he entered the room he noted the students were older than those in the first group, and he felt a twinge of hope. He started with the same introduction and was relieved this time to see that they understood.

"We'll begin with oral reading," he said, sighing as a ripple of comprehension passed over their faces. He wrote a number on the board, and the class turned to the appropriate page in their books.

Adam pointed to a student in the front row. "Please start."

The walls in the large room were blind to the outside except for an oval window in the ceiling. He watched them as they read, interrupting mechanically when a student faltered.

Adam found a chair and closed his eyes, his gaze turning instinctively inward. His fingers found the photograph in his pocket, and the touch of it sent his thoughts deeper, farther into himself. The sounds in the room grew fainter. 'What am I doing here?' he wondered again.

The day he told his father about getting a teaching job in Russia, Adam had taken the subway out to the east end of Toronto to visit his father, who was watching from the screened-in porch like a fish in a net. The porch had become the last line of defence for his father against a neighbourhood he felt had turned against him. From this spot the old man railed about the new families that had moved in on his world, writing to politicians to complain about the foreign lettering that shared or even replaced the English on street signs. "I could get lost in my own city," he often complained.

As Adam reached the door he had to wait as his father unlatched the various locks. "Can't be too careful," the old man greeted him.

It was warm and they sat in the kitchen. On the counter was a small television, and Adam sat pretending to be interested in what was on until his father handed him a beer. It was only eleven, but the bottles gave them something to hold on to in each other's presence.

The old man could not understand why his son was leaving. "You got I-don't-know-how-many degrees," he said, impatiently. "Why would you take a job teaching communists?"

He looked at his father, wondering whether to reply. "They aren't communists anymore."

"You know what I mean. If things are that bad then you should look for other work. It's not the country's responsibility to make a career for you. If you'd gotten a job when I told you, you wouldn't be where you are now."

Adam took a sip and held the liquid in his mouth, unsure of how to reply. After Clare left, the idea of another country had seemed promising. And not any country, but one which had been torn apart, had lost itself. This was a place where he could go. He picked at the label on his bottle. There were things he could not explain to his father.

The old man stared at him across the table. "Is the money any good? I can see if they're paying you well…"

"My salary is in roubles," Adam said, bracing himself.

He set down his bottle loudly. "What can you buy with roubles?"

"Lots of stuff, over there."

"What will you have to show when you come back?" Adam watched the man's knuckles go white around the bottle.

"It's a five-year contract," he said softly.

The old man stared into his bottle, the last signs of emotion retreating under his skin.

"I see."

For a moment Adam looked directly at the old man. Neither of them had mentioned Clare. Even if he had, Adam realized he wouldn't know what to say.

He glanced at his watch, and the old man nodded. "I guess you need to be going."

"It's okay," Adam said. "I can let myself out."

"No," muttered the old man, standing with resignation. "I have to lock the door behind you."

He held out his hand to his father, who squinted at it. Their hands touched.

Adam sat up and blinked. The students were standing.

"What is it?"

Someone coughed. "Class is done."

He blinked, recalling himself. People gathered their books. Students approached him, their lips moving with conversations he did not understand. Someone stumbled in the aisle and a notebook burst open. Shouts of surprise as paper flew into the air. Adam watched as the plume of pages blocked out the light above him. For a moment he was surrounded by the paper's dry, distant laughter. People helped collect the pages but Adam sat unmoving, staring at a blank page in his lap.

When the students had left he sat alone for a long time in the lecture hall. Voices from the corridor gradually subsided until everything became quiet. Looking up through the oval window Adam saw that the sky was clearing. A plane passed between the clouds on its way to some faraway place, the contrail cutting across the sky, pale as a new scar.

KATYA SAT UP, feeling for the lamp beside the bed. Pushing open the blinds, she looked out the window into the half-light. It was that time of day when the distinction between beginnings and endings is still unclear. Their apartment was set back on a hill amid the monuments and parks of the city's core. The distance was enough to dilute the noise from the street, and through her window she watched the gradual movement of traffic below. Independence Square stretched like a grey blot between the yellow and white government buildings. People stood on the bridge looking into the river, which wound leisurely among the familiar neighbourhoods – Red Market, the Old Quarter, Gorky Park.

Katya let herself pause at the window, her hand pressed against the glass. From here you could convince yourself that nothing had changed.

After washing and dressing, she went into the small kitchen, groping in the shadows for the light which sputtered indecisively before coming on. Beneath a small window sat the table. Next to it, along the wall, hummed the old refrigerator with an electric clock balanced on top of it. There was bread in the aluminum box on the counter beside the stove. She cut some for herself, toasting it beside the element while the kettle boiled.

She ate and then sat with her tea, watching through the kitchen window at the arcing clouds hanging over the city like the dust of approaching armies.

She heard her father in the hall, where he was struggling with his tie before the mirror. Katya paused to help him, and he smiled at her reflection.

"Where is Mother?" She folded the sleeve of his shirt, pinning it closed just below the elbow. "She usually helps you with this."

He watched her appreciatively as she straightened the creases in his sleeve. "She's ill, again."

"Does she want some tea?"

"Likely." He checked his watch. "But don't make yourself late."

The curtains were closed, and only a sliver of her mother's face peered out from the darkness. A clock ticked in the shadows.

"Is that you?"

Katya placed a teacup in the woman's outstretched hand. "I hear you're feeling unwell."

Lydia waved her other hand, languidly brushing away the idea. "What is there to say?"

"Are you out of medicine again?"

Her mother leaned back on the pillow, retreating from the light. "I finished it yesterday."

Like most of her generation, Lydia was ill-suited for the life they now led. She was confused by the forces uprooting their world. But where her husband responded to the changes with outrage, Lydia knew only a passive acceptance that left her daughter both angry and sympathetic.

"You should have told me. I could have gotten money." Katya squinted at the clock.

Her mother smiled faintly at her over the cup.

"I have to go."

The old woman bit her lip. "Can you manage it?"

Katya paused at the door, without looking back. "You know I can."

In the hall she paused for a moment to make sure she was alone, then slipped into the spare bedroom, returning just as quietly a few minutes later.

On the street Katya passed the corner where her father's driver used to wait for him. It was already busy as Katya joined the current of activity. A group of girls in blue school uniforms walked arm in arm, brazenly laughing and shouting. Two men loitered in a doorway, their eyes following after the girls with an air of bored desire. A woman rested on a bench next to a small dog, its head cocked at the passing world. Birds gazed down at the traffic from lampposts and trees.

A cinema was being constructed down the street, and builders had covered the windows with newspaper. Katya glanced at the pocked and yellowed pages as she passed. Headlines and pictures were pasted together like pieces of smashed teacups: tanks and flags, the grin of politicians, and, less often, ordinary people, their eyes gazing off the torn edges of paper.

She took the short tram ride up the Prospect, getting off several blocks before the university. She walked along the street, passing among the crowds going in and out of shops, a soldier haggling at a kiosk, babushkas with their smiles of gold teeth, beggars huddled like lepers on the corners.

She had difficulty concentrating in class that morning. She tried several times to focus on the professor's voice but at last she gave up. Instead Katya played with her pencil, letting it wander over the page in ever-tightening spirals, drawing a smaller and smaller orbit each time until it disappeared into itself. She was sitting next to a window, facing northeast over the courtyards and narrow lanes. Morning traffic still clogged the Avenue of Soviets as it weaved among the rows of yellow plaster flats and passed the German embassy where people queued for visas.

That afternoon Katya stopped at the small office used by the university's translation department. It was a relatively large room made tight with a meeting table and too many chairs. The fading wallpaper was overlaid with posters for poetry readings, an out-of-date calendar, and faded photographs of once-notable people.

Katya waited until she could be seen by the professor overseeing her thesis, a frenetic man who wore tired English ties and battered spectacles.

"Lovely to see you, Katya Ivanovna," he greeted, waving her to a chair, but there were books on it and he had to get up to move them before she could sit.

"The thesis committee has met to discuss your project," he smiled, trying to make her feel at ease. "I think they have made excellent choices – you'll be pleased I am sure."

Katya chewed the edge of her lip. "I am anxious to start."

"Yes, of course," he said, still smiling. "It's an exciting time. I'm very pleased for you. Very pleased. Such an excellent project."

He drew a long manila envelope from his desk, pausing before opening it to straighten his spectacles. "Now then, here are the poems the committee selected for you..."

For the next half hour, Katya sat restlessly and reviewed the documents for her thesis. It was to be the culminating task for her degree – a series of poems to be translated into Russian. It was exciting work, and as the professor talked she frequently had to hide her hands beneath the desk to keep him from seeing how they shook.

"Just remember," he said, at last, "you can consult with members of the translation committee as you require. They are here to help with your thesis." His phone rang just then, and he waved at her.

Katya stood hurriedly, reaching out for the envelope on his desk. "Thank you, so much. I'm eager – very eager – to get started."

"Yes, of course you are. Now go, and work hard. I have great faith in your abilities..."

She rushed out of the department, clutching the envelope with both hands. On the street she paused, feeling excited and overwhelmed. 'At last,' she thought. 'At last. And such an exciting topic...' But then, as she put a hand in her coat pocket, her mood suddenly changed, and a stiffness came over her features. 'I'd almost forgotten,' she thought.

She turned and changed direction, going south by the veterans' monument. At the next corner she turned into a narrow street congested with kiosks and open stalls. Behind one of these was a man with long hair held back from his face with an elastic. He sat under a canvas awning with a table of uniforms and bayonets, crests and old medals.

His lips formed into a stiff smile when she approached. At his feet a cat lapped milk from a helmet.

"Well then, dear," he greeted, his eyes never leaving Katya's. "What is it today?"

"This," Katya said, holding out her hand significantly.

Frowning, he leaned forward to examine the medal, rubbing doubtfully at the portrait of the old leader. "Yes, it's nice, but I already have one of those..."

"It was very important, you know," she said, her fingers flexing anxiously. She glanced at the bits of metal on the table. "And this one's authentic."

His smile cracked. "So is mine."

"What I meant to say is that it means a great deal to people who know..."

"It still means something," the man soothed, his mouth renewing its grin, "just something different than before."

"But these things weren't souvenirs. My father..."

"Of course you are right," he interjected. From his pocket he brought an oily roll of bills with the portraits of more recent leaders. "Here," he said. "We trade in heads, you and me."

Katya looked past his shoulder as her fingers closed around the money.

Water dripped from the awning onto the table beside her, and dark blots had begun forming on the uniforms.

On her way home, Katya decided to cut through the park. She took the path people had made where the fence was broken, following it down the embankment and under the steel arch of the bridge to the river. The air was cold and damp, and her blouse stuck to her back. Above, a truck rolled like distant thunder across the bridge. The reeds and tall grass by the riverbank swayed drunkenly over the water. Leaves, branches and trash emerged and disappeared in the tossing current. A little way up the path there was a pier where people sometimes fished on weekends, and Katya paused there and looked into the churning river. Beneath her brooding reflection coursed half-submerged water bottles, a newspaper, cigarette butts and bits of wood, a child's doll.

Katya bit at her lip as she recalled her exchange with the souvenir dealer. These transactions left her feeling ill and unsettled. Each time she had to justify her misgivings, to review the few options before her. Always Katya returned to the same conclusion – she found a quiet satisfaction in providing for her family, yet she did not know how long they could continue this way and what survival might cost each of them in the end.

When she arrived home she paused in the hallway after the door had closed. The flat was still except for the sound of her heart beat. She shifted uncomfortably, her clothes hot against her skin. The next instant her mother called to her from the kitchen.

Katya found her at the small table by the window.

"Shall I make tea?" she asked, going to the cupboard.

The old woman was gazing stiffly after her. "Did you get it?"

"I said that I would." She placed he money next to her mother's hand.

Lydia looked away, her shoulders relaxing.

That evening Petya greeted his sister in the kitchen when he came home. Katya was fond of her brother. Petya was tall like their father, and dressed carefully but plainly. He was a calming force in the home, with an air of intense concentration that allowed him to remain outwardly oblivious to the tensions around him. His quiet face held echoes of their father's pointed intelligence, yet his features remained soft and undecided, like a child's. Despite his good nature, there was behind his gaze an evasive shadow that betrayed the silent awkwardness he felt within the family.

"Was it a good day?" Katya asked as he sat.

He shrugged, biting reflectively at the corner of his thumb. "Have you seen the mail?"

She shook her head.

At the sound of Petya's voice, their mother reappeared, and she moved to her stool by the wall. "Why doesn't someone turn on the radio?" she asked, but no one did and the idea was forgotten.

Outside, the rain had started again and now and then came the complaint of distant thunder.

Katya put bread on the table, and they listened to the advancing storm as they ate.

Petya glanced at the stove. "Are we eating soon?"

Lydia hesitated. "I thought we would wait." She treated Petya with the same deference she afforded to her husband, looking on the family's oldest child with anxious admiration. He had returned from studying in Moscow just as his father's prospects were fading with those of the Party, bringing to his parents' lives the balm of new accomplishment. It was a point of pride and reassurance for Lydia that her son was one of the youngest people ever to teach at the Science Academy. He had spoken at conferences in the West, and his ideas had begun to find international favour – all things which nourished his parents' otherwise starved hope in the future. The light of Petya's career, Lydia knew, helped to allay her husband's despair at his own extinguished aspirations. Petya had become the last star in the family's otherwise darkened horizon. He was the child of promise.

But professors were paid by the State, and the State paid in roubles which were worth less each week, when they were paid at all. Petya's last paycheque had been the previous spring. Though his research made him, in the words of the university rector, a national treasure, Petya had become an unpaid one. Like many men his age, he lived at home both because he could not afford a flat, and because he was still on a waiting list to obtain one. The alternative was to bribe one's way to the front of the queue, but Petya had neither the money nor the stomach for that. The truth was he did not mind living in the cramped flat he had grown up in, though he was increasingly conscious of his inability to assist his family. For the first time in his life, Petya found himself wrestling with the confusion and futility of this new order. As a boy growing up he had been assured of a livelihood, a place to live, an income. In return the State asked that each citizen share his talents for the collective good. Petya had gained respect and made significant strides forward in his field, but the support once promised by the government was no longer there.

Lydia compulsively promoted her son's importance within the family, anointing it with the full weight of maternal deference.

Sometimes when the family was out, she went to his room and looked over the books and papers there, scrutinizing the photographs of the ice crystals and microbial organisms that preoccupied his thoughts. In one of these books she found a chapter written by him, and Lydia gazed for a long time at the oddly foreign appearance of her own child's name in print. At these times she was reminded how little she knew of him, that there was something hidden about his life, which was spent in laboratories and libraries, or in faraway places where he collected samples of ice. She had taken to teasing him about this, trying to coax out of him the mysterious details of his professional life.

"Ice is such a strange thing to study," she said one night, bringing him his tea. "What's to know? It's miserable and stays all winter. Like a bad cold."

He would begin to explain that ice, ancient ice – ten, twenty thousand years old – was like a time capsule, containing information about earlier life. "As things warm," he explained, "history is being lost. Now a century can melt away in a season…"

Just then there were sounds of stomping in the hallway and Ivan appeared. His hair was matted from the rain, and steam rose from his coat.

"Such a day!" he exclaimed, out of breath. "Historic events in Moscow!"

For months the government had been frozen in a struggle between the President and the nation's fledgling parliament of elected deputies, the Supreme Soviet. In March they made an attempt to impeach the President, and the following month the Supreme Soviet tried to bring him down with a non-confidence vote. Throughout that past summer Ivan watched despondently as the conflict began to stagnate and seemed to go nowhere. Then, in September, things started to heat up again.

A week earlier he had received word about the President's threat to dissolve the government and the implications of such a move seemed to offer new hope for the old apparatchik. With both sides insisting they were on the side of the law, Ivan hoped an opportunity would emerge for the communists to take back the power they lost after Perestroika. That afternoon came news that the deputies, led by the Vice-President, had gathered at the parliament, and had resumed the media war of invectives and accusations against the President. Ivan was thrilled.

Katya frowned at the news. She gazed out the window. If she were not so disgusted from bartering that day, she might have found the energy to follow what he was saying. But it was all too familiar now: that sclerotic vein of hope which always burst in her father, releasing his plans about restoring the Party's former authority.

'If only he would accept what was lost,' she thought. 'Then, at last, he would face the new reality.' But the next instant she wondered how she could ask him to do such a thing, and, unable to bear listening to him, she sank into her own thoughts.

"Now we will eat," Lydia said. She moved to the stove and spooned food into bowls. Ivan removed his jacket and sat next to Petya.

Katya watched.

She could remember as a girl how decisive he had been, always on the phone or rushing to some meeting. The events of the last five years had ended all that. Younger colleagues saw what the new liberties would bring and changed allegiances with the ruthless opportunism now so in vogue. But older men, whose ideas of history had been forged in the first half of the century, would not accept that you could lose the war without fighting a battle. And so they had been swept aside, not by armies or rockets, but by an enemy of a different kind. The Party had been defeated not just by the people, but also by its past. History had taught them to fear spies, armies, secret weapons. Nobody had ever thought the enemy would be a hamburger.

In the streets now people learned about shortages in breadlines, while at night they went home and watched the new television shows where the consequences of comedy and tragedy were always resolved between commercial breaks. The radio became clogged with foreign lyrics, while cinemas filled with films about plagues, Vietnam, hijackings, renegade soldiers, crime sprees, killer robots – dazzling apocalypses from a culture that flourished on images of its own destruction. In the war between communism and capitalism, only the losers really understood the ironies of defeat. Katya saw it in the streets, the new clothing with its Manhattan labels and third-world stitching; soft drinks sold for hard currency; restaurants where people queued for hours to taste fast food; and in the foreign currency stores, shelves and shelves of mass-produced individualism.

That night Ivan talked almost uninterrupted through the meal. He spoke about the implications of the standoff, who might be involved, the likelihood of a military response. To Katya these ruminations were reminders that her father was trapped in a reality that no longer existed. From across the table Petya caught her eye and winked, trying to make her smile.

Only later, as his bowl emptied, did Ivan's attention shift back to his family. "And what about the rest of you?" He leaned back and scratched the spot at the elbow where his left arm ended. "Was it a good day?"

Katya and her mother looked at each other over the table, and there was a moment of silent confederacy as their minds turned to the same thing. The clock on the wall ticked loudly. From the hall came the drip of the bathroom tap. A car passed on the street outside.

Lydia ventured to mutter something about her joints being worse.

Petya cleared his throat, nodding without commitment.

Ivan glanced impatiently from one to the other. "Now, as I was saying, if the generals intervene then we should expect to see some big things..."

Petya shifted in his chair.

Katya sat up, anger rising in her. "But don't you think the President sees his own vulnerability? Isn't it possible that – "

"Now just a minute," Ivan leaned across the table, poking a finger just beneath his daughter's chin. "What do you know about these things? Why don't you listen for a change and learn something important. There are big things going on."

Katya bit her lip to keep from answering. She sat back and crossed her legs. No matter how esoteric the topic, they must all listen to his views before they could be released. It had always been this way. By the time she was an adolescent, Katya had realized these were not conversations.

Before Ivan could continue, however, Petya spilt a glass of water. Ivan stood and stepped back from the table. "Ah, Petya! What are you doing?"

Petya caught Katya's eye as she passed him a cloth. "You can thank me later," he said in English.

She laughed before she could stop herself. "You are scheming!"

"You should try it sometime."

Ivan frowned at them. "Do you know how rude that is? Speaking that way when you know your mother and I cannot understand you."

Katya scoffed and even dared to roll her eyes. "Why did you never learn?"

"There was no need for English in my youth. Why, with your intelligence, you chose to study that language, and not something constructive, I will never know."

Lydia stood to gather the dishes, glaring at her daughter. "Why don't you help?"

"I've helped quite a bit already," Katya said, but she stood and went to the sink anyway.

"What I would like more than anything," Lydia whispered, "is a little peace. All I have around me now are battles."

"Battles?" Ivan shook his head and went back to his meal. "None of you know what a battle looks like. I could tell you about the War, then maybe you would see..." After this the family was quiet with their own thoughts. Ivan eventually finished his meal and left the kitchen. Lydia and Katya cleaned up silently, both keeping out of each other's way. For a long time Petya sat alone at the table staring at his sister, but she would not meet his eyes.

ANDREW FOUND one of the other teachers, Emil, downstairs in front of the cafeteria waiting for his breakfast.

"What are they serving?" he asked, greeting him in French.

The other man frowned. "The usual shit."

The cafeteria was a cramped room in the basement of the dormitory. After choosing bowls of porridge and milk, they searched out an empty table among the other foreign students and teachers. They scooped sugar onto the porridge with the large cafeteria spoons. When he had eaten, Emil went to the samovar in the corner and brought back two mugs.

They drank black tea and smoked, watching students come and go.

"I have to change some money this morning," Emil observed.

"I'll come along."

Andrew counted out some bills in his room then returned the rest of his money to the hollow leg of the cot.

On the street they stopped at a kiosk to buy a paper and bus tickets. Catching the next tram, they found seats at the back and Emil opened his paper, while Andrew's gaze loitered around them. It was late in the morning, and the vehicle was empty except for a pair of soldiers.

"Ever known someone in the army?"

Emil looked up from his paper. "No."

He was looking at the two soldiers. "They're big on their armies here."

"They have their reasons."

At the next stop they got out in front of a hotel. Groups of men stood about smoking and talking. Most were typical of their profession, wearing leather coats or track suits, their faces etched with restless hostility.

"See him?" Emil asked, scanning the faces.

A wide man with cropped hair stepped forward to meet them.

"Alex," Emil greeted.

"What you need?"

Emil handed him a roll of dollars. "Fifty."

He looked at Andrew. "You, also?"

Andrew nodded.

Reaching into his coat, the man counted out a handful of bills and the two retreated with their roubles.

The money changer glanced at the cigarette in Andrew's mouth. "I get deal on those."

"You don't know what I paid."

"Yeah I do."

Andrew grinned. "Another time."

Instead of catching the tram, the two decided to stop at the café inside the hotel. They ordered coffee and sat by the window, watching people as they came to change money. It began to rain.

Andrew played with his spoon.

"You're fidgety."

"It's nothing."

Emil glanced at his watch. "I have class in an hour."

"Okay."

"You?"

He picked up the spoon again. "I'll probably look around for a while."

"Still planning to take the new teachers for a drink?"

"Of course. I'll come by and get you."

When Emil was gone, Andrew ordered another coffee and read some of the papers until it was almost lunch. Once, he tried lighting a cigarette but his hands shook. He took out his wallet and removed a worn piece of paper. He set the paper beside his coffee cup, so that his finger brushed against it now and then as if by accident.

Andrew caught a tram to one of the old neighbourhoods across the river, getting off in front of some neglected shops. Using his newspaper to shield himself, he sprinted through the rain past a lonely statue. On the corner, Andrew stood for a moment trying to determine where he was. He waited under the arcade, thankful for the rain.

A man came along the street, and he questioned him about the address he wanted. The man was not sure, but the next person Andrew asked knew it, directing him to a squat building with wrought-iron balconies and tall, narrow windows. At the front door, Andrew unfolded the paper from his wallet and checked the address.

Inside, he found the correct flat, but the tired-looking woman, with a child on her arm, who lived there had never heard of the person he asked after.

"How long since he lived here?" she asked.

"Many years," Andrew admitted. "When I was his age," he said, nodding at the child.

The woman shook her head. "What did you expect?"

"I thought someone might know where he went."

She shrugged. "Sorry."

"How about the neighbours?"

"They all moved in after me."

Andrew looked from her to the child.

The woman sighed. "Where did this man work?"

"The theatre."

"That is down the street. You might go there next."

He looked up. "I'll try that."

Andrew found the theatre but it was not open, and he had to wait. Several people were standing about waiting to buy tickets. It started again to rain and they sheltered in twos and threes in the surrounding doorways.

He found himself with a man in a soiled coat leaning against the doorframe. Andrew offered him a cigarette. The man took one and, after it was lit, said something about the weather.

Across the road a girl in a blue sweater leaned from a window, where three or four pigeons sat on the sill below her. Andrew waved, but she continued to look down the street. The apartment was still impressive, with its mullioned windows and arched doorway, though up close you noticed the disrepair. The masonry was pocked with neglect. Shingles were missing in several places. At one end a drainpipe had come away from the wall, and yellow water leaked from it like a sore.

The man in the coat said something and Andrew thought he understood.

"You are right," he said in Russian, and he tried again to get the girl's attention.

"You're not from here." The man stated this in a matter-of-fact way, though Andrew took it as a question.

He told the man where he was from.

"Nice city?"

"I guess so."

"Nice as this city?" and the man winked.

"Nice as any city."

Andrew offered him another cigarette and they were quiet for a while. Rain dripped steadily from the doorway, where it pooled at their feet. The man took a roll from his pocket.

"Have some?"

"I will, thanks." They sat on the step to eat.

"Where you learn Russian?"

Andrew chewed thoughtfully for a moment before answering. "My mother," he muttered, unaware that he was frowning.

"She is Russian?"

"She was."

"Was?"

"Was, yes."

"She was a teacher?"

"A musician."

The clouds came on steadily, and Andrew watched the rain fall into the street. The puddles swelled, and ash from his cigarette glided delicately on top of the water.

The man stood to brush crumbs from his pants. "Your mother was born here?"

Across the street, the girl in the blue sweater suddenly reached down and caught one of the pigeons just as its wings opened.

The man whistled, still staring though the girl had disappeared. "Did you see that?"

Andrew turned away.

The man frowned.

"Do not be like that."

He faltered, forgetting to speak in Russian. "I didn't say anything."

One of the large doors at the theatre opened, and those who were waiting began to emerge onto the street.

He glanced at his hands.

The man pulled the dirty flaps of his coat about himself. "If your mother was here," he said, speaking now in English, "she would tell you that it was not for this girl that you were embarrassed."

With the rain still coming down, he stepped into the street and turned to Andrew.

"She would tell you that this girl is beautiful."

Andrew looked again at the window where the girl had been. He stood in the doorway for a long moment and watched as the man crossed the street, his face lifted to meet the rain.

Inside the theatre no one knew of the person Andrew asked about. There was a woman in charge at the ticket booth, but she looked harried and had no time to listen to this foreigner. Instead she sent for the stage manager who chain smoked through Andrew's story and offered no

61

help. It was a woman at the coat check who suggested that Andrew look at the photographs in the lobby. "They say that everyone who has ever performed here is on that wall," she explained. "It is not the help you are looking for, but it is something."

Andrew walked to the end of the lobby where a long series of frames hung on the wall. In each one were photographs of actors and musicians arrayed with costumes or instruments, standing in poses at once plastic and significant. Each frame was dated, and Andrew moved along the wall until he found the picture he wanted. 1970.

He frowned, feeling aloof and hostile toward the impassive faces of the people in the photograph. They stared at him knowingly, seeing as everyone who poses for a photograph does the invisible but expected viewer in the future, seeing him there in the empty lobby of that theatre. Andrew gazed at each of the faces, searching their features for some hint, but in the end none of them would yield the clue he sought. For a moment he shivered as reverberations of panic and rage pass through him. He felt suddenly as though he was a child calling for help to these adults who only stared through him.

What he wanted would have been so little for them at the time they stood for this photograph: a nod, a lifting of their finger, two or three words, and he would know at last.

What he had was a name. What he wanted was a face.

Behind him people busied about, polishing handrails, setting out playbills. A chandelier flickered on. Somewhere overhead he heard instruments being tuned, instructions coming over a microphone. Someone started a vacuum.

'He is here,' Andrew thought, still staring at the photograph. 'He is here, staring at me, waiting for me to recognize him. But of course, I don't.'

For a long time Andrew stood before these photographs, searching them for a face he ought to know.

AT THE END of that first day of teaching, Adam left the campus exhausted. It was late in the afternoon, and the Avenue of Soviets was congested with commuters as he made his way back through the city. The rows of linden trees along the street stood against the sky, wind dragging their leaves among his feet. At the end of the block he came to Victory Square, walking until he was in the centre where he stopped to look about. A pair of soldiers strode in parade uniform, the air ringing with the report of their boots.

He gazed around uneasily, aware of a sudden weightlessness in this place. It was as though he had reached a pole, an axis of something larger than himself.

He watched people passing across the square like distant sails. Beyond them was that centrifugal pressure of life, everywhere that deep, rhythmic momentum. At the far end of the square stood the immense obelisk carved with figures in heroic postures. It reminded him of an Emily Carr painting – totems looming among forests and derelict longhouses, gods whose names had slipped back into the shadows.

A tram approached, and when it stopped he got on and clutched at the railing as it pulled forward. Two boys sat talking in the seat next to him, and when they stood to get off Adam sank into one of their seats. He rested his head against the window and tried to let go of the day's strain. He stared through the glass at people on the street, his thoughts punctuated at each stop by the mechanical clap of the doors behind him.

When he got back to the dormitory, he found Andrew waiting for him. "How was your first day?"

Adam shrugged. "I'll get the hang of things."

"Sure you will," he said. "Now come on, we're taking you out."

His shoulders sank. "Out where?"

The others were already in the taxi. Andrew leaned into the car. "Make some room for the new guy."

The bodies in the back pressed closer together, and Adam managed to squeeze in. The inside of the cab was dimly lit, but then Andrew shut the door and everything went dark.

Adam squinted through the window, noting a park on the other side of the street, the rusted skeleton of a swing set.

"Hi," said a voice beside him. "I'm Troy."

"Adam," he nodded, though with difficulty. "I'm new."

"Where are you from?"

"Toronto."

"I'm from Montreal."

"Small world."

He winced as he tried to get comfortable. "Would you mind moving over just a bit?"

Andrew sat in the front between the driver and someone named Ford. He turned to face the backseat, the white finger of a cigarette in his mouth. "Everyone comfy?"

The cab sped away from the curb, quickly carrying them into streets and neighbourhoods Adam did not recognize.

"So what are you teaching?"

"Conversational English."

He made an empathetic clucking sound in his throat. "Sorry."

Adam felt himself frown as he searched for something more hopeful. "They asked me to help with the translation board, as well."

Troy shook his head. "Strike two."

Someone spoke from the other side of Troy. "My name is Candace. I'm new, too."

"Anita," offered the person by the opposite window. "How do you like it so far?"

Adam tried to smile over Troy's head. "I'm sure it's nicer in the good weather."

The car shook with sudden disembodied laughter, like the House of Horrors ride at a fair.

"You really haven't been here long."

"This is the good weather," someone finally explained.

The cab pulled up to a row of shop fronts. Adam looked around. The only evidence of light was a blinking Sanyo sign in a window. The flashing neon stunned him for an instant and he weaved slightly as he got out of the car, feeling unsteady. On the other side of the road was a row of emaciated trees with crows stirring in the branches like dark leaves.

They entered an unlit door, passing several figures in the funk and shadow. Adam stopped.

"A couple of my students told me about this place," said Andrew. "Isn't it appalling?"

Adam made an effort to grin. "Words fail me."

The bar was cramped and foul: bare sweaty walls, the air heavy with offence. The floor around the bar was congested with tables and mismatched chairs where a collection of indistinguishable patrons sat, faces veiled by blue cigarette smoke. Ten years on this place would be a 24/7 cyber café with nineteen-year-olds drawn there by videogames and wide-screen televisions. At that moment, though, all of this was not yet imaginable, and the place still belonged to the past.

Ford draped an arm over each of them as they looked about. "Comrades, the fat lady has definitely sung."

Several people from the university waited meekly at a table next to the wall, each of them noticeably relieved as the others arrived. Everyone sat while Andrew went to the bar for a bottle and some glasses. When he returned he stood at the end of the table and poured everyone a drink, measuring out the vodka like quinine.

People held their glasses until Andrew was ready. "To the fat lady!" he yelled. And as one the group took back the first drink.

Adam found a chair in the corner, and listened as the others settled into conversations. The wood was hard against his back and smoke stung his eyes, but the voices of those around him were comforting in this faraway place and he listened to them with tired appreciation. Bethany was coaching a guy named Ethan on where to buy souvenirs. Bethany, who did almost all of the talking, was carefully put together and carried herself with an air of agonizing perfection. Looking at her, Adam had a feeling she was just slumming here to escape some tyrannical mother, to see a bit of the world before returning home to marry a bond trader and have some kids. In contrast, Ethan, the guy she was talking to, appeared waifish, lacked style, and was apt to say very earnest things. Ethan was that guy you knew at college who wrote appallingly open-minded columns for student newspapers, and dated women in hemp dresses and the clunky wooden jewellery found in Oxfam catalogues. He attended sit-ins at Deans' offices and other benign locations in the hope of being arrested. When he first arrived, Ethan announced somewhat prematurely that he was there to understand communism's utopian vision, only to find that Russians just wanted to listen to Nirvana.

Gradually though, Adam's attention strayed and he began listening to the others at the table as they got progressively drunk. Their conversations formed in earnest, voices cutting in on and interleaving one another, reaching him in fragments. "...and the band is coming here. Of course, they're mostly here for the tour, but I heard they're doing part of a video as well." "I keep getting these whiny letters from him. To be completely frank it's just making me sick..." "– well, technically I didn't, you know, *finish* my thesis. Not per se. Though I'm really close. Only three more chapters. I just needed to get out. I had this fallout with my advisor, and it got to be too much. She was just such a theory guru, you know?" "...that group they had opening for them – Rupture – their last CD was so affected, if you ask me. You know, like when a band just gets so self-conscious. So full of itself. Like David Lee Roth thinking he was Van Halen." " – and anyway, I was choking on all of that quote-unquote *oppression* which you have to locate. If you ask me –" "So I told him: if it's true love I'll worry about the damn orgasm. But of course he never called back..." "– started grad school because I used to like reading, and I ended up doing my dissertation on *The Simpsons...*" "...they've been together since, what, eighty-five? I was in grade nine. My dad's been divorced twice since then. Think about it: grade *nine*, man." " – and anyway, well, I'd heard that this place had fallen apart, and there was a faculty position, and, I just had to get out of that neurotic treadmill of tenured people lecturing on proletarian radicalism – "

After several minutes these shards of conversation began to chafe at him, and Adam decided to ignore it all. He glanced distractedly at Candace who sat across from him. Even in the strained light of the pub she appeared iridescent. Enormous green eyes staring out from under a shelf of dark hair. She wore a suede vest over a t-shirt with day-glo lettering. As she lighted a cigarette, he noticed that her hands gleamed with brightly painted nails.

"Are you settling in?"

She nodded in a perky way that made him

71

more tired. "Do you know many people here?"

"I don't know anyone."

"You should meet that guy at the end of the table."

He looked at Andrew, who was leaning back in a chair.

Candace poured herself another drink. "See his pants. I think they're from the *Bundeswehr*. They're the same ones they wore on the Wall."

Adam avoided her gaze, unsure of how to respond. "The wall?"

"The *Wall*. Like in Berlin."

"That's –" Adam was going to say something ironic, when he suddenly noticed her necklace.

"Are those from actual bullets?"

"Real ones." Candace smiled profoundly at the string of spent shell casings around her throat. "From Africa."

"Wow."

She blew smoke into the air. "Some war they had."

"That's something."

Her eyes widened. "Totally."

He ran a hand over his face. 'I should be drunk,' he thought, looking into his empty glass. Jetlag had sped up the alcohol, and he seemed to have skipped the good part and gone directly to the hangover.

"Hey!" He jumped, squinting at a flash of bright light.

Andrew had produced a camera from somewhere, and was going around the table taking pictures. "Have to get some memories."

Adam turned to face the lens, noting the bright jewel on Andrew's school ring just before it was eclipsed by another flash. A ruby.

Three months from then he would find the pictures from that night among Andrew's things. He would be stunned at the sight of himself in those pictures: his left eye just visible behind Troy's head; other shots full on him, features overexposed, blurred. Ford with an arm thrown over his shoulders, the bewildered crescent of his own grin. A side shot while he listened to Alice. His recurrent place among these people still so clearly random, tenuous.

Andrew moved with the camera to the other end of the table, and Adam's attention turned back to Ethan, who was well into an apology for Castro.

Across the table, Troy was making an effort to stand and people instinctively grew quiet. "Well folks, we just wanted to say welcome to Candace and Adam. Most of us don't know you yet, so why don't you introduce yourselves?"

Candace waved to those around the table. "It's so nice of you to welcome me. This is my third overseas gig. The first was to Antwerp, in high school, which was great because they had just opened a Hard Rock, and it was hilarious because they served us, but like if we'd been back home there would have been no way. Then I sophomored in France the year EuroDisney opened. And well, I just love living in foreign places, though this place is the strangest one *ever*. Still I'm glad to be here, because I think it's really important to travel."

"Couldn't agree more," endorsed Troy, his head teetering sagely. "They can be challenging, but these sorts of experiences will change you.

People nodded in a non-committal way. Things became quiet again, and Troy squinted at Adam. "What about you?"

There would be times when Adam would remember this moment, recalling it through the lens of an impending middle age. Gone then were the jetlag, that first day of teaching, the strangeness and disorientation weighing on him at that moment. Instead what he would recall were the faces around the table, and where they ended up: Troy, who eventually returned to finish his degree in Montreal, where he teaches; Alice who went on to work for UNESCO at a Kenyan *posho*; Candace who disappeared the following winter with a Belgian guy, emerging now and then on postcards from towns and cathedrals throughout Europe; and, of course, Andrew, for whom things would always be different. But all this would come later, when they had gone back to the familiar pursuit of their own lives. At that moment they were still mourning stalled careers, evading student loans, and looking for the opportunities that seemed to have vanished after graduation. They were still a group of strangers on the edge of a place they had hardly begun to know, none of them realizing how they would be changed by that country whose consciousness is dominated by an inexorable awareness of what might have been. For Adam, that night in the shitty little bar, like so much of what happened to him in that place, would be one of the gradual revelations which for years afterward came to him in the stillness of long afternoons, in the light that was still left to the day.

He blinked self-consciously at those around him, his eyes coming to rest on Andrew who stared from the far end of the table.

"Not much to tell, actually," he began, speaking without enthusiasm. "Born in Toronto; always lived in Toronto. Lit major. Couldn't find work at home after I graduated, so I came here. Much like the rest of you."

Troy looked around, trying to decide if Adam was done. "Is that all? Are you sure? Are there any other things, anything at all that you want to share?"

"Those are the bones."

"It's always so nice for us to meet another disappointment," Ford said, placing an arm over his shoulder as Andrew took another picture. Just before the flash Andrew smiled in a disappointed way, so that Adam knew he hadn't believed any of it. It was as though Andrew already knew about Clare.

Soon afterwards they left the bar, deciding to take a cab back to the dormitory where they all lived.

It felt good to be outside in the cold air, and for a moment Adam forgot where he was. Only a few people were around, and there was a kind of tranquillity in the street. Night hung upon the city, broken only by the streetlights which spread moth-shaped patterns over the pavement. Adam concentrated as he walked, consciously keeping within the light's ragged edge. He could hear the others speaking together on the periphery of his thoughts, and it seemed nice to him to be with these people.

While they were walking someone saw a cab and waved it down. There wasn't room for everyone, though, so Andrew and Ford agreed to walk.

"I'll come too," offered Adam.

Alice waved out the window. "Awfully nice of you fellas."

When the cab had gone they began to walk, following the intermittent trail of streetlights. It was late and everything was still except for the occasional hum of distant vehicles. Kiosks sat along the curb in small clusters, the curious gaze of their proprietors following the three foreigners. Along the street beggars slept in the foetal position of road kill. Adam stopped before a man wrapped in a fouled military coat, and stared at the limp cloth of his pant leg. He felt mesmerized by the limb's absence. The empty pant leg was like a shrine or a monument, not to the missing part but instead to the broken whole.

After a while the street came out at the river, and Andrew pointed out the onion dome of a church on the far bank.

Adam rubbed his arms in an effort to hold off sleep. "Are we close to a subway or something?"

Ford shrugged. "What's your rush?"

"It isn't that late," Andrew agreed.

"That's odd," said Adam, squinting at his wrist.

"What is it?"

"My watch is broken."

"No, they just go backwards here."

"Really," he insisted. "I think it's broken."

"You can find another in one of the markets."

Andrew was looking at him. "You okay?"

Adam held the watch to his ear, and he realized for the first time that he was trembling. "One of you knows where we are, right?"

Andrew stared at him through the dark. "How do you mean?"

"What do you mean, how do I mean?" his voice rising. "I *mean*, do you know where we are?"

Ford laughed. "You mean exactly?"

Something sank in his chest, and Adam stopped. "What I'm *saying* is do you know how to get us home?" And through the dark and exhaustion and the sudden panic he became aware that Andrew was frowning at him.

"Calm down," Ford muttered.

Andrew's eyes narrowed. "Home?"

Adam stepped away from them, sticking a hand under each arm.

After several blocks they spotted a sign for the metro, and as they went down the stairs into the station they were surrounded by a draught of scorched air. At the base of the stairs a woman stood beside a pail, her mop sliding across the floor in a repeating arc. Adam paused for an instant, remembering the woman he'd tripped over that morning at the university.

"Don't stare," Andrew hissed, dragging him by the arm. "You look like a tourist."

It was late, and on the platform a few people were waiting. Several soldiers stood talking loudly next to Andrew and Ford.

When the train arrived, there was a squeal from the tunnel, and a sudden rush of air and steel ripped the voices from people's mouths. Andrew waited as the others on the platform boarded before leading Adam and Ford to a less crowded car. The subway started to speed up and Adam found himself staring at his reflection which looked coldly back at him.

At their station they got out and climbed a broken escalator to the street. Andrew was hungry, so they stopped at one of the kiosks where he knew the vendor. They bought Pepsis and sandwiches of cold sausage and cucumber wrapped in pages of newspaper, eating as they walked back to the dormitory.

When they came to their building, Ford went in while Adam waited outside with Andrew, who wanted to stay up. "Not too many nice nights left," he said. "The cold will come and that will be that."

They sat on the stairs, Adam holding his head while Andrew smoked.

"How are you holding up?"

"I'm just tired."

"Ever travelled before?"

"Not like this."

"Wanted to see the real world?"

"I needed to change some things."

He laughed. "I don't know what you were expecting, but I guarantee you this place is not what you had in mind. The country used to be a superpower and now it's having problems feeding itself. The only thing they have left to swallow here is pride, and that doesn't digest well. Remember this before you go judging the place.

"Some foreigners laugh when they see the way things are, but they don't *see*, you know? It's as though they think that everything in the West is superior, and everything here is crap. Of course, back home they'd all be driving Toyotas."

Andrew finished his cigarette. "There's a reason why they call it culture shock. This whole place is swamped – the dyke they set up finally broke and everything is flooded with foreign stuff: smokes, televisions, jeans, fast food. You and I."

Adam shivered, pushing down a cold sensation that had been growing inside him. Everything he knew had disappeared, and he found himself now alone with only the memory of the things that were gone.

"The truth is I don't know what I'm doing here."

The ember from Andrew' cigarette glowed faintly on the pavement. "Really?"

It was quiet and from the stairs where they sat they could hear the murmur of voices inside the dormitory. The thin wind sent a stray piece of paper rasping along the street. A car door shut somewhere in the darkness.

'What *am* I doing here?' Adam thought. He watched the dying cigarette, faint ideas emerging from its light, and staying with him long after it had burnt out.

TO KATYA, life seemed almost good again. Her father was caught up in the country's new political turmoil and he spent longer and longer days at the Party offices. For a time this change in his mood lifted a cloud of anxiety and apprehension from the family. Her mother's health improved and she began to go out again. Petya threw himself into a new project at the university, and when he was home seemed only interested in the mail. Katya allowed herself to set aside the family's money problems and turned to the slow but satisfying work on her thesis, and began translating the English poems into Russian. After classes she went to the library's fourth floor and sat at the long wooden table near the stairwell. Here she could work beside the shelves with dictionaries and other reference sources for dozens of languages. From her canvas bag, she removed a collection of pencils that she sharpened over a metal wastebasket next to her chair. She set out her copy of each poem across the top of the desk. When this was done, she surveyed the papers, savouring the private pleasure of the moment before setting to work. Soon she was oblivious of everything else, including the small smile that crept upon her. The work was a protracted and excruciatingly detailed process, and the intensity it required allowed Katya to forget the world. She spent hours each day searching the old poems for difficult tropes or images, problematic words. Through the window beside her the afternoon sun drew over her work, passing softly across her face like an open hand.

One afternoon as she was leaving the library, Katya's thoughts were interrupted by a funeral procession making its way through the street. A man with a tuba strode a little ahead of the casket. In front went a priest, his palms held open toward the ceiling of clouds. As he walked, his beard trailed in the wind like dry grass. Next to him walked two boys in white cassocks.

Though droning and discordant, something about the music stirred a strange sympathy in her, and she followed at a distance as the procession wound through the Old Quarter with its narrow streets and shabby buildings still marked by the scars of now-distant wars. At Poets' House the procession swung past the spot where a famous writer was killed by a firing squad, then proceeded briefly to the river before turning into the open square of the market. The crowd parted at the sight of the coffin. Fish hawkers and babushkas standing behind baskets of cabbage grew quiet as they passed. A boy with a pig's head on his shoulder stopped to take off his hat. Animals looked on from cages. The procession passed a small charcoal grill, the smoke drifting among the line of mourners. The wordless canticle of the tuba resonated through the square, turning the heads of those at the back of the crowd who saw only the brass Cross and the open casket over a sea of heads.

Church bells began to ring as they approached, the measured sound reverberating along the streets and alleyways. Two children appeared on a balcony, staring down at the face in the open coffin. On each side of the road people watched with the old gestures of faith.

At the back of the church stood men who had come down from the scaffolding where they worked. Katya looked on behind them, unnoticed. As she watched, she noticed a giant eye staring at her from between the bars of scaffolding. She felt herself held in its gaze, and she changed her place among the other mourners to evade the pressure of its stare. Katya looked at the floor, but she felt it still, looking at her between the skeleton of platforms, equipment and ladders that lined the church walls. Glancing up again Katya saw the eye was part of a woman's immense face painted on the far wall. She saw evidence of other figures too behind the scaffolding, and she made out ears and hands and wings, swords and fire. As she looked about, Katya noticed alcoves and darkened recesses where large figures stared, revealed intermittently by the nervous light of candles. In other places, the murals were all but gone. On the arch above her she noticed a head with no mouth, while on the opposite wall nothing remained except a single arm with delicate fingers, like a child's.

When the funeral was over Katya remained in the shadow of the archway while the repair crews went back to work. She stood aside as they passed, their skin and clothes so pale with dust they almost blended into the afternoon light as they climbed the scaffolds. Great coils of rope rested on the ground, and from where she watched Katya could smell its straw-like odour. Pulleys began to work, lifting pails and equipment to the men. Voices called to one another as the workmen rose into the dome.

She stepped into the adjacent antechamber, retreating from the noise and work. Cribs of two-kopeck candles sat beneath icons. Behind them the saints shuddered to the chanting creak of the candelabra. Katya looked around before taking up one of the long wooden matches. A wick sputtered with life. She examined several murals around her, finding them ugly – the mouths smug, eyes darkened with cataracts of mildew and soot, bodies peeling and crusted with the lesions of age. Fissures had formed in the walls, running across limbs and features, severing the murals into fragments of themselves. In places plaster had come away, carrying with it some body part – a king's toe, the eye of St. Michael. Yet for all this there was an enduring existence about them, they were of the past and yet present, as if the paint had bled deep into the centre of the stone, beyond age.

There was a shuffling of feet and Katya started.

Behind her a man nodded shyly.

"You are new at this?"

She glanced over her shoulder. "Am I doing something wrong?"

The voices of workmen lingered about them like smoke. Someone laughed, the sound echoing in unseen passages.

"One normally prays."

Katya stiffened. "I am not here to pray."

"Then you are doing fine," the man shrugged.

Katya looked at him from the corner of her eye. His head was lowered, hands pressed together. She tried to do the same thing, but after a moment she grinned and a laugh escaped her.

The old man remained motionless. "Is there something the matter?"

Katya coloured, but kept her head lowered. "Doesn't it feel a bit silly?"

The old man's position did not change. "It

does not."

"What I mean is, don't you feel strange with all these old faces staring at you?"

He opened one eye. "What do you think you are looking at?"

She frowned. "I do not understand."

The man's head turned until he was looking directly at her. His stare was stern but expressive beneath his wild hedge of eyebrows. "You look but do not see." As he spoke, he shifted about to gesture at the ceiling. "Do you recognize that mural there?"

Katya strained to make out the image: a row of faces, expressionless and rigid like people in a breadline.

"It was inspired by a much older mural which lies within a convent built in the year nine hundred. For all that time it has been guarded by nuns who maintain a vigil over it. The mural has endured tyrants and invasions, famine and deprivation. Yet, after a thousand winters, they are gone while it remains." The candles shuddered as a draught circled the chamber. The man's face softened. "An icon emerges out of time like a diver from the ocean, it brings forth a consciousness of places that exist hidden from our common existence."

He looked at Katya, who was staring at the faces around them. "I don't know what to say," she said at last.

"You are not here to talk."

She smiled. "I'm not used to that."

His expression changed then, and for a moment Katya thought he was going to speak again, but instead he turned away and went back to his prayer. And after this they were quiet, Katya and this old man, and the lengthening silence seemed to filter into her thoughts, like deep breaths of calm. For a long time Katya remained like this in the shadow of the great arch, listening to the whisper of an old man's prayer.

That evening after dinner Petya and Ivan each withdrew to their rooms while Katya helped her mother in the kitchen. Lydia began humming by the sink, a thing she did whenever she was preoccupied. Katya cleared the table, but as she opened the fridge she coloured.

"What is this?" she said, unaware that she was whispering.

Lydia hesitated, and when she spoke her voice was tentative. "A rouble does not buy what it used to."

Katya sickened.

"But I just –" she paused, calculating how far the money should have stretched. "There must have been enough," she said determinedly.

The old woman held her breath before speaking again. "The heating bill."

"What heat?" She threw the towel on the floor. "Half the time we are freezing!"

Lydia opened her hands, attempting to share her daughter's anger. "Of course, this is how I see it. I will talk with them tomorrow. Perhaps they will listen to me this time."

Katya turned away, afraid suddenly that she might hit something. Her hands contracted and opened as she looked into the sink. "What will we do?"

She gripped the counter to steady herself and closed her eyes.

"You *know* what you will do," Lydia whispered, pinching the girl's elbow.

Through the kitchen window Katya watched as night drew in upon the city, the tops of buildings lost in the low sweep of clouds. The days were shortening. Katya set her jaw.

The room where her grandmother had lived now sat empty, the air stale from disuse. No one went in here anymore except for the winter clothing stored in the closets. When her grandmother was alive, the room enjoyed the tacit openness of a living room. But since her death the room had become like a guarded memory, sheltered and unchanging.

Katya glanced wistfully about, her eye taking in the furniture and small items she knew so well – two narrow beds with high wooden backs, a writing desk, the samovar, slim book shelves on either side of a wardrobe, a pair of gossip chairs beneath the window.

It was the latter of these items that held the warmest associations for Katya. Here she had sat in the long afternoons of her childhood, singing along with the radio, doing schoolwork or listening to her grandmother, who so often spoke to the girl of her family's past.

"Did your father ever tell you how he lost his arm? Of course during the War, but do you know how it happened? He was still a boy then in Leningrad, during the siege. For nearly three years they starved the city. Those inside were unprepared, and after a few months the city was like a morgue. People just fell over in the street. Often the graves were not deep enough and in the spring you would find bones rising through the ground. Pushed up like stones by the frost. You should ask your father more about these things. He was there..."

As a teenager, these speeches always made Katya roll her eyes, and the old woman would upbraid her for her flippancy. "You don't know any better than your brother. To your generation it never existed. You don't understand what it means to be born when you are."

These conversations, though easily dismissed at the time, rushed back upon Katya after the old woman's death. Standing now in the half-darkness of that room, she recalled the final image of her grandmother's body, the lifeless trunk of their family tree. She had stood by the edge of the bed, holding the basin of water for her mother who washed the woman.

Katya had at first looked away as the body was stripped, but gradually succumbed to curiosity. Between the limp creases of flesh lay evidence of toil and strain – the protrusion of a poorly healed rib, a pale scar about her abdomen ("That is from me," Lydia explained), and exhausted breasts sinking into her frame.

"She had a life much different from mine," her mother said, tenderly washing out the cavity of the old woman's navel.

Katya was affected by the sight, her mother's pink hand touching the body with such intimacy. For a moment her mother was drawn from the periphery of life, as if by caring for the dead she became more alive. Watching at the edge of the bed where she stood, Katya felt a new sympathy for her mother that she would never completely forget.

When her mother stepped out of the room Katya leaned over the body, with its oddly dry smell. Taking a fold of skin from the cheek, Katya pinched the old woman, holding it between clamped fingers, watching as her flesh whitened with exertion. She thought of her own body – its capacities, its blemishes and alleged potentials, the concealed impulses. She saw the traces of the dead woman lurking beneath the flushed outline of her mother's face. 'How different they were from each other,' Katya thought. 'Their identities have been moulded by forces which neither could ever understand.'

As the youngest child, Lydia had been sent east when the War started, returning only after peace and reconstruction had hidden the worst of that time. Alive and unscarred, Lydia's mother had protected the innocence of her child, who never learned the very practicality and strength so badly needed now.

Each day Katya felt the loss of the old woman, sensing that her grandmother, who as a girl had watched the carriages of the nobility in the streets of Moscow, would have understood this time they were living through. The climate of Katya's own life had changed dramatically. Winds from the world outside now shook and finally pulled up the roots of her daily existence, leaving her exposed and unmoored amid the storms of confusion which fell on them. Inflation, crime, unemployment, shortages of food and fuel: all these were to Katya both personal affronts and national misfortunes.

Not long after her grandmother's funeral, she had come home to find Lydia weeping at the kitchen table.

"It's all right," Katya had soothed. "We all miss her."

"It's not that," Lydia said, shaking her head woefully. "I went to the store but prices rose again. What am I to tell your father?"

Katya had been put out by her mother's disregard for the dead, but as the implications of her complaint sunk in she too became caught up in the significance of it. Rather than tell her father, Katya convinced Lydia to keep silent. Several days later Katya handed some money to her mother, who eyed it suspiciously.

"Where did this come from?"

Katya shrugged.

Lydia continued to question her daughter, but in the end she accepted the new source of income. As the months progressed, prices in all the kiosks and *gostronomii* continued to rise, doubling sometimes in a week, and all the while her husband's salary bought less and less.

"We must not bother your brother," Lydia explained. "He contributes his entire salary when they pay him. If he does well he is bound to get an increase…"

And so it was Katya, in the end, who had to find money to make up the growing shortfall in the family's income.

Now crossing the room, she opened the wardrobe and withdrew a worn box from one of the drawers. She removed two bundles. In the first was an assortment of rings and jewellery, and, in the second, fraying pendants and tarnished medals – each embossed with the familiar profiles of the old leaders. From among these items, she selected a ring and a pendant, returning the others to the drawer as she had found them. There were stories attached to these things, the echo of her grandmother's voice trailing behind each piece like a shadow. Her grandmother had guarded these things; each one was for her like a chapter in a larger narrative of their family, and at first Katya had shrunk from the idea of pawning them. But necessity had hardened her resolve, and as the months wore on the rings and medals and ribbons had less and less nostalgic value. Instead, they had transformed into a different kind of currency. With these things Katya now purchased time for the family to find security in this new world of terrible certainties.

She paused for a moment in the hall. Outside, a fine drizzle seeped through the gloom, tracking the window with fissures. Her own face stared back at her from the pane, and behind it, her home, as faint as her own reflection.

A light was on in her father's study, and her ear caught the tune of a faraway song stretching out to her from under the door. Katya stood and listened, and for a moment she was far away from there, in the gentler past. There was a time when the sound of music would have drawn her closer to him, and she would have knocked on the door, gone to him the way she had as a child. Music was the one place of entry into her father's heart, besides the Party, and it was a key she had used in the past to be closer to him. When she was a girl, her father had let her sit in his study, where they talked about the great composers, about opera and ballet. He was more human in these moments, without the hardness he usually wore. She grinned to remember the emotion that would erupt from him, at the same time understanding that she owed her own passionate nature to him.

There in the hallway the memory kindled in her but then, almost as quickly, extinguished. Katya pressed her cheek against the doorframe, closing her eyes to concentrate on the music. 'No matter what happens to me,' she thought, 'this music will go on existing, will be beautiful. Its beauty is oblivious to me, even though I feel it. It will be no less when I am lost –' But then she stopped herself thinking this way: it was like capitulating to the darkness which threatened her. 'No,' she thought, pushing away from the door and straightening. 'We will not be destitute. I will not let it happen.'

Catching her reflection again in the window, Katya allowed herself an instant more with the image of herself, then turned away and was gone.

THE MORE ADAM and the others knew about Andrew the less they understood. Most of them were there because they couldn't find work at universities in the West. As Ford observed, "I woke up one morning to find my career had gone bad for some reason or another. Like a carton of milk before its expiry date."

Andrew was different. He went through school on a series of good scholarships, and after graduating he was offered a research fellowship in London. At a conference some publishers got wind of his thesis, and when the dust settled he had signed with Rotterdam for that book and the next one. By then it was clear he was being groomed for a spot in a big school, one of which offered him a position for the following spring. That was the summer of 1993, a year when you could have listed the university appointments in the country on a cocktail napkin.

But instead of doing what anyone else would have done, Andrew turned down the job and left to teach in Russia.

Of all the places he could have gone.

Just as everyone with an education was leaving that country, he signed a five-year contract with some school no one had heard of. Five years. In academics that's a bullet in the head.

One of the big universities tried a final time to bring him back into the fold, faxing to Russia to offer him another position. But by then he had already met Katya, and it was too late. That was at the end of September, when the trouble in Moscow was worsening and everyone began talking of leaving before things blew up. Andrew declined the second job offer with a letter in hand-written Russian. This was all too precocious for the university, which would never have understood Andrew's decision to throw it all up and go to Russia. Certainly Adam never understood, though he continued to think about it long afterwards.

Even now people maintain that the defining moment for Adam's generation was the fall of the Berlin Wall. After he'd returned from Russia, Adam continued to read new books celebrating the 'coming together' of East and West. But they never meant coming *together*, so much as they meant when the East moved west – the exodus of people who left Russia for America and Israel and Europe. What the politicians and the historians, those from the generation before Adam's, what they never discuss, and do not seem aware of, is those who left the West to go east. With all the gloating euphoria that accompanied the fall of communism, no one in the West fathomed why anyone would leave for a defunct Workers' Paradise. Yet, people went.

In the autumn of 1970 Andrew's mother, Nadya, who was a musician, became pregnant. She and the father, Andrei, agreed to marry before the child was born. This plan was interrupted, however, by her decision to defect while the orchestra they played with was touring in America. Nadya had never in her life

102

demonstrated such guile or recklessness, and certainly none of the authorities would have allowed her to leave the Soviet Union had they thought her capable of something so bold. But a child can make even an ordinary person do extraordinary things, and for Nadya the chance to create a new destiny for the child was too tempting for her to resist. No fear she could conjure of a new life in the West was enough to shake her resolve to escape history's grip on her unborn child. And so the plan to defect began to grow in her alongside with the child. In the time before the orchestra's departure, the child and her dreams of freedom became entwined together in her mind. Before they left Nadya did not discuss her intention to defect, but, like the child's existence, she kept it secret and hidden. Even Andrei, though aware of his impending fatherhood, did not suspect her plan to betray the Motherland. He was stunned therefore when she announced her intentions to him in a Boston hotel.

"You aren't serious, Nadya."

"I am," she said, lowering her voice significantly.

They were in the hotel coffee shop waiting with the others for the Greyhound that was to take them to the airport. The dark-suited men who watched over the orchestra were arguing with some of the hotel staff.

Nadya stirred her coffee loudly, the spoon rattling in the apple-red cup until coffee splashed onto the tabletop.

"You aren't being serious," he said again, stressing each word this time, insisting them onto her.

"This is our chance." She yanked a napkin from the aluminum dispenser, as though she was plucking a bird. "No one is expecting anything."

Together they glanced through the glass doors at the vehicles and bodies on the street.

Andrei looked at her again. "Have you thought about this?" From her expression he could see she was wavering. Nadya could not truthfully say when she had first considered the idea, but at that moment she felt no surprise at what she was doing.

"What is there to think about?"

"Our families."

Her eye twitched, then firmed. "They'll live."

"Yes, but their *lives*..."

She shook her fist at him, bits of napkin protruding from between her fingers. "What about our lives?"

"You would punish them?"

She rose, holding her bag tightly. "I would save myself."

"Nadya..."

She released the crushed napkin, leaving it on the table. "My family will understand the choice I am making."

He stared, dumbfounded at her recklessness. "Nadya – the child."

"Precisely," she said. "The child."

After pausing another moment in case he changed his mind, Nadya passed through the glass doors of the hotel, and a moment later she was gone.

When he was two, Andrew's mother met and married a professor in Boston, where they had been living. He was older and without children. Their marriage took place at the campus chapel. After concluding the vows, the professor embraced her with uncharacteristic fervour. "There, there," he whispered. "You are safe now."

Nadya looked up at him, alarmed. "Safe from what?"

In the first months of their marriage, her American husband often recalled to his friends how he had met Nadya. "I had just paused in front of a shop to check my hat in the window, when my focus shifted, and I saw this woman inside who was looking into the street, right at me."

He paused each time at this point in the story to shake his head. "I couldn't help it," he always confessed. "I loved her right away."

For a long time after they were married, the professor waited for her to reveal to him the great trial or tragic misfortune in her past, from which, he believed, he had certainly rescued her. But when it was clear that no revelation was coming, he began to suspect that she had not emigrated for the reasons he anticipated. As his expectation waned, it was soon replaced by disappointment and a vague sense of betrayal. She would not confide her past, and so he began to suspect it. But the professor was not a demonstrative man, and rather than openly reproach her with his disappointment, he resigned himself to sulking discontent.

Even as their marriage cooled, the professor remained fond of his wife's son, though Andrew could not bring himself to return this affection. Instead, the boy thought only of the absent identity of his father. He bothered his mother for details about his father in that faraway country, and practiced spelling the man's name in Russian. All that she would tell the boy was that his father had been a musician.

"In our country," she explained, "they do special things for artists and other people. Sometimes they even name streets after them. In the city where we lived there was a park dedicated to musicians..."

Later Nadya regretted telling even these small things to the boy, who became more devoted to the father he had never seen. He found a photograph of his mother when she was younger, but the second half of the picture had been torn away, leaving only the side of a man's face – dark hair and an ear. "Yes," she admitted, when he confronted her with the photo. "That was a picture of your father and me. I felt betrayed when he would not stay here with me, so I tore him from the only picture I'd brought."

Andrew had not replied, but after this he set the torn photograph on a table with a candle. When he was twelve, Andrew began writing letters.

"The police will read your letters before he sees them," she warned, trying to deter the boy.

"What do I care?" he retorted. "I'm not writing anything bad."

"That won't matter."

"He will be happy to hear from me. He should know about me."

"We can't even be sure he still lives at this address. He may have moved. He may have a family of his own..."

"I am his son."

"You are," his mother said, as if confessing something.

But after a year of sending letters there was still no reply, and Andrew wrote no more of them.

Like so many women disenchanted with marriage, Nadya found consolation in her child. He was intelligent and happy, attractive and successful, and she gazed on him with that parental pride which is also a kind of envy.

For all her attempts to dissuade Andrew's new interest in his past, Nadya was committed to the idea that he learn Russian. She wrote out words on cards – Russian on one side, English on the other – and hid them where he would discover them at unexpected times. Each evening, she would quiz the boy to see how many he had learned. Opening a textbook he would find the word труд in his mother's fine hand, or, at lunch, next to his sandwich, хлеб; from his pencil case emerged карандаш. Other children laughed when this happened, and the boy grew cautious when opening things for fear of spilling his mother's words into the open. But in spite of the embarrassment this caused him he never complained to her, sensing that this game was part of something more earnest between them.

Each day after school Andrew was always a little surprised to find his mother in the kitchen making dinner. She seemed so distracted and intent that it was hard to believe she had been waiting for him. But it was always the same. When she saw him, she went to the stove and wiped her long fingers on the cloth. Then she sat at the table and asked what he had learned that day. She brought him close so she could look directly into his face as he recited the words she had hidden for him. Her expression changed with each word, depending on his pronunciation. When he finished, he went to his room and placed the pieces of paper in a box where he kept things closest to him.

When he told Katya of his mother's notes, she grabbed at his arm and shook him. "Don't you see," she exclaimed. "She was trying to explain something important. She was telling you that you can rename your world. She was giving you the gift of translation."

In 1989, on a weekend during the final year of his doctorate Andrew came home to find his mother in the kitchen. The table was cluttered with photo albums, yellowed newspaper clippings and other things she had saved from his childhood. Next to it was that day's newspaper with the news from Berlin. The trees in the yard were almost bare, and the sky was streaked with birds flying south. That day in November he found her wistful, brooding, and as they talked her thoughts became more and more backward-looking. She had been informed of her illness by then, though she would not tell Andrew until after his exams.

"You understand why I had to leave my country, yes?" she asked, speaking to him now in Russian.

Andrew blinked, considering her face frankly. "Not really."

"I left for myself. And for you."

"Yes, but you gave up my father..."

"I thought he might come with us," she said, squinting as she remembered back to that day in the hotel. "I have often wondered what it cost him when he got back," and Andrew watched as the image behind his mother's gaze drifted away from him to a man he had never met.

"Still, I had to go," she started, suddenly returning to the present. "It was how I obtained my freedom," and even as she said this, Nadya couldn't help but glance around the kitchen.

Andrew bit his lip. "Then it was worth it."

She smiled with vague bitterness. "It is a terrible thing when you cannot bear your country, when you must flee from it to reclaim yourself. Even if you leave, you are never entirely free of it. Even after a lifetime away, that place has a claim on me," and here her voice lowered to a whisper, as though there was something she distrusted. "I am Russian," she said. "This means that the country is part of me, the way people's surnames connect them to a family. You never truly leave a place that was your home."

She stared for a moment, her gaze coming back into focus. "I look at you – " she hesitated. "And I wonder who you would have been in my country, what you would have become." Nadya sighed. "It is something lost that we will never know."

Andrew often remembered this conversation after she died. He was working in England by then, and the news of his mother's death unmoored his life in a way that both transcended, and hinged on, geography. It was because of the conversation that day in his mother's kitchen, more than anything else she ever said to him, that Andrew decided to leave his future in the West, to go to Russia and search for the life hidden there.

AFTER HIS failed effort at the theatre to locate his father, Andrew used a second address he had found among his mother's things. He hesitated at first to use this address, the last piece of precise information from her life in Russia. For more than a week the paper with the address stayed in his pocket. In the evening it came with him to the bars and restaurants he explored with the other expats. At night he took it out and placed it on the chair beside his bed. At breakfast he found himself sometimes turning the paper over in his fingers, imaging the person whose name was on it.

The address on the paper was the last obvious course left for him. He brought along a photograph of his mother. Her face was the only proof he had of who he was and why he was here.

Like so many of the city's streets, the one he was looking for had been renamed. An old couple he asked still knew the address, and Andrew found himself in front of a door with casements of scarred glass. The door was ajar, so he went in, climbing the unlighted stairwell until he found himself before a leather-covered door with the flat number he sought. There were sounds from behind the door – soft pad of feet and the clank of a dish – and for a long time Andrew stood motionless, listening. His knock, though, brought silence, and for an instant he thought maybe he had imagined the lives behind the door.

"What is it you want?" A woman's voice.

Andrew glanced around before realizing the voice came from behind the door. "I'm looking for someone."

"Who are you?"

He said his name. "I'm from America," he added.

"What do you want?" the voice asked again, this time in English.

Andrew looked at his mother's face in his hands. "I am looking for my aunt. She used to live in this flat. Maybe you know where she is. Maybe she is still here..."

A sliver of light fell across his face. "What is this person's name?"

The woman was suspicious of the foreigner at her door. But as he explained himself, holding out the photograph of his mother, her distrust melted and, after a moment of disbelief, two arms appeared and then a face and suddenly Andrew was being embraced.

Aunt Lena was a small, older woman with features which became delicate when she was emotional. Her blue eyes were overcast with black brows that contrasted with the whiteness of her hair, which she wore back from her face with the help of unnumbered pins.

Taking her nephew's arm, she spoke to him in a voice that was brittle with shock, ushering him into her flat. As Lena moved about the kitchen, Andrew sat self-consciously on the end of a bench next to a window looking over the street. It was a small, bright room, with pieces of framed embroidery on the walls, and a shelf with a round clock and wooden candlesticks. Every few minutes, his aunt stopped what she was doing to look at him and smile.

"I always wondered what happened," she began, glancing at him apologetically. "And now you are here, from so far away..." She moved closer and touched him demonstratively, still unsatisfied with his realness. After this she excused herself, slipping out of the room, and returning with a photograph that she placed before him.

Andrew was quiet for a moment, trying to imagine his mother's life as it appeared in this picture.

"That is a picture of her at your age. Look at your own face, it is her. Here in my kitchen. I can't believe it, no really I can't. But here you are all the same..." and she resumed touching him.

He stared at his aunt's hand in his own.

Andrew was overwhelmed to find someone at last who remembered his mother, who recalled the pieces of her which he had never known. The risks he had taken, the professional setbacks he had brought on himself, were suddenly justified by the presence of this small woman with her own photograph. Here was a person with memories and knowledge that completed his own. It was like discovering someone with the other half of a torn letter. It helped add to the story of her that he kept in his mind, adding new colour, pieces hidden by time.

Though at that moment he had no words yet for this realization, what Andrew comprehended there beside his aunt was that his mother was not fully known to him, that she had layers of existence that he only now began to glimpse. It was at that moment that his mother became for him Russian, a part of this strange new place he had come to in search of her. She had sat at this same table. She had lived in this city. She had known its streets and faces. And one of those faces belonged to his father.

Andrew was looking out the window. "There is so much to tell you," he said, his thoughts returning to his aunt. "But first, you should know what has happened..." and he went on to tell about his mother's death, recounting her life in reverse back up to the point that she had left his father. Lena listened in spurts, interjecting with abrupt questions or comments. She was eager to hear about her sister's life.

"What about her music? Did she play in an orchestra in America? Did they appreciate her? What was her husband like? Were they very much in love? Did she travel the way she wanted to?"

Andrew felt heavy with answers. His aunt's comments seemed naïve and unexpectedly silly. They were spoken from a memory of his mother that was young and idealistic and passionate – characteristics that Andrew was unable to imagine. His aunt similarly had difficulty reconstructing her sister from what Andrew had told her.

Only when the front door opened did Lena and Andrew return to themselves, letting Nadya slip back into the past.

"He's home in good time," Lena observed, staring at the round clock on the shelf.

Andrew started. "Who?"

"Ilyin."

"Who?"

"Of course. How would you know?" Lena stopped, a sad smile passing over her face. "Come and meet your cousin."

Ilyin's first response was one of surprised hostility toward the stranger in the kitchen. He stood with his arms crossed, ignoring his mother's explanation as he assessed Andrew.

118

"I can see he is a foreigner," he interjected, addressing his mother. "But what is he doing here?"

Andrew backed into the table, uncomfortable under the man's stare.

Lena put her arm around Andrew, and confronted her son. "This is your aunt's son, from America. He has come home. Your cousin has come home."

Ilyin blinked. "My cousin?" and then all at once his demeanour melted and he grabbed Andrew's arm.

"It's what I've been telling you!"

Ilyin embraced the foreigner. "My cousin!" he exclaimed. "I can't believe it!"

"Hold him again," Lena encouraged. "You will see."

On his second visit, Andrew brought a photo album of his mother's, and together with Lena and Ilyin he recounted for them the people and places depicted in its pages. Like an old door, the cover creaked when he opened it, releasing faces from the past into his aunt's kitchen. Here was his mother, young and alive, the way she must have looked when she was his age. Photos of her American husband, their faces around Christmas trees and Thanksgiving turkeys in Boston. There were photographs taken at Niagara Falls, the Empire State Building, the Lincoln Monument. And on these pages Andrew was a child again, when the centre of the only world he knew was her. The more photos he showed them, the more uncomfortable he became. There are pictures of yourself which can be almost hateful because of the ignorance of the future which rests on every face. You recognize in a person's expression the seeds already planted for what is to come, and there is nothing you can do to change this. You can only see and know.

"Just think of it," his aunt said, looking up from the photographs. "You arriving here so unexpectedly, after your mother gave up so much to leave..."

"Yes," Ilyin said, becoming quiet. "Why have you come back?" He was tall with dark hair that he wore flat against his head. His chin had a slight cleft that appeared when he frowned, which he did now.

Andrew shook his head, suddenly defensive and self-conscious. Then, in halting, broken sentences, he tried to justify, as he would so often to Adam and the others, his decision to come to this place that so many, including his mother, had fled. The explanation always began with his mother's death, but invariably eroded into a disconnected litany of new and unrelated convictions that had begun to preoccupy his life.

"I'm not sure," he said, when he came to the end of his explanation. "Only I had hoped to meet my father."

Lena and her son smiled at the same time. This seemed enough for them.

After that Andrew became a regular visitor to his aunt's flat. On these visits he tried to explain his mother to them, and he came to understand her in the process. His efforts were often reciprocated by his aunt, who recalled memories of her sister as a girl growing up. Sometimes as he was listening, Andrew would sit in a chair and think that his mother too had reclined on the same furniture. The thought would bring an oddly gratifying sensation. His aunt showed him old books with his mother's handwriting in the margin, in a closet was a sweater she had worn – one or two hairs still clinging to the back of it. All about him were traces of her life, like echoes that did not fade away. If he could no longer touch his mother, he could still locate items that once had. Lena had all of his mother's music, even a recording made by her orchestra, and often in the evening they would sit in the living room and listen to it.

Sometimes Andrew went to his aunt's flat just for the pleasure of having a bath in the middle of the afternoon. Lena owned a large iron tub and, unlike in the dormitory, you were able to get hot water in her apartment at any time of the day. On these occasions Andrew scrubbed himself with the bar of harsh yellow soap they used, and after he was clean he lay in the steaming water, listening to the radio which drifted through the transom. The tub had a small board that fit across the sides and improvised as a table for cups of his aunt's black tea or Ilyin's chessboard. His cousin, if he was home, would sometimes appear and they would talk together, or check newspapers for soccer scores. After, Andrew would dress and wander about the flat. The apartment was filled with books: on tables and in doorways, spilling from shelves, even stacked under a chair missing one leg. In the tiny family room there were two old sofas with frayed arm rests, and always the cat, Alfred, who liked to sleep on a faded copy of Balzac's *Père Goriot*. Drifting through the flat Andrew lost himself to his aunt's idiosyncrasies: the toilet fixed with a clothes peg and wire, the bench in the kitchen that transformed at night into a bed for Ilyin, the television with tinfoil on the aerial to improve reception.

"You don't mind all this disorder?" his aunt once asked him.

"I don't see disorder," he said.

"Blindness can be a gift," she smiled. "If I had to see everything I would simply go mad."

"Yes," he said. "That's what happened to my mother."

Lena reached out and touched him, the way she so often did to Ilyin.

"Thank you," he said. "Thank you for still being here."

Late one afternoon when Andrew arrived on a visit, Lena ushered him into the flat and he found Ilyin shaving in the hallway wearing only his pants. He was arguing with his friend, Mitya, who sat before the television in the family room. The two men nodded to him as he came in, and then went back to their discussion.

"He has the authority to dissolve the parliament," Ilyin yelled from the washroom. "Why should this offend you?"

"This is the man who says he wants democracy for the country. But how democratic is a government that fires its elected officials? It only shows that nothing has changed."

"If he doesn't stop parliament there can be no reform – do you want to give our new influence back to the government?"

"Give back?" Mitya frowned. "They've never given it up!"

"Someone has to be in control. If it isn't the President, then parliament will end up returning power to the communists and then where would your new rights be?"

"You're speculating."

"This would happen."

Lena was listening from another room. "Why doesn't the government step in?"

"Ma," Ilyin said, gesturing at the television with his razor. "They *are* the government!"

Mitya made a face at the television. "Is there nothing else to watch?"

Ilyin tried the other channels. "Maybe they will show a soccer match."

Andrew went into the kitchen as they were talking. He leaned over the stove, watching as his aunt dropped a handful of buckwheat into the pot.

When Mitya left, Ilyin went back to the bathroom. "Don't let him get you down," he called. "Like everyone, he thinks too much about politics right now."

"Things are getting tense here..."

"Ah, you're from the West. What do you know about these things?"

He gestured at the television. "I'm just saying there is real unrest."

"Stop worrying," Ilyin called. "There's a party tonight. You should come along."

Lena was setting the table. Ilyin came in buttoning his shirt. They sat and began to eat. Andrew tried to get Ilyin to talk about politics again. Lena interjected, explaining that she had to go out because of her job at one of the city's hotels. "It's good for us," Ilyin explained. "There are many foreigners there, and she gets tipped in dollars."

"Yes," she smiled wryly. "Every time prices go up, I get a raise!"

Andrew stared into his soup. "I don't understand."

Ilyin frowned, feeling that this talk about money had gone on too long. "When prices go up the rate of exchange rises, and she can change the dollars for more roubles."

Andrew coloured, embarrassed. He'd never thought about it.

His cousin shook his head. "For a capitalist, you don't know much about money."

After eating, they took a tram across town, but traffic was heavy and there was a lot of waiting. "Not far now," Ilyin assured him.

"It's all right," Andrew said. "I like looking around."

The sun from that morning had been pushed aside by a shelf of storm cloud over the city. Traffic gradually moved them into the suburbs. The road became flanked by uninterrupted rows of apartment blocks like giant boxcars, their concrete forms blending into the grey sky.

"We should get out here," Ilyin said, standing. "We need supplies."

"Supplies?"

Ilyin tapped his chin. "Oh yes."

Andrew laughed.

At the next stop they stepped out into the crowd waiting for the tram. It was Friday afternoon and commuters stood with that relaxed fatigue that comes with the end of the week. Parents held hands with their children, who always seemed well-behaved and bright in their school uniforms. People brushed you as they passed, but not roughly. Two students asked Ilyin for directions somewhere then offered him a cigarette for his help. Despite all of the activity there was calm in the crowd, everyone enjoying the cool of the evening and thoughts of the weekend.

Andrew followed Ilyin to a row of red kiosks, where they searched the greasy windows. Each kiosk was a bazaar of merchandise – cigarettes and candy, women's underwear, baseball hats, Folgers coffee, a radio, watches, cheese, Oreo cookies, even a holster. When he found someone selling vodka, Ilyin bought a bottle and held it under his arm as they walked.

They followed a stream of people making their way through the massive apartment blocks. The sheer size of the buildings seemed to subdue individual voices, but as they walked Andrew became aware of stray conversations and the smells of cooking. Between the mazes of buildings were a school and playground, and open stretches of uncut grass. They came to a smaller concrete building, and Andrew followed his cousin across the empty yard and into the building. The lift was filthy and smelled of cigarettes and urine, but Ilyin seemed happy that it was working. When they entered the flat Ilyin introduced his cousin to those he knew. Andrew looked around, recognizing people from the university.

Someone offered Andrew a cigarette, and for a while he smoked and tried to follow what they were saying. There were several conversations around him, and it was a moment before he found one that interested him.

"It's really terrible. We can't even keep our government from tearing itself apart."

"You make too much of it," someone said dismissively. "These are birth pains. They may be messy, but they're necessary."

"To look at us you would never think it was possible to find a single country in all this mess. I've heard the capital is a circus. There are too many voices now to hear anything."

"I see it like you. All of us are trying to construct a new state, a new reality. But what is needed is one identity, as Russians. Not all these individual interests."

A woman stood shaking her head. "There are larger allegiances to consider. The whole world is at our door now."

"How can you be so eager to trust the foreigners? Already they are in our streets like burglars, buying up our country with dollars and then renting it back to us. What we need is leadership. I support the President. We have always known that our country requires a strong ruler. For without strength there is only chaos."

Ilyin turned to his cousin. "What do you think?" he said, drawing their attention to the foreigner.

Andrew was thoughtful, locating his words in Russian before speaking. "These reforms will occur whether the state sanctions them or not. And you're wrong – the world is not at your door, it's already behind it. You're wearing the world, you drink it and smoke it and watch it. You sing it in the shower. It's too late to turn back now. And that's lucky, because no government will ever again dare to hide the rest of the world from you."

"Well now, that sounds so fine, when you put it that way," a thin man at the edge of the group interjected. "Yet I always become uneasy when someone from the West tells me how lucky I am to be just like him. Are you one of those missionaries we meet so often now?" he sneered. "You seem to forget that the miracle of capitalism has come to my country through a series of disasters."

Andrew colored but found the words coming more easily. "Say what you want, but your life is better than it has ever been."

"Better? Why, because you begin to recognize the things I eat and wear? I don't like the way you in the West talk about your lives. You go hungry on full stomachs; you call enough too little. To excuse your indulgences you call them civil liberties."

Andrew crossed his arms. "Your country has joined the rest of the world. Like it or not."

"I do not like it. We don't want your bits of plastic, your milkshakes and pop music. I am not free, surely, just because I can now wear blue jeans. Please do not tell me that the West's ideals go no deeper than that."

"Those things come with freedom. And besides, people do want these things," he said. "They come with new words like *parliament, democracy, constitution, elections.* The country's future is being built on these words. Without them all you have are the old, tired words of the past."

"You do not understand," the thin man gestured dismissively. "None of these ideals will ever survive a firing squad in this country. Until they do, you and your idealism are just visiting. When the cameras turn off people will discover there is nothing there. The show, as you say, will be over. All of your white-gloved manners shall not hide the fact that there is someone else's blood on your hands."

People stared into their drinks or moved away. Someone changed the topic. To smooth things Ilyin took his cousin over to a friend who studied at the university. She sat away from the others, though from the look on her face Andrew could see she had been listening. Ilyin introduced them with characteristic generosity, thinking that each would like to practice the language of the other.

"This," he said, "is Katya."

"You made some people angry."

Andrew glared before replying. "I didn't mean to."

"I think you did."

"I wasn't going to back down, if that's what you mean."

"You knew you would upset people before you spoke."

He glanced at her defiantly. "Don't tell me you're afraid to speak your mind in public. You should be shouting what you think everywhere you go."

Her smile thinned, and she sipped at her drink without breaking his stare.

Ilyin reappeared beside them. "What's this?" he mocked, handing a bottle to his cousin. "Can I take you nowhere? I leave you alone with my friend for a minute and once again you're on some glum topic."

Andrew grinned, glad suddenly to have his cousin there. "You haven't heard my side."

"Be careful," he cautioned, talking into his cousin's ear. "You do not know about her."

After this they moved to the kitchen where Ilyin had found some chairs and they talked above the music and other voices.

"You are not like the others," she observed in English.

"What others?"

"All those professors on lecture tours. They arrive for a week or so. They look about and have their pictures taken, then do some preaching. Academics in your country are certainly looked after. Are you another idealist with radical ideas about us?"

"You know, it occurred to me once that the real difference between our countries is the way we treat radicals."

"These people are not radicals."

"Oh yes they are, or were at any rate. Here if someone challenges the state, officials send him to jail or worse. In my country we'd give him a book tour. Our biggest export is entertainment, most of which is written by left-wing folks. Instead of shooting these people, someone in America had the bright idea of handing them a microphone and selling tickets to people who wanted to hear them. You know who makes the real money from our radicals? Guys in suits.

It's the same in universities, we have tons of Marxist intellectuals in America. Probably more than you have. But they're not in jail with the drug pushers. They have research chairs endowed by companies on the stock exchange. The last people who want to see capitalism end are American radicals. They'd never find a better patron than capitalism."

"I'm not sure you can be called a radical if you're fed by the state."

"You're right," Andrew said, looking into his glass. "I'm not like them." The alcohol had exaggerated the events of the evening, and after his argument with the thin man he now felt restless and uneasy.

Katya glanced at the collar of his shirt. "Are you certain?"

His face grew serious. "I could have been," he sighed. "There was a time not long ago when I was really close to becoming one of those people. But not any more..."

"And who are you now?" She smiled, her voice reassuring, as though speaking to a child.

Behind them the noise of the party seemed to press against their conversation, and he concentrated on the space between them. "I don't know. I am waiting to see."

Katya handed her glass to Ilyin who had appeared again. "Good luck." Then she slipped away among the people in the crowded kitchen.

Ilyin shook his head. "What did you say this time?"

Andrew found her at the door. She was wearing her coat. He called to her over the music, but she did not seem to hear and before he could speak again she had left.

The chill air in the hallway startled him. The door shut, and the noise of the party was replaced by a self-conscious silence.

Katya was waiting at the elevator.

"I'm not like that," he started.

She stared at him for a moment before answering. "How would you know?"

The elevator's gears groaned somewhere in the building. Andrew flexed his hands, fighting back a shiver along his skin. "I'm not like the people you mentioned. That's not why I'm here."

Katya raised her eyebrows. "Of course not."

"My mother is gone," he continued. "She left Russia so we could have a better life, but it was not how she expected it to be. She died not knowing how to live outside her own country. She didn't know what to do with her new life. She was so excited when the Wall came down in Berlin. It vindicated her reasons for leaving, but it didn't change the fact that she'd never been able to be herself in another country." The cold crept over him and he stepped toward her, as though for warmth. "I am not like those other people. I gave up a good job. I've left that world behind me. I've come to find my father. That's why I'm here."

For the first time Katya appeared unsettled, and it was a moment before she spoke. His breath hung in the air between them, almost reaching her.

"Why did you tell me this?"

The elevator opened.

Andrew blinked, seeing something change behind her eyes. Then spontaneously, as if in reply, he leaned toward her.

Katya moved away as his breath touched her mouth, and she stepped into the waiting elevator.

The doors closed on his eyes.

After that day Ilyin often invited Andrew to go out with his friends from the university. Each time she saw him, Katya observed with a sense of uneasy satisfaction that the foreigner remained drawn to her. Her own interest grew too, and she began to brood on the possibilities confronting her. Like most vain people, Andrew was oddly open to new things, his outlook expansive. She sensed his unconditional nature, and she found its possibilities tempting. There was something appealing about this quality next to Petya's aloofness or her father's frugal affection. The foreigner did not believe he could be hurt, but in this vulnerability Katya recognized something that might be called courage. It gave him an atmosphere of unexpected independence: his foreignness offered a novel kind of immunity from the expectations and constraints that accompanied the other men she knew. But it was Andrew's outburst that night in the hallway which ultimately assured her response. She was drawn to Andrew's need to redeem his mother's life, to discover his father. This connection between them found assurance in the meeting of glances when they met, where everything was still unspoken between them. In that space where people's eyes meet, their mutual attraction became a kind of first knowledge. A recognition of something that was still unnamed.

Then one evening when Katya left the library, she found Andrew outside waiting for her. It was already dark and he walked with her across the campus to where she caught the tram.

"Are you feeling settled here?" she said, knowing already why he was there.

"My aunt and Ilyin have made me welcome."

"You like your job?"

"I suppose I do."

They crossed the open square and stepped into the street, walking slowly along the Avenue of Soviets with its rows of bare trees. The air was cold and smelled of autumn. Standing under streetlights you could see your breath. Farther down they watched as people queued in front of a restaurant, their bodies stained with the glare of neon.

Katya glanced at him. "I saw some of your friends go in there the other night."

"They go there a lot."

"They like these new places."

He laughed. "They like what they know."

"Not you?"

"It's different for me."

"I don't understand."

"Even when I was a kid growing up, a part of me always knew I was from here. My mother left Russia to have me, but my dad was here." Andrew realized that he wanted badly for her to understand why he was here so that he could understand it himself. "My father did not go with her, though he could have. I always wondered why he chose not to. He knew she was pregnant, but he still wanted to go home. To be here. He was in the orchestra here." Andrew looked at his feet. "I guess it was a pretty good job."

They paused at the corner where the tram stopped. The streetlight here was broken, and they stood together in the shadow.

"You are angry with him."

"I'm not sure," Andrew looked up the street, weighing out his answer. "I guess I'll know when I see him."

"You are sure you want to do this?"

He shrugged. "I've never seen my father. Not even in a picture. I would like to meet him."

"Do you look like him?"

"I don't know," he shook his head. "But my mother gave me his name." Andrew smiled in spite of himself.

Katya tried to make out his expression in the darkness.

Just then a tram turned at the corner, revealing them in the unsteady glow of its headlights. A small smile passed across Andrew's face and, his head lowering, he appeared to look beyond her.

She squinted at the approaching brightness of the tram. It drew to the curb next to them. She felt Andrew's mouth on her own.

As the door opened he mumbled something in a mixture of English and Russian, and for a second she did not know in which language to answer. Instead she reached out and touched his face. A moment later she was inside the tram with all of its light, looking into the darkness to where she knew he must be standing.

When Katya came home that evening she found both her parents out. From the living room, she observed her brother on the balcony, and for a moment she stood at the window unseen, watching him. Her breath formed a film of mist on the glass, and as her brother began to fade from view she drew her palm across the pane. She stood watching the sadness in his face.

Petya smiled as he noticed her, and she opened the casement door and joined him.

"What are you doing out here?"

"Just watching."

Below them a crane was erecting one of the new billboards appearing around the city. On the horizon similar signs proclaimed running shoes and beer and denim clothing and restaurants in flashing lights.

"Foreigners are sprouting up everywhere."

"I wish sometimes they had not come at all," she frowned, immediately regretting her words.

"They are worrying," he admitted.

"They act as though they are saving us from ourselves. They don't understand that there was something here before they arrived..."

Her brother was quiet for a moment, and Katya knew he was thinking about what she had said. "Things had to change," he said, at last. "Yet I find it ironic that they come here preaching about economics and finances and markets when so few of them understand the real cost of things."

"Yes," she nodded. "Precisely."

"Still, I've met quite a lot of them and they're not bad people. You must see plenty of them at the university?"

Katya leaned over the balcony and closed her eyes. "I do."

"Besides, it will not always be this way."

She looked at him. "You don't think so?"

"All of this will cease to be special at some point," he said, his tone reassuring. "And we will finally stop seeing them as separate from us. There will come a time when we will forget that there is an east and west, that a border could keep us from everyone else in the world. These foreigners bring ideas that used to be banned. If their being here means anything, it is that nothing is forbidden anymore."

Katya squinted to make out her brother's face in the darkness.

His hand came to rest on her arm. "Are you all right?"

"You really think people will change?"

Petya paused, as though holding his breath before answering her. "Most of us will have to."

She turned again to see him, but this time his face was completely lost. "But not everyone."

142

"No," he murmured. "Not everyone."

The following week Lydia asked, as she usually did at that time of the year, if her daughter had friends who could help at Yasna Danielovna's *dacha*. Yasna Danielovna had been a childhood friend of Katya's grandmother, and every summer that she could remember Katya and her family had been invited to holiday there. As Yasna Danielovna grew older, the arrangement came to include helping the woman look after the gardens she kept. This agreement always included a share in the food. That past spring, Lydia and Katya had planted vegetables throughout the entire yard, and they now planned how to harvest the bulk of it with some help.

Katya asked Ilyin to help as he had in previous years, and he pointedly suggested bringing along his cousin.

She agreed, but tried to appear tentative. "Tell him he must work if he comes. This is no holiday in the country."

Andrew accepted the offer when Ilyin mentioned it. Andrew asked Emil, who could not go, but Adam agreed. Andrew reasoned that the Canadian would provide a buffer between him and Katya if things did not go well.

They left on a Saturday morning, having decided to make an early start. Katya and her mother had gone the previous evening, and would be waiting for them. When Andrew and Adam arrived, the station was just becoming busy and they found Ilyin in the crowd next to the entrance. Andrew introduced his friend, and after a few words they bought tickets at the blue kiosk next to the gate.

"You will like the *dacha*," Ilyin said. "It's a fine place."

They showed their tickets at the turnstile and went to find the train. By then the platform was crowded with people going to the country for the weekend. "There is time to walk around," Ilyin suggested, glancing at the large clock at the end of the station. "We won't get a seat now."

"I'm going to find a newspaper," Andrew said, but almost as soon as he left the conductors began letting people board.

Ilyin grabbed Adam's arm. "Hurry now."

They moved toward the closest car, pushing through the elbows and luggage until they reached the door. Inside they spread themselves out on a berth to keep others from squeezing in. "Don't let anyone sit," said Ilyin, and he hung out of the window to wave at Andrew who was looking for them on the platform. He joined them, negotiating a path amongst those forced to stand in the passageway.

Adam settled down for the ride, feeling cramped and hot, but happy to be seeing new things. They watched as their car drew away from the station, and soon they had passed out of the city. Ilyin was smiling and looking out the window at the fields and trees. "I like the country," he said.

For a time the train followed beside a river with small boats and people fishing, and everything was bright. The river gradually grew closer to them until the train seemed to be on top of it and then they were passing over and it was gone.

Andrew, who had been reading his paper, showed his cousin the front page: a photograph with the President looking heated and righteous. "What do you think of this?"

Ilyin waved dismissively. "What is there to think? It will all come to nothing."

"How can you be sure?" Adam wanted to know.

"When the crowd is holding guns, then I will think something is about to happen. But without guns there is no change. This is how things are." Ilyin produced a bottle from his bag and they passed it between themselves. Andrew set his paper aside, though he was not done with the topic and after a drink he launched his own retort.

No, Andrew maintained, if things went on like this the government would have to act. Perhaps, Ilyin conceded, but the President didn't have to worry because no one really wanted another revolution anyway. Of course they did – everyone needed the occasional revolution. Only someone from the West would say this. What did that mean? No one wanted an uprising because it meant bloodshed – had he not seen the monuments? He had seen the monuments. They seemed like bad advertising. Advertising? For the tourists, of course. Who cared about the tourists? No one cared about the tourists. Still, reminders of tyranny and bloodshed were not a big draw for outsiders. Beaches and amusement parks; these were more appealing. Ilyin didn't know about this, but he was sure history was not reassuring. Andrew was convinced something pleasant must have happened – surely Stalin, or Khrushchev at least, had helped a babushka across the street – why not a monument for this? No, it would be out of character – only tyranny and oppression. And don't leave out the winters. Who could forget the winters?

Ilyin turned to Adam, who, through all of this, had been looking out the window. "Your friend is quite something."

"He's drunk."

"You are drunk also?"

"Too early for me."

Ilyin shook his head. "People from the West cannot drink."

Andrew took exception. "I assure you, his are not the habits of the free world."

More denunciations were made, each followed by a drink and retorts of increasingly sloshy logic.

Sometime later a conductor appeared and moved up the crowded aisle. The man wore an ill-fitting uniform, and without his cap he looked squat and incomplete, like a roofless house. He demanded to see their tickets.

Ilyin paused, his amused expression replaced with suspicion. "Someone already looked at them."

"I will check them." The man had shallow eyes, and to Adam his voice seemed to be mocking them.

"You're checking everyone's tickets?"

"Do you have your ticket?"

"No."

"Then there is a fine."

"A fine for not having a ticket?"

"Five hundred roubles."

"Then here is my ticket."

The man did not bother to look at the ticket. "Also for being a disturbance."

"How much is that?"

"Five hundred roubles."

"Some coincidence."

He turned to Andrew, licking his lips. "For you, also. And your friend," nodding at Adam.

Andrew stared. "What?"

There was a flicker behind the official's eyes, and for an instant he wavered before mustering. "Come on then."

"He knows you're a foreigner," Ilyin said in English.

"How?" Adam asked, but no one bothered to answer him.

Those in the aisle watched with interest.

Ilyin glanced at the man's uniform and made a sound like a pig. "Get lost," he said, and winked at Andrew.

The conductor frowned, not comprehending. "Well?"

"Piss off."

"That's right," Andrew said. "Piss off."

The man glared, his face growing red. "There are consequences. You cannot flout the law..."

Ilyin sneered. "You mean your thief's law?"

A man across the aisle laughed. "That's right, piss off."

The conductor glared at those about him, then backed away.

"Look at him – pickpocket swine. *Every citizen must carry out his duty with honesty,*" Ilyin quoted and made more snorting sounds.

The conductor did not turn around until he reached the end of the car.

Andrew stopped laughing. "Will he make trouble?"

His cousin shrugged. "What can he do?"

"We should tell someone at the next station."

Ilyin scoffed. "This is what I was saying. There are thousands of people like that man in my country, and most of them have the guns. People can protest all they want. Go ahead and tell someone. But to take away a man's gun you need one yourself. It is like this in every country. Even yours."

They did not see the conductor again, and everyone forgot about him as soon as they stepped off the train and onto the wooden platform where Katya was waiting in the morning sun.

Yasna Danielovna's *dacha* sat in a group of similar cottages, each with its own fenced yard of gardens and fruit trees. It was a small, carefully managed lot, with a storage shed and privy. The outbuildings were painted yellow to match the cottage, which was constructed after the War in the old style with heavy working shutters, and a roof of wood shingles that had turned green on the south side with moss. Katya took them inside, showing them a room where they left their things. There was a large bed that they would share, and a table and basin for washing.

They went out to stand behind the buildings where her mother was working next to Yasna Danielovna. Lydia smiled tautly at these foreigners, and with some stiffness she introduced their host.

Though bent with age, the old woman held herself with an air of significance when she met them. Her hand extended to each of the guests with unconscious poise, and Adam felt he should bow as he touched it.

Yasna Danielovna seemed pleased to have so many guests. "You are all from the university?" she inquired in English. "How thoughtful that you have come to help. Do you speak Russian?" she asked, nodding to Andrew and Adam.

"Only my cousin," said Ilyin, who had been waiting for a chance to speak.

The old woman looked over the American. "Very good."

Ilyin grinned daringly. "It would be, except that it means we must all listen to him."

Yasna Danielovna smiled. "And you?" she said, turning to Adam.

"*Nyet*." Adam shifted as her attention settled on him. He shook his head.

She clapped her hands. "Why he speaks Russian just fine!"

People laughed in a way that made Adam feel relieved.

Only Lydia felt uncomfortable. She seemed to Adam to be dry and very thin compared to Yasna Danielovna, like a dead twig next to a living branch. Soon however Ilyin and Andrew made her easier with their joking, and she went off with them to see the garden.

Katya and Adam stayed behind and talked with Yasna Danielovna under the birch trees.

The yard was dominated by three plots in various stages of harvest, the tendrils and branches and fruit tangled about one another in a defiant embrace against the fall. At each plot Lydia paused to point out particular plants to the guests, who listened and looked about. Andrew asked questions intended to please her. When they returned to the house, they found

Katya and Adam putting out bread, pickled tomatoes, cheese and tea. They sat on benches beneath the birch tree and ate. Afterwards Andrew and Ilyin shared a cigarette while Katya discussed the work that needed to be done, showing everyone where the tools were kept and the place where baskets were stored.

Crouching in a corner of the yard that afternoon, Adam felt the satisfaction that always came over him when he worked in the soil. Using an old nail, he pried beets from the earth, separating leaves and roots into different baskets. Now and then he paused to look at the high waving grass along the fence.

"I like this place," Adam told Lydia, who had come by with a clay jar. It was cold water, and he drank until the top of his head hurt. The old woman's eyes narrowed as she watched him.

When she was gone he glanced about the yard at the others, who seemed to him still and serene in the pale light. Shadows stretched across the path like sleeping dogs. The air vibrated with the last hum of insects. Leaves collected in the grass; everywhere it smelled of autumn.

"It is nice that you are here," Katya observed to Andrew, who was working next to her. "I mean that I'm glad you could help."

He looked up and smiled self-consciously. She wore her hair back, and her face was pink and hot from sun. She looked away before he could speak, and for the first time he was certain that she also felt this thing which drew him to her.

"I knew what you meant."

It was late in the afternoon when Petya arrived from the city. He already knew Ilyin, and together they went with Andrew to look at the gardens. Adam stayed back to finish washing the potatoes he'd dug up. When he was done he carried them to the shed, but stopped at the door. Lydia stood looking at the food they'd collected. As Adam set down the basket she looked away, but not before he caught the look in her eyes.

That evening they talked over bowls of soup with sour cream and bread, boiled carrots with onion, and afterwards tea. Everyone was hungry and the food left them with the satisfied sensation one has after working outside. Birds called to one another from the birch trees around the cottage. The sun hung low in the west, its light falling gold and red on their faces. A breeze carried the smell of leaves and grass, the sweet odour mingling with the sound of their voices. Throughout the meal Adam found himself watching Katya's brother. Though he spoke often enough to the others, Adam sensed a reserve in the man's gaze as he talked. 'This is a good chess player,' he thought.

Petya had brought some vodka with him that revived Andrew and Ilyin, and even Lydia found herself enjoying the cousins' effusive but erratic banter. As the meal came to an end, Petya grew quiet. When Petya spoke, Adam had the feeling that he'd been waiting with a calculated patience before beginning.

"So," Petya began, looking across the table at the two foreigners. "Are we Russians what you expected?"

Ilyin rested back on his stool and glanced at his cousin.

"A little," Andrew confessed.

Petya stretched across the table to pour everyone another drink. "Can you explain?"

Andrew looked at Katya. "I expected you all to be different from the way you are. I thought you would be mysterious and vaguely hostile. Certainly more closed than you appear now." He glanced again at Katya in a way that made her frown. "But I've come to see that the differences between us are just in the words we use."

Yasna Danielovna clapped her hands. "What a diplomat you are! You have replied with something polite and enigmatic, and yet I'm sure no one here knows what you have said."

Ilyin grinned. "Yes, what was all that about? Do you mean that we are just the same as people in the West? Or that you are the same as us? I don't understand you, but I think I should be offended. Katya, can you translate my cousin's murky statement for us?"

Katya was very still, careful not to move her fingers which stretched like pale cracks across the weathered surface of the table. "I think in this case we should allow the speaker to explain himself."

Andrew looked around the table. "Of course there are differences between people from different cultures, just as there are between individuals. What I am saying though is that when we come together as we have today, these differences seem less obvious, less important. We must all work. We must all love."

Yasna Danielovna smiled. "My American guest, I cannot decide whether you are a Communist or a Romantic."

"Or just a fool," Ilyin finished.

"I am none of these," Andrew interjected. "I am a cosmopolitan, if there is really such a thing. There are contrasts between both our countries, to be sure. But when you strip away the flags, it is a similar life which each of us is living, wherever we are living it. We all work and love and die. We are all someone's child."

Petya became quiet, staring thoughtfully into his glass. "What you say is well meant, I am sure. But the psychology of a country is a special, even immutable, thing."

Andrew looked at him. "Have you been to the West?"

"Of course."

"Was it as you expected?"

Petya offered the thin smile often used by his sister. "There are many contradictions in the West, if you will forgive me for being candid. I have noticed that most of these contradictions come from your ignorance of others. I will give you an instance of this. I remember I was on my way to a conference last year. There was a couple from America in the airport and they were commenting on the prevalence of pornography in Russia. They seemed to me very serious, moral people – and they no doubt would have much that was good to say about my country's new politics – but the ubiquity of pornographic material clearly offended them."

Andrew raised his eyebrows. "Not everyone in the West shares this attitude. Most people would just ignore it."

"I'm sure that is the case," Petya said. "But this is not to say they would be any closer to understanding why Russians are condoning of pornography."

Andrew shrugged.

"What no one in the West seems to understand," he continued, "is that only a few years ago such things were banned, precisely as that couple at the airport wanted them to be. Pornography was illegal here. It came to my country at the same time as milkshakes and denim jeans. It appeared with German cars and Japanese televisions, with British music and American movies. It seems that we could not have grandmother's apple pie, as you say, without also seeing her daughter's tits," and here Petya looked hard at Andrew.

"A cosmopolitan must, above all things, understand the implication of differences. I hope you will come to see that many things you knew in your country can mean something quite different in mine."

Andrew emptied his glass.

Katya suggested taking a walk.

Dew had fallen, and the air was fresh and chill with it. They left the *dacha* and followed a road past a farm and climbed a hill, where they sat among the grass and watched the sky grow orange. They spoke in hushed voices, unwilling to break the silence around them. Below them was the huddle of cottages, half hidden by the smoke loitering over the roofs.

After a long while they all stood and walked back to the *dacha*, darkness coming at their backs.

Lydia and Yasna Danielovna went to bed when they returned, and the others sat up talking in the kitchen. Petya had a short-wave radio, and they listened first to the BBC and then to a jazz station from Vienna. They were tired after their day, and the music had a soothing effect. One by one people began to turn in. When Petya went to bed, he took the radio, its faraway voices trailing with him down the hall. Only Katya and Andrew remained.

Insects sang to each other outside. Katya watched a spider in the kitchen window. After a moment they became aware of the buzzing of the light above them.

Andrew stared at her hands on the table.

Katya watched him, feeling her own attraction collapse the last obstacle between them. He began to speak but she placed a finger on her lips, giving him, in her own way, the reply he sought.

They stood and went together into the night. It was dark, and as they stepped outside Andrew wondered where she had gone. Finding her hand, he drew her closer. The darkness became a space between them and the cottage, so that the sound of the radio seemed to come from a great distance.

Already half asleep, Adam listened in his room as Petya searched for a clear signal, bringing into the cottage rags of voices and music quilted together with static.

Outside, the radio was all but lost to the quickening of their breathing. Trying to be quiet, Andrew struggled with her as they found one of the benches. Katya shivered as his hand slipped inside her shirt, and she exhaled into his neck. Around them floated the distant sound of the shortwave radio – Latino dictators and Baptist preachers, a Nebraskan conspiracy theorist, Bowie and Berlioz, a Munich cooking show featuring Thai rice dishes.

To Adam, who turned restlessly in bed, these voices seemed like the salvo of distant guns in his dreams.

The next morning Katya woke and dressed in the silent cottage. She took a jar from the kitchen cupboard and went outside where she found someone standing beneath the birch tree. "You are up."

Adam smiled at her, though without surprise. "You, too."

She turned from him and looked toward the road.

"We need milk."

"May I come along?"

"Of course."

They passed out of the yard and followed the road into the countryside. There had been a frost which glazed the fields of turned earth.

"Our host is quite something."

Katya smiled. "Yes. She is an old friend of ours. I have known her my entire life. But I think I like her most because of – how do you say it? Her *charm*. She is like a whisper from the past. When she speaks I sometimes think I hear in her voice an echo of long ago. I hear its mutter as she walks in the garden. She went to school with my grandmother – I love her for this. They saw the carriages of the nobility in the streets, princesses in the park. They remember the Revolution, and what came after."

Adam whistled. "I hadn't thought of her life in that way."

"People her age have lived in such different worlds. I know only what is around me. Of course I remember how things were before the changes, but not like they do. Yasna Danielovna lived through war and upheaval, invasion and starvation. I wish she would talk more about those things. My grandmother tried to tell me, but I was still young and would not listen."

"I like to think that we are still young."

She smiled sadly. "Not in the same way. Not innocently young. I cannot be oblivious the way I used to. I miss being innocent. I miss not knowing."

Adam looked into the fields. "You miss feeling clean inside."

"Yes, that's it, isn't it? I would like to be like that again. But I won't. That feeling is gone. It has been taken away. Life takes that from us. We are only clean when we are young, when we are beginning.

"That's our problem, I think. Yasna Danielovna is old enough to be comforted by what she knows, though she has seen so much that could not have been good. Still even in the difficult memories she must find comfort, because she survived them. But people our age don't have that. We must find our way without such perspective. We know about the danger, but we don't yet know if we can endure it. When I think of myself becoming old, I think of my grandmother and Yasna Danielovna. I hope to be like them. I would like to know life, and yet not turn away from it. I don't need to see the whole world. But I would like to know the part of it I have lived in."

Adam listened as they walked, uncertain how to respond.

"I like this time of the day," Katya said suddenly. "There is a special stillness."

The clouds had moved on and the sky was open. Leaves scattered along the road. Poplars stood young and tall, their bark silvered by the paleness of the morning light.

"Sometimes I can't stand such quiet," Adam blurted, feeling that he must say something. "All that silence is just the surface of something deeper. It's like staring into a well. You can look in it and see your reflection, but below that there are things which are way over your head."

She turned as they walked so she could face him, the empty jar between them. "You are a poet, Adam."

He smiled. "No, but I wish I was."

They had come to a farm. There was a small house with a yard and, behind it, a barn and the sound of animals. A dog barked at them through the fence. Katya looked over his shoulder. "Here we are."

A woman appeared in the yard with a metal pail, and Katya went to her while Adam stood at the gate. She knelt over the jar as the woman filled it from her pail. A baby's cry came from inside the house, angry and accusing. Katya paid the woman and they headed back. Adam offered to carry the milk.

The jar was warm, and on the road they stopped to drink from it. They stood for a moment, neither speaking, and watched the hastening clouds.

"Are you enjoying being away?"

"I haven't travelled much, really."

"I meant, do you enjoy the adventure of being away from your home."

He glanced into the jar. "Nothing's the way I expected it would be."

"I see."

"I didn't mean to offend you."

"I am not insulted."

"But you're angry. I see that you are."

She hesitated, weighing her thoughts before speaking. "We see your faces every time you find something embarrassing in a stairwell or you are bothered by something that is different from the way it is in your country. You make us self-conscious in ways that we do not like. We know, each of us, that ours is a great country at its heart. We sense our capacity for future greatness, but also the mistakes that weigh on us. Of all the peoples in the world right now, we are perhaps the ones most uncertain of ourselves. Yet you foreigners, you come here and you do not understand any of this. You are contemptuously ignorant of your own mistakes, your own travesties. You can see only the ways we are not like you, and that has an effect on us. Especially now," and Katya paused, sensing he wanted her to stop talking, then continuing anyway. "People like you come here and disturb things, but soon you find what you wanted or you don't or it's too hard, and you leave."

"Is this why you hate us?"

"You don't know what we hate."

"Be careful not to blame us for everything that is wrong."

Katya flushed. Then, without knowing why, she said to him, "My family is in trouble." The words slipping from her mouth, like a note under a door. "We are almost destitute."

Adam became still and he saw that she was looking at him. "Your mother knows. Doesn't she?"

"She is the only one."

"It's because of the changes?"

She nodded. "We are not who we used to be."

"Could your father find a better job?"

Her eyebrows joined with irritation. "You do not understand. He works for the Party. He's a *communist*," she said, over pronouncing the word in English. "His whole life is the Party. He cannot abandon this. It is unthinkable..."

Adam was quiet for a moment. "And your brother?"

Katya made a sound like a leaking tire. "The university pays him in roubles, which buy less and less all the time. No, my mother and I will make life work until we cannot. I sell things and the money lets us continue. I want to do this, you understand? It is the first real thing I have ever done for my mother. She counts on me to keep the others from seeing. But one day, perhaps soon, it will not be enough and they will all have to see."

"Do you know what will happen then?"

Her face softened. "It won't be good. I can see that much."

He stopped in the road and looked at her, watching the way she walked through the light. "Why are you telling me this?"

She had turned and was gazing at him now with open fear. For a moment it was as though Clare was staring at him. Katya opened her mouth to speak. Adam was very still, waiting to hear the words she would say.

But she turned back to the road. "The others will be up soon."

That day they worked in the garden. There was a new urgency in Katya, and she spoke very little to the others as they gathered food against the coming winter. When they were done, the baskets and burlap sacks were stacked next to the door like a wall of sandbags.

PART II

Now, my co-mates and brothers in exile....

Shakespeare, *As You Like It*

IVAN SAT at the small desk in the extra room he used as an office. The only sign of emotion on his face lurked in his eyes, where thoughts seemed to seep along the capillaries. Lydia came in to ask him something, but, recognizing the look on his face, turned and closed the door. He was sometimes overcome with these moments of paralysis, brought on by thoughts that hung about the back of his mind, where fragments of faces and voices waited.

He had blacked out next to the truck on that July afternoon on the outskirts of Leningrad. He would have bled to death if it had not been for a fleeing officer, who, seeing the boy, carried Ivan as they retreated, staunching the wound with his own belt and the shirt of a dead soldier.

It was almost a week later when the boy emerged from unconsciousness in the basement of a hospital glutted with casualties. He lay on the floor among broken and unlimbed bodies. The place was poorly lit, and the passing of days was marked only by the appearance of orderlies who arrived each morning to remove those who had died in the night. Voices and faces materialized in the gloom, and then the boy would be moved or adjusted in some way. The rest of the time, Ivan lay in a darkness clotted with unbodied pleas, stench and his own fevered raving. Old women with water passed among the wounded like grey memories. Their dresses were torn and ragged where men had grasped them seeking comfort. Voices in the dark called for mothers, wives, God.

For two weeks Ivan remained in this basement, his existence, like that of the city, oscillating between death and survival. At last a face, haggard though oddly familiar, appeared before the boy.

His name was Anatoly Sergeiovich Subov, a Red Army officer. He had carried the boy from the battlefield. His visit to Ivan was brief, though over the month which followed he returned twice to see the recovering child. After the officer's third visit, Ivan was moved to a hallway in one of the upper floors, where the air was better and there was daylight and activity. This move, he was told, was a sign of hope.

"Either they believe you will live, or there is no more room for you to die," Subov laughed. "However you look at it, this is good news for you."

Reports of the fighting passed through the hospital, brought by ambulance drivers who paused long enough to swallow cold tea and update a nurse or doctor on the struggle. The information was sometimes encouraging, other times desperate.

All this the boy watched through the terror and pain which wracked his small body. If casualties were heavy he was forgotten, and when the nurses at last returned they would find him pale and sweat-soaked from the pain which burned through his missing arm. Then a nurse might kneel by him, whispering in his ear and running her palm over his hair until the morphine soothed the coals in the lost limb. When Ivan's dressing was being changed, the boy turned his face from the stump, gaping through his tears at the stars which looked down at him in the window.

During the long stretches of loneliness, he was left to stare in awe at the terrible fragments of men who lay about him. During these times his thoughts yearned for his mother and father, and in the night he would sob for those primal bonds by which one is known to and belongs in the world. One night his grief was interrupted by a soldier's cries for his own mother, and the next morning Ivan watched as the nurses buttoned his uniform and combed his hair before orderlies took the body out to the open grave behind the hospital.

The slow misery of healing was interrupted only by Subov, who wandered the crowded corridors looking for Ivan. The officer always brought news, though he seemed to seek information more than he was willing to share it, and he inquired often during his visits about the boy's background and family. But it was weeks later before Ivan's release from hospital, that the purpose of Subov's questions became clear.

"I have made inquiries about your parents," he said, speaking with what Ivan would come to recognize as the soldier's matter-of-fact approach to awkward subjects. "Your mother was evacuated just before the rail lines were cut. This area is now behind enemy lines. Your father's unit was assigned to a position which fell in August. As to his fate we can only guess..."

For a moment Subov looked at the boy, hesitating. "We have a flat, my wife and I. You are alone. Winter is coming. Your chances will be better with us."

The boy's journey to Subov's home two weeks later revealed the urgency of the situation. It had been months since Ivan had seen the city, and he was shocked to find it so altered. He gaped at his own reflection in store windows pasted with strips of newspaper, the antiaircraft guns on buildings, sandbagged entranceways, and apartment blocks gutted by fire. Trenches and rifle positions were set up throughout parks, while intersections and major streets had been cluttered with anti-tank obstacles. Walls and tram stops were covered with placards:

> Citizens! During the artillery shelling, this side of the street is especially dangerous.

Lampposts stood contorted by blasts, while the horizon was striped with ribbons of smoke.

People went about with anxious glances at the sky. A film of ash and dust rested on everything. At one corner the boy stared at the wing of a plane which jutted like a limb out of its own ashes.

"What is that?" he asked, pointing at the charred insignia.

"That," Subov replied, "is the enemy."

Subov lived in a modest flat which sat beneath a music school. The building stood in a cluster of grey tenements which looked down on one of the city's canals. As they entered the stairwell, the boy met with the sound of a piano and someone singing. Subov waited at the landing while Ivan caught his breath. The boy stood panting, watching Subov, who had the same harried look as the doctors and nurses in the hospital. His face was creased and unshaven, and wherever he stood his eyes moved restlessly from one thing to another, betraying dark preoccupations. The officer's gaze met the boy's, and each stared at the other in the half light of that stairwell, the distant music hanging between them. And then the agitation in Subov's eyes stilled, and Ivan knew that the man was seeing only him.

A feeling of warmth came over him and the boy felt a tremor of emotion that threatened the grip he had on himself. "I am frightened," said Ivan, his voice a whisper.

Subov nodded, still holding the boy's gaze in his own.

"My mother – my father…"

The officer reached out to comfort the boy, inadvertently grasping the empty sleeve of Ivan's coat. But even so the boy felt the pressure of Subov's hand on the lost arm and the ghost skin prickled at the man's touch.

"You saw the city, boy. You know what is happening. You are not the only child to be separated from your family."

Ivan bit at his lip, but did not let go of the officer's stare. "My parents are dead, aren't they?"

Subov set his jaw. "Yes. They are."

Ivan held the man's eyes for a moment longer, finding security in the honesty of Subov's gaze. There, in that dark stairwell in a city under siege, Ivan began the orphan's intimate, tentative transfer of trust.

For the rest of his life, Ivan never forgot the moment he stepped into Subov's flat. At once he left the damp and dark of the hallway and was met with a succession of sensations that stopped him where he stood: there was the humid smell of boiled potatoes and tea, the sudden amber light of a small table lamp next to the door, and, from a different room, the sound of someone humming. The next moment the voice stopped, and then a woman was before him, kneeling so she could look at him face-to-face.

"This is Larissa Ilyinichna," Subov said. "My wife."

She leaned forward to get a closer look at the strange, damaged boy. She had dark hair that fell below her shoulders, and a pink round face that reminded Ivan of his mother. She smelled dry and sweet, like new paper. Her gaze was intent but slightly aloof, the way adults looked when thinking something quite unrelated to what they are saying. She was disquieted by the boy's wound, and her eyes paused at the empty sleeve of his coat. When she spoke her voice was soft and uncertain, as though approaching an injured animal.

Ivan flushed. He held out his hand, at the same instant noticing the fraying sleeve of his coat.

She felt the boy flinch as they touched.

"Don't worry," Subov said to his wife. "He talks eventually."

That first night, Ivan lay in a small cot listening to the breathing of Subov and his wife. He felt disoriented without the commotion of the hospital, the rushing of nurses and doctors, the conversations of the wounded. From another room he could hear the dog moan in its sleep. Ivan stared at the new ceiling, tracing its cracks and patterns as his mind tried to absorb this new situation. His life – which only three months ago, had been populated by the familiar faces of his family and friends – was now irretrievably lost, those people obliterated, inexplicably ripped from him like his arm. Since coming to the hospital, Ivan had stopped trying to anticipate even the simplest events of life, like the next meal or who would be in the bed beside him when he woke. And so as he lay there, he instinctively resisted thoughts about the next day, though he found himself trying to picture the flat in the daylight, the sound of Larissa's voice, the dog playing on the carpet, Subov's stare.

'Stop it,' the boy thought. 'It may all be gone when I wake. Everything could be gone.'

But the next day Subov and Larissa were there. In the washroom, Ivan found his clothes dry on the line, and he dressed, smelling of soap for the first time since his life changed. After they ate, Larissa took him with her to walk the dog along the canal, speaking to him softly of life in the city since the siege.

"I will get you a ration card," she informed him. "But first you must find some sort of job. I know people who can help," she added. "You shouldn't look for just anything. One receives larger rations for jobs related to the city's defence."

Within a few days the boy was assigned to help at the Winter Palace where Larissa worked, while at night he joined a squad organized by tenants to protect the building during bombardments.

Ivan met the others from his squad on the roof during an air raid. From here the squad could see the city's chimneys and church domes, as they searched for planes. His first turn on the roof was a clear night, the air a dark blue and smelling of leaves. Blimps hung in the sky, their bellies pale and silver like the bloated carp you saw floating in the canals. During the third hour there came bursts of flak from the centre of the city. Soon they heard the approach of planes. Shock flashes appeared as the bombs landed, followed a moment later by the hollow concussion. Yellow blades of flame cut open the darkness. The glow exposed entire streets, so that you could identify neighbourhoods which had been hit. The dome of St. Isaac's shimmered like a moon on the horizon, while the waters of the Neva were lit up like a vein of fire running through the city.

If the view was not so horrible, someone admitted, it would be beautiful.

In the following weeks a strange casualness pervaded these gatherings on the roof. It became an opportunity to trade gossip. Friendships developed, advice was exchanged, books shared. A chessboard appeared. One woman read aloud to them during the attacks from Pushkin and Byron, Blok and Milton, her voice a wavering candle against the night's violence:

I sung of Chaos and eternal Night;
Taught, by the heavenly Muse, to venture down
The dark descent, and up to re-ascend,
Though hard and rare; thee I revisit safe,
And feel thy sovereign vital lamp; but thou
Revisitest not these eyes, that roll in vain
To find thy piercing ray, and find no dawn...

Ivan remained alone among his squad. His mind began to absorb what had happened to him, as he stared at the city's destruction. His arm was still only partly healed, and in the phantom pain which echoed from this lost limb he found a prosthetic voice for the emotion inside him. A terrible cramp, like a burning sensation, sometimes swept up the space where his arm should be, and he would clutch at the empty sleeve, massaging the absent muscles and tendons until the pain faded. From the rooftop he looked into the horizon, imagining the battlefield that circled the city. Sometimes he felt sure his arm was still under the shattered truck. And then he would wonder if he could move his dead fingers out there beneath the vehicle. The feeling of his arm was real. One sense told him it was alive, another that it was no longer part of him. Perhaps somewhere was his arm, the fingers wiggling in the mud. This thought left him feeling unstable and frightened with hope.

For a child living safely with his parents, fantasies of abandonment are a dream of escape. But Ivan had fallen headlong into nightmare. Sitting on that roof surrounded by the darkness and the fire, he wept not only for his phantom

182

arm, but also for the family taken from him, wondering where they could have gone. His parents' faces were no longer certain, their images broken and fragmented in his mind. The new world created by war did not include his parents, and so on that rooftop it seemed as though they might never have existed. Why could he still feel his arm but not see their faces? The question wrenched him with guilt. Were his parents farther from him than his lost arm? Could a person be farther from you than something that was gone – what was farther away than death? Did his arm have a stronger claim on him than his mother, whose own body he'd once been part of? Did this mean his parents were dead, but not his arm? Had it been rescued also, by some retreating person? Maybe it was waiting for him in a hospital, waiting for him to come looking for it... But why hadn't his parents found him? Were they looking for him? Were they in the city, too?

The lasting horror of pain is the aloneness. Survivors of calamities – the burned, the accident victim, the bereaved – will seek each other out because of this. They find not only an echo of their own pain, but the language of shared grief.

Only in childbirth is the sufferer accompanied. The first thing we do to a trauma victim is touch, that first and last of languages. Of course suffering loves company.

A morbid longing often overtook Ivan, and he sometimes thought that if he could remember his parents' faces, then they might see his hand wherever they were, and touch it, and he would feel them again. He began to dream that he could find his parents through his lost arm, which wasn't really lost at all but still trapped under the truck somewhere. He could see his mother and father in the crowd, searching for him, and he waved and cried out their names. His mother always reached him first, kneeling with him in the mud and stroking his arm, though it lay under the truck. Always his father was farther behind, but coming. But each time his father fell over the body of the screaming soldier, and at that instant Ivan would wake to the concussion of bombs falling on the city. Surrounded with darkness the boy waited for the shells, feeling his arbitrary place in the surrounding disorder. He stared into the sky of stars, each one a potential plane, an angel of death high above.

One night he watched with the others in his squad as a plane fell out of the sky over their neighbourhood. It came down on fire, rolling slowly in a death fall. Those on the roof cowered as it passed over their heads. But the boy did not flinch. For an instant Ivan saw a man in one of the gun turrets which glowed with the flame and hell inside it. Pressed against the glass the man's face looked out at him. An instant later he was wrenched into darkness with the primeval scream of the dying plane.

Ivan followed the plane as it fell among the buildings behind him, waving to the enemy with his invisible hand. The plane exploded, and Ivan felt something hot and dark spread across his chest and he shivered with the special warmth of hate. The other members of his squad watched dumbly as this usually remote child laughed and gestured at the flames. Whoever Ivan had been up to that moment, whatever portion of what we call innocence still remained in him, passed away that night.

But if the world outside was on fire, in Subov's flat Ivan found the shelter he craved. The couple took an active interest in the boy, including him in the routines and rhythms of their lives.

Larissa gave him jobs to do around the flat, books he might read. She introduced him to the woman who ran the music school above their flat, showing the boy the rows of pianos which stood along one wall.

"You could take lessons," Larissa offered.

"Yes," Ivan agreed, though inside he resisted the idea. He flexed his phantom fingers. The thought of such a thing was too difficult to imagine. It was a future that belonged to the past.

Larissa still met with her students at the university and arranged research projects through the museum. Recitals for new compositions were organized, lectures were written and attended. She went to every event, careful to miss nothing that life offered. The small, unappreciated things of life before the war suddenly became incredibly important, as though people sensed that you could hang on to these things, like pieces of a sinking ship. A journal was planned, and Larissa was asked to sit as one of the editors. Around them the city burned.

Larissa, who was an anthropologist, worked cataloguing and researching the collections in the Winter Palace. Through the summer of 1941 she had been busy along with the rest of the museum staff packing the most valuable artefacts for evacuation. Two trainloads, carrying one and a half million pieces of art, had been sent deep into the country for hiding. A third trainload had been boxed, though the rail lines were destroyed before it could be sent. Like the rest of the Palace's staff, she now spent much of her time trying to protect its remaining treasures. Each morning Ivan went with her to the Palace, where he was put to work in the massive chambers and storage rooms. By then even a one-armed boy was useful.

They boarded up windows in the Palace's rooms so that the galleries, parlours, dining rooms, salons and halls gradually became caverns, shutting out the world and locking the museum in shadowy grandeur. Ivan worked alongside students from the Conservatoire and the Academy of Arts who piled sand for firefighting in each room of the Palace, later filling the entire Athena gallery to protect its porcelain collection from the shelling. In September he helped to dismantle the gun collections, which were used to outfit various battalions set up to defend the city.

Using a sack slung over one shoulder, Ivan hauled sand from a barge on the canal, carrying it among the academics and curators still busy removing paintings and sculptures. Here the boy's modest origins were eclipsed by the ceiling of the Jordan staircase, the hundreds of crates sandwiched between the white pillars of the Rastrelli Gallery, the sombre forest of marble in the Hall of Twenty Columns, the canopy of chandeliers and skylights. On these trips back and forth through the Palace, he was overwhelmed, never before having seen such fineness, such opulent space. The hallways he traversed each day were cluttered with hundreds of busts – politicians and prophets, mistresses and poets, dukes, ottomans, philosophers and heretics, sovereigns, gods – stacked together in corners and along walls for their own protection. During one raid, a shell landed so close the blast knocked Ivan unconscious, and when he finally woke the boy found Rousseau staring calmly at him.

In the Palace there was room after room of gutted grandeur. Thousands of vacant frames hung on the walls, or lay on floors like dry bones. These empty frames looked now onto a blank horizon, so that, like the boarded windows around them, you wondered what lay beyond, what you were supposed to have seen. For the boy they became monuments to things that no longer existed, like his arm. Without the canvases which they once held, these frames were left void of denotation, clocks without time.

The boy sometimes spent weeks alone with Larissa, accompanying her in the queues for food or running errands. Subov's unit of engineers was assigned to inspect and maintain the city's defences, and this meant he was rarely at home. Larissa was more and more anxious and upset, though Ivan also sensed the deep vigour and courage that sustained her.

As the siege went on, Ivan became affected with attacks of nervousness. He was sometimes overwhelmed with panic, unable to stop shaking or stuttering. When this happened Larissa calmed him, pressing back his hair and whispering to him until he was still. Ivan became anxious about his proximity to her, so that he always knew how many steps he was from her, the way people now gauged their daily errands in relation to bomb shelters. He leaned against her on the streetcar, took her hand when they were walking. At night, if the shaking returned to him, he would crawl into her room to touch the bed on which she slept. Ivan found he could endure the destruction, the bodies in the street, even the aching of his lost arm by concentrating on the memory of her touch.

When Subov was home everyone strained to be happy. They would sit and play records, clapping while he and the boy took turns dancing with Larissa. Sometimes Subov would return from the front with a bottle of vodka, and he and his wife would drink and smoke Pamir cigarettes and he would tell her about the fighting. To the boy, Subov talked always about the Party. Ivan's own parents had had little interest in politics, but he found in himself a natural enthusiasm for the officer's messianic visions.

"The Party does not just shape our lives, it gives them meaning," he counselled. "It is like a lens through which an individual's actions are magnified by the effort of all members. Its accomplishments are the accomplishments of all who participate in it. And so each citizen becomes great, part of an army destined to change the world..."

Subov took Ivan to a mass meeting in Tauride Palace, where veterans of the Revolution spoke to the Young Communists. Here the moment of patriotism caught Ivan, who thrilled at the speakers' stories of sacrifice. As the meeting ended he joined the others in an oath to die defending the city. They turned him away, however, when he tried to enlist. He watched, downcast, as hundreds were organized into units and marched straight from the rally to the front. Later Subov intervened and the boy was given a place as a propaganda youth officer. His first assignment involved going through the city with cans of paint, changing street names, or concealing the numbers on buildings. It was said that the fascists had collected hundreds of maps of the city before the invasion. The propaganda unit was sent to confound the enemy's plans. Street signs were moved or completely changed, entire blocks had their addresses altered. If the enemy came, they would find the language of the city erased.

As winter approached, starvation came like a slow rigor mortis upon the city. Hunger worked like a maggot that crawled from belly to limbs to brain, hollowing a person from the inside. During a bombardment, Ivan saw a horse get struck down by a shell. He immediately fell upon the animal with a dozen others, cutting away limbs and flesh and smuggling them home furtively like treasure.

By then the Luftwaffe had been diverted to the campaign on Moscow, and air raids were replaced by artillery barrages which descended on the city.

In November, starvation and disease took more people than the shelling. That month ten thousand died of hunger. By December it was fifty thousand. In January three or four thousand people perished each day; February, the shortest month, ended with the deaths of two hundred thousand. Each week was worse. Amid the ice and snow appeared drifts of bodies stacked in courtyards or outside of apartments. Others lay for weeks where they had died. Research animals in universities and hospitals disappeared. Pigeons and crows were trapped and eaten. Bark was stripped from trees and used in bread making. Ointments, oils, pastes – anything derived from seed or grain or fat was consumed in one form or another. Lipstick was used for frying food; glue was stripped from wallpaper and made into a jelly; plaster, linseed and paper were mixed with flour to bake biscuits; leather shoes, gloves and belts were boiled for soup. At Larissa's request, Ivan drowned the family dog, and then helped her butcher the tiny carcass into strips of meat which she froze on their balcony. People perished in doorways, heads resting in their hands, brows creased with their final thoughts. Trolleys and buses sat in the road at their last stops, sometimes with passengers still frozen inside. Any form of central heating had long since halted, so Larissa constructed a makeshift stove from sheet metal and bricks. To stay warm in the evenings they sat around the stove, feeding it with pieces of furniture or scavenged wood. Ivan took daily foraging trips, searching bodies for bits of food, ration cards or valuables. Entire buildings were emptied by starvation, and the boy joined the gangs who pillaged abandoned flats – stealing home with fuel and blankets left behind by the dead. Larissa passed all of the valuables she owned to the boy, who took them along with anything else he could salvage to a squat building near the Turkish market, where he traded these things for single slices of bread made with sawdust. A family watch or ring preserved for generations was exchanged now for a single day of survival. A twenty-year-old necklace now bought you as many hours of existence, a hundred-year-old samovar could extend your life by five days. In those months, inheritances were traded for a few moments of the future.

One evening as he was coming home, Ivan met a girl in the doorway tying up her boot. A bombardment had started, and he was hurrying to join his squad on the roof. As he passed he noticed a piece of her hair had fallen lose from under her hat, and the simple beauty of the girl's hair against the snow and blue light of dusk drew him for a moment away from himself. He stopped before her, wanting to speak but feeling foolish. The piece of hair swayed delicately. The girl did not look up and, embarrassed, he moved on.

That night he watched from the roof with his squad as the bombardment streaked overhead. Fires started nearby, and Ivan stared as buildings he had walked by that day suddenly took shape in the darkness, trembling in the light of their self-consumption.

"My uncle used to live over there in that neighbourhood," observed a man beside him, as though commenting on the weather.

Ivan remembered the girl in the doorway, and he wished then that he had spoken to her, had stopped long enough to think of a word to describe her strand of hair. 'I could recall her by that word,' he thought. 'I could always see her again if I had a word to remind me.'

Someone lighted a cigarette, exhaling smoke out over the city.

The next morning when Ivan left to gather their rations he noticed the girl was there again, just as she had been the night before. Ash had collected on her head, covering the hair he had admired. He stopped again, this time feeling no urge to speak. Kneeling beside her, Ivan saw that the boot laces still rested in her fingers.

He put his arm around her, almost tenderly, and lifted her out of the doorway. The hat she had been wearing came away and her hair fell, dry and soft, against his face. The touch of it staggered him, and he went down on his knees, pushed by a strange and sudden weight in his chest. He closed his eyes. Tears ran in cold streaks against his skin. He smelled her then, a final fleeting intimacy drawn into his lungs where it existed for an instant, made momentarily alive like memory, before being exhaled, passing into and then joining the winter air.

As death's broom swept through the city, people's anger rose. Discontent was most palpable in food lines, which always stretched farther than the food. Even when the sirens went off people remained in their queues, more afraid of losing their place than of the bombardment. The likelihood of death increased, and they became less afraid and began to speak openly against the authorities who seemed powerless to help them. Rumour passed like a bad smell among crowds during the long hours spent in breadlines. Some talked of seeing explosives placed on the city's monuments and buildings, and people whispered of a plan to blow up the city to keep it from the fascists. Many of those who lived through the siege pondered in secret the harrowing subtleties of their new liberty. The eye of the state was necessarily focused on the enemy, and citizens were able to complain and question where before they feared open speech. For Ivan this liberty was linked inextricably to the siege itself.

The boy listened with silent awe as mothers and old veterans raged against the Party, the generals – anyone who might be blamed for the suffering around them. Even those guarding the local bakeries began to mutter. In November a soldier standing in front of Ivan had gone mad – taking off his clothes and running in the street shouting obscenities. No one stopped him. He swore and gestured at the police guarding the store, then stood on his head and sang a song. Only when two of the guards approached him did the man stop raving. Scurrying back to his clothes in the snow, he pulled out a pistol and shot himself.

The next time Subov was home Ivan told him about this incident and the things people were saying. Subov listened closely, not speaking until the boy had finished.

"Do you see what is happening, Ivan? People would never have been allowed to say such things before the war. Look what happens when we let our guard down even for a short time! Never join in such talk," he cautioned. "Stay away from those who participate. There are some who sympathize with the fascists. They try to attack us from inside ourselves, and so they are more destructive than the bombs. The only responsible reaction is to be firm. I do not pity this man you talked of – he was weak, and in conflict weakness is death. I would have shot him myself."

Subov leaned forward then and stared at the boy. "Have you ever wondered why I stopped for you that day, during the retreat? It was not because you are young. You are not the first child I saw that day. Many children were left behind. What stopped me was the sight of you cutting your own flesh in order to survive." He placed a hand on the boy's shoulder. "You could have kept your arm. But you gave it up. And why? Why, Ivan? That is the great mystery of you. That single terrible choice you had to make. I could not let that strength perish. I would have carried you across half the world after what I saw you do. You will survive, Ivan. Always remember that you chose to live on and fight. And never, never forget what it is you are fighting for," and here Subov clutched his arm just above the stump, drawing the boy close and pointing to the hammer-and-sickle on his uniform. "Never forget the Party. It is not enough to be strong. You must attach your strength to something larger than yourself. The Party, boy. Remember the Party will save you."

Ivan took a dark comfort from this conversation. He had lived because he had been ruthless. And only ruthless people – like Subov, like him – could stop the madness that had brought everything Ivan knew to the edge of obliteration. Families could be killed, armies could evaporate, homes bombed, an entire city starved. But the Party – the Party survived. People like Subov, those who belonged to the Party, could hold back that terrible emptiness in people's eyes, that hollowness which drove them to speak out, to find new names for the darkness.

In December Larissa began staying in bed. Subov did not come home all that month, and she had to send the boy on his own to collect their rations. One morning Ivan was coming back with their food when the sirens began, followed almost instantly by the brittle keen of shells. Too weak to run, he bent double and stumbled along the street. Fire appeared in buildings, and the street began to fill with smoke and cinder. A trolley passed him, people leaping from its burning hulk as it continued to roll along the street. On the next block he was knocked down by a shell that landed in the road behind him. Pulling himself up, the boy clutched the bread and staggered forward. His only thought was to get back to the flat. Shells whined overhead, shaking the ground as they landed. The concussion shattered windows around him until the air glittered with glass. Skeletal figures appeared in doorways, while those too weak to leave their homes leaned out of windows, handing down children to those on the ground. As the Subovs' flat came into sight there was a roar above him, and in the next instant the adjacent building burst, vomiting the contents of entire flats into the street.

The boy pushed through the debris, calling Larissa's name, stumbling over rubble and blackened bodies. Above the smoke he saw members of his squad on their roof, shovelling sand into the fires. As he got closer there was a groan and the walls of the building which had been struck toppled, falling into the structures around it. Several of those from his squad dropped headlong from their roof, and Ivan watched as the side of his apartment collapsed under the new weight, folding in upon itself.

One by one the windows on each floor burst as the levels above it buckled. When it came to the fourth floor a thunder of notes rang out as pianos from the music school plunged through the flats beneath it – notes splintering, breaking apart. On it went, floor by floor, the terrible music forming a death chorus, continuing even after the building disappeared behind a plume of smoke and dust.

The next day the boy found himself with a group of orphans and other evacuees in the back of a truck – part of a new caravan bringing food into the city across the frozen lake. The departure point was a series of bombed-out warehouses by the dockyard, where trucks waited restlessly in the moonlight beneath the smashed scaffolding. Subov found Ivan here.

Leaning into the back of the truck he handed Ivan a bundle. "There is some bread in there," he said. "And my last scarf." For a moment he held the boy's stricken face between his hands. His stare moved desperately over Ivan's face, as if trying to remember everything about him.

"Subov," the boy gasped, his voice dry, a broken whisper above the commotion and engines. Ivan clutched at the officer's arm, feeling the muscle and tendon. Even in the dark he could see the man's eyes were bloodshot from suffering, his face haggard.

The driver shut the back of the truck. Voices around them called to one another. People rushed about. Someone pushed Subov back from the truck.

"Remember," he said, his voice harsh and emotional, breaking off as the vehicle started up. "Remember why you are alive!"

Ivan gazed numbly after Subov until he dissolved into the dark. The trucks moved away from the shore, passing the moon-bleached hulk of a sunken ship, just its top deck and turrets protruding from the frozen lake. As they drew away from the city a figure appeared for a moment stumbling along the pier, calling to the disappearing convoy.

"Remember!" the voice reached them, now hardly recognizable in the rushing air. The boy leaned out of the truck, staring after the figure until the convoy turned its back on the city and the flaring arc of shells already dropping silently out of the night sky.

AFTER THAT weekend at the *dacha* an awkward suspense settled between Katya and Andrew, during which each waited impatiently to resume what had begun between them. Katya was almost relieved, then, when he appeared at the table where she worked in the library.

"We should talk."

She did not even smile. There was no need.

They went together through the streets where people had come out to eat lunch and enjoy the unexpected sun. It was one of the last good days. There was a park at the north end of the university, and Katya led him past the sculptures that stood beside the gravel path.

"These figures," she explained, "come from children's stories. Parents bring their children here."

A woman was selling candied apples, and Andrew paused to buy one for each of them.

They stood eating and enjoying the afternoon. "What should we talk about?" Andrew asked.

She raised an eyebrow. "I don't know."

"Tell me about your father."

Katya tossed away the rest of her apple. "You don't want to know such things."

"Why not?" Andrew persisted.

"Let's walk…"

In the centre of the park stood an iron climbing gym, rust bleeding through the paint. Children played here while their parents watched or lounged on the long wooden benches. Two women with a handkerchief between them ate cucumber and cold sausage. A middle-aged man sipped tea from a thermos as he read the newspaper. On the grass students lay reading and smoking.

As they walked, Andrew noticed a building which stood away from the path, and he asked her what it was.

"This —" her voice fading off as she searched for the word. "This is a place for keeping birds, but I don't know how you call it in English."

"An aviary."

It was a white clapboard building with a pagoda covered by screening. A small turret sat on top of the building, crowned with a vacant flagpole. Andrew saw that the paint had begun to peel and come away from the boards, while the pagoda itself was congested with leaves and garbage.

"Where are the birds?" he asked.

"The supervisors could no longer afford to keep them, so they were released."

He looked at Katya as she spoke. With a single finger he drew the hair back from her temple.

"Some flew away. Others were unwilling to leave their cages. The people who used to come here continued to feed them. When winter arrived these people took the birds home."

He was staring at her. "You came here in the winter, didn't you?"

"I did," she said, lowering her voice. On the path behind them a woman went by pushing a stroller. "I took them home and we ate them."

Andrew leaned forward and kissed her, tasting the sweet trace of apple.

Katya stepped back. "You should be careful," she whispered. "You do not know the things I know."

A vague anxiety rose up in his chest, and he felt suddenly like a child caught at something.

"Do you see how difficult this is going to be?" He heard her sigh, an unwilling sound.

Andrew stared at his feet. Something in the bland frankness of her voice prevented him from looking at her.

But she did not let him answer and instead leaned into him, pressing her mouth to his.

The next day he appeared as before at the library, and they walked together into the adjoining neighbourhood of the Old Quarter.

"You know this area?" she said, seeing how he looked about him.

"I came here not long after I arrived," and he showed her the torn photograph with only the side of his father's face. "I need to find him," he whispered. "That is why I came here."

"It's unfortunate that he moved," Katya said. "He could be anywhere now."

"I know," Andrew admitted. "It was a long time ago that he lived here."

They came to a narrow road called Granatny Street. There was no traffic at that time, and their feet sounded on the pavement as they walked. Part way up the street Katya stopped at a little building, and she led him to the third floor. At the end of the hall they stopped and she took out a key. Andrew saw what they were doing, and he struggled to contain his surprise.

"What is this place?"

"It belongs to a friend of mine."

"You've thought about this," he said.

She stopped at the door. "Haven't you?"

"Of course."

"You are alright, then?"

He coloured. "Yes."

Together they looked shyly about the flat, which was narrow and dark, the curtains drawn in each room. The place was mostly bare – empty closets, a few books, no plants. There was a vacant spot in the cabinet where a television used to sit. The refrigerator was unplugged.

"Your friend lives here?"

"This was her grandparents' flat."

Andrew nodded, understanding. "They are gone."

"Yes."

"And her family keeps it?"

Katya shrugged. "No one has bothered to take it back."

He looked up from the bookshelf. "The government lets them have it?"

"For now," she said, adding tentatively. "Of course someone will come for it eventually. None of this will last."

"I suppose not," he said, touching her hand.

Adam opened his eyes and was immediately aware of being in an unfamiliar place. He sat up feeling panic. Through the window he noted the billboard at the end of the street, and the sight of it brought a sinking sense of remembrance. He felt the wave of emotion rise up as it did nearly every morning when he woke. He reached out to the chair beside the bed, where he found the photograph and for several minutes he lay clutching it until his breathing slowed.

When he was ready, Adam stood on the cold floor and began looking for clothes. He paused at the door to pick up the roll of toilet paper he kept there before walking to the lavatory at the end of the hall.

Squatting over the hole in the floor, he tried to make out the mosaic of messages carved or scrawled on the wall. The bathroom stalls were like bottles into which a hundred voices had been squeezed, bits of poetry, names, song lyrics, slogans, drawings, cartoon heads. Strings of thought overlapped one another in a rigmarole of alien statements. The majority of the graffiti was elegiac, left by those who had come from other countries to work at the university, the fugitive thoughts of aliens brought here to teach a language that immediately began to fail them.

The graffiti fascinated him, as if it were written by people he already knew. In those cramped stalls he found a fraternity of voices echoing his own isolation, speaking with a crude eloquence of the same desperate loneliness. During those first weeks in that place he got in the habit of copying out a graffito onto toilet paper each morning, pocketing it until later that day when he got to his office at the university.

Previous occupants had left books related to their particular subjects, and from among them Adam gleaned a number of dictionaries: Harrap for Italian and Spanish, the Le Robert's formidable *French*, Oxford for German (backed up with a rather slim Larousse for cross-referencing), Hebrew in a Bantam-Megiddo edition, while Russian and Polish stood out in Langenscheidt's bright yellow binding, as well as a nearly complete set of *Hippocrene Practical Dictionaries for the East Asian Languages*. With these books he translated the day's piece. The majority of this graffiti was brief and simplistic, riddled with possessive pronouns, usually bereft of adverbs, and with few, though exceedingly precious, adjectives. Language stripped to doers and doing.

vai tomar no cú

Each graffito, Adam found, contained traces of its owner's identity – linguistic trappings and blemishes that formed a sort of fingerprint – through which he sometimes discovered that the writer of a message was the same as someone he had translated days before.

Occasionally he found he'd copied incomplete artefacts, utterances mangled by age or the intrusion of another hand – the chorus of a Dylan song interrupted by the name of someone's girlfriend, or the logo of a rock band cleaving some private confession – forcing Adam to reconstruct the skeleton of the message from its fragments. These transcriptions were often unsatisfying, discovering only the expletives and discriminatory remarks of the jilted and the bigot. Other times there were examples of humour, which, though usually lame, made Adam laugh at their stumbling invention.

Ultimately, though, this melancholic communion had a disillusioning effect, and eventually Adam left off reading the graffiti. These same words became now like scattered shrapnel, bullet holes – the insignia of old battles – and he fled from them for his own preservation. His thoughts existed in the void left by what he had known, that coded ellipsis between him and this new country. As his own language became less useful in the outside world, it also came to have less control over his inner one. Here even the consolation of books betrayed Adam, their sentences strung now across each page like barbed wire. He was lost within the vacuum of his own presence. Conviction and belief had evaporated before him. His thoughts became like marrowless bone.

Adam's time was moulded by routines, which, though uninteresting and predictable, provided assurance. There were assignments and essays to mark. His lectures progressed with uninspired method through textbooks. He took his meals alone as often as he could, sitting in unobtrusive corners or on a bench in the courtyard. He became a remote fixture in the halls around the dormitory and university, walking the same daily paths between classrooms and the little office where he kept sporadic hours.

A few weeks after he arrived, Adam decided to send his father some token to say that he was okay. A souvenir, a life sign. What he wanted was to tell the old man what had really happened with Clare, to explain to his father what had been lost. He started writing a letter, but each time he went back to it he couldn't find the words that were in him. So instead Adam went looking for a souvenir, a piece of this place to hang on a fridge, for his father to look at when he thought of his son. With this in mind Adam had stopped at a store he'd noticed from the tram. When he arrived there was a line of twenty or thirty others, who stood with resignation in the drizzle.

Pulling up the hood of his coat, he listened to the confederate silence of those around him. Only now and then did he catch the trace of hushed and recondite voices.

The rain soon permeated his clothing and shoes. Puddles of water had formed like bruises on the sidewalk, catching up stray leaves and bits of litter. Adam watched as a man stepped from the store and walked to a green Volga parked at the curb. As he started the car, the engine turned over uncertainly before cutting out. There was a ripple of interest among those in line, who watched as the engine revved and died a second time. At this the driver got out of the car and, pausing purposefully, hit the vehicle three times in the centre of the hood, then restarted the engine. Again, it jolted to life only to die just as abruptly. This time when the man got out he took a moment longer to aim his blows, however the engine was no more responsive than his previous efforts. By the fourth attempt, his audience was losing interest.

Adam drew the edges of his coat about him. As the line stepped forward he became aware of a sign over the store, its letters staring down like dark birds.

Rummaging in his coat, he brought out the dictionary he carried, and began looking up the words he would need. As he found each one, he wrote it on his palm, then practiced his request as he entered the store. The woman in front of him was gesturing to a shelf behind the counter, where two women in white smocks waited on her. They seemed to be arguing, and the staccato modulations of their voices fell like stones, jarring his concentration so that his tongue seemed to lose the words he had rehearsed. When he consulted his palm, he saw the ink had smeared in his fist.

The woman paid for her goods, and squeezed past him to get outside. Someone nudged Adam in the back but his feet refused to move. He stared at the larger of the two women behind the counter. He gaped stupidly at them, the rehearsed phrases dissolving in his throat. There were voices behind him, and an older man in a sweater heavy with rain stepped forward, speaking now to Adam who looked at him blankly.

"*Izvenitia, izvenitia...*" he repeated, hoping to hold them off as he searched his dictionary for something to say. He scanned the pages vainly until, panicking, his eye snagged with random desperation on a word. Without thinking he collected it in his mouth, the syllables slipping awkward and giddy from his tongue like marbles.

"*Gemmoroii*," he said, making an effort to sound confident.

There was a sudden pause, which was filled with a moment of open-mouthed mystification from those in the store.

One of the women scratched her temple, leaving a blot of flour in her hair. "*Schto?*"

Adam stared back at the women with faltering resolve. "*Gemmoroii*," he repeated, drawing out each syllable with deliberate emphasis.

The look of confusion on their faces turned suddenly to insult, and he gasped as one of them reached for a broom behind the counter.

He hurriedly glanced at the dictionary to see what he had said, pinning the offending word beneath his thumb so that it could not escape. He felt lightheaded, struggling to grasp the word's meaning. His mind fumbled with the letters, and, to steady himself, he sounded it aloud in English.

"Haemorrhoid."

The women at the counter shouted and gestured at Adam, while the man behind him laughed and pushed him out of the way. The cramped store seemed to swell with the flux of their voices, fragments of sound passing back and forth between them in some random pattern he could not decipher. Several people shouted behind Adam, who responded with more apologies. Someone bumped him and he dropped the dictionary. In the melee he bent down in time to see it kicked under the counter, where it hit one of the shop women in the foot. She yelped with surprise and kicked the book back.

Adam fled the store, hands over his ears. As he stumbled into the street, he nearly collided with the man who was still hitting his car. Adam pushed through the queue of people, instinctively crossing his arms as he headed back to the dormitory.

The cafeteria was an inconvenient room of long tables picketed with benches. In the absence of alternatives, the cafeteria served to nourish the collection of foreign teachers and students who lived in the dormitory. Throughout autumn the air had become increasingly humid and tired, so that water formed on the walls and overhead pipes leaving strata of calcium and mildew. The food was uniformly bad, prepared by four overworked women who also served and cleaned up.

Meals in the cafeteria only strengthened the feeling the teachers had of being shipwrecked. Those from abroad generally ate together on islands of their own making – the Chinese teachers in one corner, next to but not speaking with a table of North Koreans, whose backs were turned to a number of Sudanese, Ethiopian and Egyptian professors. Against one wall sat Europeans with the handful of Americans and Canadians and a guy from New Zealand. From day to day there was little or no variation in this arrangement, strangers preferring to remain strange to each other.

"What this place needs is a total overhaul," Alice began. "Seriously – new everything."

Ethan, who was always ready to be affronted on the behalf of others, frowned. "Where's the money going to come from for your renovation?"

"There's always tourism," she offered.

Emil smirked. "Yes, that defibrillator of obsolete economies."

Alice shook her head insistently. "It has worked in other places."

"But who, besides Ethan, would actually pay to visit a communist state?"

"Oh, it's very chic right now." Alice insisted. "We went to Cuba at spring break last year expecting to find everyone wearing berets and fatigues. All we saw were other students looking for cheap pot, and wearing Ché t-shirts."

The conversation was halted suddenly by the arrival of Ford, who appeared at the table with a large FedEx box. His face was radiant. "Santa came early kids."

Andrew grew pale. He set down his fork. "It's here already?"

He nodded eagerly. "Can you say Mega Channel?"

Those sitting around the table stood at once and made for the door, almost lifting Ford who kept yelling at them over his shoulder. "Who can spell MTV? Anyone?"

Adam remained at the table. "What's going on?"

Ethan looked up from the piece of meat he was sawing. "I guess you hadn't got here yet, had you?"

He looked after the others. "For what?"

"Ford convinced everyone to chip in for a dish."

"A dish?"

"You know, for satellites."

"Really?"

He nodded to him sympathetically, misreading Adam's response. "Appalling, isn't it?"

Adam reached for his coat.

"Don't tell me you're going?"

"Why wouldn't I?"

"I thought you were past all that."

"What made you think that?"

Ethan chewed absently on his meat. "We're the ones who don't fit in."

Upstairs Adam found them laughing and talking together around one of the windows in the lounge. Andrew and Emil stood holding Ford's legs as he leaned out the window. From the next window his progress was monitored by Candace, who provided regular updates to those inside. "He's nearly got it!"

Adam squeezed beside her to see what was happening. Ford had managed to reach one of the flags that hung at the front of the building. Grasping its pole, he tossed it into the yard below him. Then, using both hands to wield the dish he inserted its arm into the empty bracket. "It's like they were made for each other!" he exulted.

"Now you should face it toward the west," Gertrude read, squinting at the instructions.

People stood about excitedly, their concentration alternating between Ford and the television. A bottle of wine appeared from somewhere. Gertrude and Gunter were at one of the couches reading out the instructions which were in German, while Alice and Hillary searched the channels for signs of life. The blank screen flickered. A tube of toothpaste appeared, and the room filled with an English accent singing a familiar jingle, "...*a revolutionary kind of clean!*"

There was applause from the people standing around, while those holding Ford nearly let go as they tried to join in. When he came in from the window he was greeted with backslapping and a can of warm beer. Alice was flipping gleefully through channels, ignoring the others' calls to turn up the volume or to stop at a particular show.

When people had settled down to watch, Ford approached Adam. "Where's your fifty bucks?"

"Sorry?"

He gestured at the others with his beer. "We all kicked in for the dish."

Andrew came over. "He can pay you later."

"It's okay," Adam said, withdrawing. "I'll come back when I get the money. Anyway, I've seen all these shows before."

Candace looked up from the television. "I know, isn't it great?"

In his room, Adam sat and took out one of the textbooks he taught from, letting it fall open part way through a lesson. Down the hall came laughter and voices. He glanced at the page in front of him and tried to concentrate on the vocabulary list. His eyes strayed over the words on the page for several minutes, then he closed the book.

It didn't matter, he realized. These words were not real here.

Growing up he had noticed those opaque people who existed in the background at high school or on the subway because of their clothes or a smell that belonged in a restaurant. At the time Adam wondered why these people didn't change themselves to fit in, why they clung to things that made them echoes of another life. They had to, he realized. It would be like cutting off a piece of yourself.

He rested his hand on the textbook, with its catalogues of grammar, uses of punctuation, its

221

pages of words. It was filled with mechanisms for expressing thoughts, for extending consciousness into the world, as easily invoked as a finger is moved. But in this country these same tools became the very lock which trapped him inside himself. Outside his classroom, on the street or in stores, he was lost, crippled and incomplete, left to mutter at the edges of this new world in which he found himself.

He looked up as laughter echoed in the empty hallway beyond his room. From the street came the weary moan of metal from a tram staggering its way along the street. People passed beneath his window, their voices reaching him in pieces, a confusion of syllables carried by the breeze, fragments unrecognizable to him.

The afternoon drew on. The voices in the hall scattered themselves like dry leaves in his room. At last Adam stood and walked to the window where he stared at the long shadows of strangers, his gaze following their varied gaits and postures until each in its turn faded beyond his reach.

IT WAS ONE of those rooms found in libraries or the older sort of university. Here silence becomes a voice you hesitate to challenge and even the floors creak with discretion. Along the walls was a series of bookcases and some faded prints of socialist painters. There were several windows and a set of glass doors which opened onto a balcony. Over the doors was the hammer-and-sickle, and from the ceiling hung a fixture with eight bulbs, seven of which were missing. In the centre of the room was a table.

Katya stood to greet Adam as he entered, crossing the room to shake his hand.

"Nice to see you again," she said, irritated by the unexpected flush of self-consciousness she felt.

He was struck by the ceremony with which she carried herself, an almost austere politeness that was so different from how she had been at the *dacha*. Adam sensed her new discomfort around him, and he wondered what had changed between them. He shifted awkwardly in the chair as soon as he sat. "What is it you need help with?"

Katya hesitated. "It is a collection of old poems they have asked me to translate as the final project for my degree. I am afraid I have not grasped the nuances in some of these verses. Regular prose is one thing, but poetry is so often elusive," and she handed him the list of poems she had been working on. "You can see the ones I have marked."

Adam examined the list.

"You know them?"

"Oh, yes."

"If you look at the first one, you'll see what I have tried to do." Katya reviewed her notes at length with him, referring Adam to the esoteric passages and other idiosyncrasies she had found in the poems. For the next hour, their discussion paused at sporadic intervals, like an overseas telephone conversation, while one person's statement passed through the time zones of the other's comprehension. Outside the shadows began to stretch.

"I don't understand you," she complained, at last. "The dictionaries I consulted were very clear about this phrase."

He shook his head. "Put aside the dictionary for a moment – look at what the poet is saying. Here the poet focuses on a woman's physical beauty in order to reveal her spiritual appeal. It's all a cliché now, but the affect is still poignant. The woman described in this poem is in mourning. The trivial excesses of her life have been burnt away. There is a sense of the terrible purification which her grief has purchased. It gives her a sense of grace. And it is this metamorphosis, I think, which the poet is trying to articulate, and which your translation should reflect."

There was a pause as an idea came to her and Katya made a note on one of the pages. Adam met her eyes as she finished. He pointed to the paper. "May I see this?"

"Of course."

It was a long piece of newsprint folded in the centre. The English original was written out on one side, while on the other was the draft of

Katya's translation with her notes in the margins.

Adam looked at her. "I have never seen this done." He held her work a moment before giving it back to her.

"It is sometimes frustrating," she said. "Our poet, Pushkin, said that translators are the post-horses of civilization. I think this is why people distrust what I do. When they read something that has been translated there is a part of them which struggles to accept it. They think: 'How do I know this is what the author wrote?' And of course they are correct. I have changed it. I know I have." Katya was staring at a pencil on the table, and her eyes grew distant as though she was concentrating on something else. "Meaning is a reflection of the writer's intention. A translator is a kind of shadow on the page; the more transparent the shadow, the better the translator. But a shadow is always there. Decisions have to be made when a work is transferred from one language to another. It can be an uncomfortable process for me. Some of my professors speak of finding equivalences between languages, but everyone admits that this is often an illusion, to believe that two languages can truly speak to one another. In the end, the professors tell us that translation is about fidelity – but fidelity to whom?"

Adam watched as her eyes saddened.

"When I began translating, it was the book I loved, not those who read it. But something is changing for me. I struggle now to be faithful to both," and as she said this Katya closed her eyes before going on. "I do not like this contest for my allegiance. It leaves me feeling complicit. Like a traitor."

Adam cleared his throat. "Aren't you being too hard on yourself?"

"We go to a doctor because we do not know why we are ill. That ignorance obliges a patient to place faith in someone with understanding. Reading is an act of faith, as well. A translation collapses when readers do not trust its source. In this is the translator's dilemma. What is more important, the faith of readers or the veracity of the words in which their faith is placed?"

"Aren't they the same thing?"

"No."

"I don't understand."

"You cannot cure yourself with a lie."

"*What?*" Adam became frustrated, but he could not look away from her.

"The final redemption of translators' work is our proximity to the truth. We almost never fully reach the author's complete meaning. Languages hide from one another. A translator reveals the hiding places, brings light to words and thus to those who read them. But people want some things to stay hidden. Perhaps this is why we are mistrusted. It is not that people think we have left something out, but that we have revealed too much. This was true for the great translators. They took astounding risks to do their work. Think what it must have meant to translate Adam Smith into my language, or Lenin into you yours. The first people who translated the Bible were burned with their translations. People do not burn lies; they cannot be bothered."

He leaned back, taking in all that she had said. "They burn the truth," he murmured.

She ran her open hand across a blank page, as though caressing it. "In my profession, revelation is always followed by flames."

Stepping off the tram that evening, Adam decided to walk through a small park near the dormitory. Leaves and trash lay sodden and matted underfoot, while overhead thunder rallied among the clouds. Dusk drew like blight across the ground, bleeding colour from the street. He walked beneath the lengthening shadows, passing a monument to some forgotten battle. At a news kiosk Adam noticed the papers and magazines from America, and he paused to purchase a newspaper and a copy of *Time*.

When he got to his room, he found a note on the door from Andrew: *Gone to movie. Come if you can.*

He looked about the room at his own things. His belongings seemed vacant, meaningless there without him. The empty room reminded him of the day Clare left, how ordinary objects could become suddenly foreign.

After she had gone he found items she'd forgotten at the back of cupboards, under the bed, in closets. Without her their purpose was gone, leaving these things looking incongruous in his hand, flattened. Like photographs of themselves. So he put them in a box of other things she had forgotten to take and gave it all to the Red Cross which was collecting aid for some disaster somewhere.

That same month Adam saw a flier at the university advertising teaching jobs in Eastern Europe. At the student development office he met the woman in charge of these things. She was surprised by his impatience, and it took her a moment to locate the contract.

"There is a lot of paperwork," she apologized.

Adam sat as she explained the details until he could not stay quiet any longer. "Just show me where to sign," he insisted.

Adam took off his coat and went about making tea. As he plugged in the kettle, a murmur of voices could be heard from one of the other rooms and for a moment he stood quite still, straining to hear them. He listened and they seemed to die away, and soon he was left with only the sound of water boiling.

It had been like this between the old man and him after his mother died. Adam had gone back to stay with his father, thinking that he might be wanted to help around the house. But the old man had retreated behind a wall of monosyllables and, finally, total incoherence.

Adam spent evenings in his room trying to interpret the grunting and clatter through the walls. But as the days passed, it became clear that his father did not know the words for the things he felt, that he was trapped with experiences he could not articulate. Without these words, there was no bridge between father and son. After a month of this Adam went back to the emptiness of his own apartment.

On the small table next to his bed was the letter he was still trying to write to his father. Near the top of the page was a blot where he had written Clare's name and then scribbled over it, not stopping until the pen had formed a hole in the paper. Now he stared at the letter wondering if he should resume it, but the effort felt suddenly too much for him.

Adam glanced about his feet. The newspaper he'd bought lay where it had fallen: Middle East Under UN Microscope...World Bank to Discuss Africa...Tokyo Bounces Back. He left the paper on the floor. All this was biopsy and diagnosis, a hasty cutting open and naming. The appearance of completeness was really just familiar abbreviation.

231

While the tea steeped, he ate on the edge of his cot. There would be a proper meal in the cafeteria downstairs, but Adam wanted to be alone. Around him the glow of street lights mottled the walls with irregular forms, vague and edgeless. The trees outside his window stood against the night like veins of frost.

He closed his eyes, trying to push back the rubbery penetralia of memory, its fingers wiggling about for something to grab onto, a piece of him. Between the silence and the darkness there was a heaviness in the room, and at times it was as though someone was sitting on his chest.

Most of the women he had dated before Clare were a mess in one way or the other. The wispy, hemp-wearing types who hung around the Arts building wearing black clothes flecked with cat hair. Those whose lives reeked of self-consciousness, who had turned disappointment into a kind of addiction, shamefully stashing self-help magazines around their apartments like bottles of gin. It got so he could find these caches instinctively, recognizing the glossy covers and the frantic assurance of their headlines: Simple Ways to Feel More Love

Every Day; 5 Tricks to Flip His Listening Switch; or, Instantly Gorgeous and Totally You. These women inevitably went out with equally neurotic guys, like him: men who had never really gotten over being laughed at through a decade's worth of gym classes, who went about with that lurking righteousness they excused as a symptom of being smart. And so when Clare landed in Adam's world, she seemed to him like another life form, an artefact of that world he was so intent on critiquing from a distance. She changed everything.

There was something tangible about her that drew him, while at the same time making him afraid of the possibilities that accompanied her, this self-understanding of who she was and what she believed. He was certain that she had never once tried to explain herself.

The first time they slept together she showed him a scar over her abdomen.

"As soon as I saw the knife, I ran," she said. "So he only got a bit of me."

"Didn't it hurt?"

"Later," she nodded, "when they were stitching it up."

Adam looked away.

"You can touch it if you'd like."

"That's okay," he said, already looking about for his pants.

She terrified him with her willingness to suffer. It made everything possible, assented to all potentialities. Once he watched as she held her hand over a match and counted to twenty. The objective, she said, was to get to twenty before you pull away. "It's to remind you that pain can be survived," she explained. "That it ends."

It was out of this courage that Clare exposed him to the stark meanness of everything he had previously been offered as love. Only after would he comprehend what it had meant for him to be with her. Clare moved boldly in dark rooms, reaching out and clutching the unseen things in life. She was one of those rare people who understood that darkness was just the shadow of something bigger than your vision, that revelation is not in seeing something new, but what has always been there unnoticed.

For this – because she showed him how to be free, if he wanted to – Adam punished her with his fear, used it trap her, too, though not for very long.

Almost from the beginning he struggled to draw borders around her, telling himself that it was for her own protection. In turn she would become impatient with him, trying to insist her practical independence upon him, while he wished she could just accept the broken state of the world as fair warning. Clare often spoke of the places she wanted to see, maybe live. Adam retorted with a list of atrocities: human rights abuses, political upheaval, *coup d'état*, crimes against humanity.

"These things are real," he would insist. "They happen."

"Of course they do." Clare shook her head at him, as though he spoke a different language. "That doesn't mean we can't go there."

Adam turned off the light next to his cot, and lay on his side. Against his ear was the deep footfall of his own pulse. He sighed heavily, his body like wet paper.

Trams went by every few minutes now, their lights opening holes in the darkness of his room. On the wall photographs hung like rags cut from the fabric of a moment. As though place and time were things you could preserve.

Closing his eyes, he gripped the picture he always kept in his pocket, struggling now to recall the faces from it in his head.

He drew the blanket over himself and tried to sleep. Gradually he became aware again of sounds behind the wall, the resonance of other lives, and for a time he lay listening. Soon though, he noticed a child's cry amid the others. It grew louder, filling Adam's head until he was unable to concentrate on anything else. He sat up and tried to plug out the sound, but it clung to him, joined him in the darkness, found him where he hid beneath the blanket, in his small room, in that vast country. 'Why won't it leave me?' he thought, before realizing the cry was not a child's at all.

That night they went out onto the balcony, naked against the dark. Andrew wanted to go back inside right away, but she stood feeling the air on her body.

"Let's go in."

"In a moment."

"Aren't you cold?"

236

"I am," she said, flinching from the sudden warmth of his hands.

Katya stared out over the city to where the constellation of lights merged with stars on the horizon. Noises came to them faintly from the distance. A car engine. Voices in the street. A plate in someone's sink. The brittle sound of wind in leafless trees.

"It is peaceful, seeing it this way," she said.

He was quiet for a moment, and she concentrated on the warm spot where his hand rested on her back. Someone emerged from a doorway and began walking up the street.

"Can I meet you here tomorrow?"

"Of course," she said, smiling to him through the darkness.

They had begun coming during the week through the narrow streets and cluttered arcades of the Old Quarter to the flat on Granatny Street. Here they fell into one another with that obsessive concentration of early love which denied existence to anything outside itself. In the slow darkening of those afternoons Katya found in this borrowed flat a reprieve from the world. For her desire was like a jewel you hid in the part of yourself you could not afford in the outside world. When she returned to this place in herself Katya always felt righteous and self-justified, as though she was stealing back what she already owned. To Katya, the flat was a spot on a treasure map, a place where she could not linger for fear of being found out. The bed with its cambered mattress and fraying sheets became for her a place of acquittal from the trials outside that flat. Here she found peace amid the scent of almost-forgotten things, to which she and Andrew now added traces of themselves. They quickly became comfortable in the flat, began drifting to other rooms to read, to listen to the radio, to eat. Began to leave traces of themselves. Their fingerprints joined others on door handles. A chip in one of the plates became evidence of their second meal in the flat. She started reading a novel from one of the shelves and found a bookmark waiting between the pages. At the sink she discovered a grey hair next to one of her own. A pillow on the couch kept the impression of Andrew's head.

Katya smiled to realize these signs of their time in the flat would linger, messages for whoever came after.

"What do you think of this place?" she said one evening, propping herself on an elbow.

"It's great," he murmured.

She found a match and lighted one of the candles next to the bed. "I mean, is it enough for you?"

He was staring at her in the glow of the candle, its light filling her eyes. "What else would I want?"

She felt his mouth on her neck.

"Something more?"

"I hadn't thought that far," and his mouth paused over her skin. "Is that wrong?"

Katya rolled over and watched the candlelight dance on the ceiling. In the street a door slammed. The sound of feet on wet pavement. She began to speak without looking at him.

"I was very sick once as a child. For several days my parents thought I would not live. I recall very little about being ill, except that after the fever broke I remember waking to a strange stillness. My father was sleeping in a chair beside my bed. Through the window I could see the sky was pink, the sun only just holding sway against the dark. I could not tell whether it was the coming of day or the coming of night. I lay watching this contest for what seemed a long time." She turned now to look at him, to see if he would understand. "I have thought a lot about that moment. Often now I stare into the darkness and do not know if it is passing away or about to engulf me."

He searched her face. "Why tell me this?"

She watched the candlelight on the walls. "There has been a great deal taken from me, Andrew. So much of what used to be is now gone. You are the first thing that has been added to my life in a long time. It has been like a gift. But gifts have a cost." She glanced around the bedroom. "I cannot give more than this. Do you understand?"

The candlelight shivered on her face.

Andrew smiled, reaching out with his broad confidence. "Everything's going to be okay."

Outside a tram rambled up the street, its moan filling the small flat that was theirs. The radiator gurgled, and warmth began to pass mysteriously into the room. Beside them the candles shuddered.

Katya stared at Andrew, and she wanted to believe.

KATYA STOOD outside the lobby of the Planeta Hotel. She had seen people do this before, girls sent by their mothers with trinkets and heirlooms to sell for dollars.

Unfolding a cloth in her hands, she held out several bracelets of her mother's, a ring of her own, and some items she didn't think her father would miss. She had picked this spot on purpose, waiting until the afternoon when she knew the foreign businessmen and tourists often stopped for a drink on the way back to their hotel rooms. Standing in the cold, she waited.

There were others at the hotel that day. A boy with a radio. Next to him some women selling a variety of items: a flute, two fur coats, matching candelabra, a serving plate. Together they stood arm-to-arm, looking dry and slightly bent. Like a field of autumn corn.

People came and went from the hotel, some pausing to glance at her while others ignored them as they passed. The woman with the candelabra was the first to find a buyer, followed by the boy. After another hour, just as she was losing hope, a tall man in a black overcoat stopped.

At first he only wanted to buy one of the bracelets, though Katya explained to him in English that they were a pair.

He glanced at her from beneath his fur hat. "How much do you think they're worth?"

"Thirty," she said, without blinking. "Dollars."

"That's an awful lot, isn't it?" he asked.

She stared. In an attempt to improve the items, she added, "They were my mother's."

He looked at her. "They are pretty."

After the man paid her, he paused for an instant, glancing over her shoulder at the people going into the hotel. "You should get warm," he smiled. Perfect teeth.

"I am fine where I am."

When he had left, Katya turned away to stare into the street. People brushed past, carried on by their own importance. Two men hurried by, voices trailing behind them. Someone paused in front of her to butt out a cigarette. A Zil limousine deposited a woman onto the curb, and she disappeared into the hotel. Lowering her head, Katya pushed her face into her sleeve. Beside her, the woman with the serving plate offered encouragement.

"Do not be upset," she consoled. "That was a very good price."

Katya came home that same afternoon to find her mother asleep. Careful not to wake her, she placed the money in the drawer of the bed table and left. She felt unpleasant and upset, and she yearned for someone to talk to, for distraction. The silence in the flat irritated her and she moved, agitated and miserable, from room to room, aware that she was searching for things to sell even as she was trying to forget the events of that afternoon. At last she came to her father's office at the end of the hall. There was a forlorn precision to his things here, like in a neglected museum.

It felt wrong to be there without her father, but in her restlessness she resisted the urge to leave and instead let her gaze wander over his shelves. Close to the floor she noticed some slim books with worn spines. She recognized them right away, and as she opened each in turn, the pictures and words stared back at her like forgotten acquaintances. It was in these books, Katya remembered, that she had learned to read.

The paper had faded, but other than this the books were unchanged. She turned over the pages, their odour drifting up to her with the stale sweetness of old paper. She could still hear her father's voice folded between the pages. The first book was a story about a boy and a girl riding in an automobile. Katya smiled as she remembered herself looking at the picture of the girl beside the great leader as he cheered the workers. On the last page a soldier pushed over a throne while the great leader looked on approvingly.

Katya leaned forward in the chair, and as she surveyed the book her thoughts turned gradually back to herself.

The world had changed. She almost did not recognize the country she had inhabited as a girl when she had listened in earnest to her father's sermons, and the political lessons of her Komsomol leaders as they preached about the country's future under the Party's guidance.

Then as an adolescent this future had seemed increasingly plastic and ridiculous, and she had turned from it with half-hidden ambivalence. Yet now, sitting there in her father's chair, Katya felt a wave of nostalgia for that future she had once been promised.

After Perestroika, her father's message had changed, and the future he'd foretold was replaced by the very chaos the Party had promised to protect them from. For Ivan, capitalism represented a sort of fraud which had begun to infect his country even before the Party lost power. Katya had known even as a girl how easy it was to buy a car if you could bribe the right people to avoid official waiting lists. Communism, though full of immense irritations for the individual, purported to treat everyone on the same economic plane. That was the choice for every society – glacial inefficiency or moral corruption. Now they had both.

The second book on her father's shelf was Lermontov's *Borodino*, and she recalled the way Petya, as a boy, had adored the soldiers – on one page smiling with long pipes beneath their moustaches and cocked hats, on the next charging the French cannon. Even the dying were set in postures of defiance, bleeding for the Motherland with gallant resolve. Toward the back of the book, Katya paused, noticing – it seemed for the first time – a group of soldiers being blessed by a priest with an icon.

She heard the chime of the clock in her parents' bedroom, followed by sounds of her mother stirring.

Katya stared at the picture of the icon, wondering if she had noticed it as a girl. She thought back to the funeral she had watched, recalling the tuba's dirge and the coffin's slow march through the city. The ceremony in the church afterwards had seemed so indulgent, the body surrounded by the songs and paintings from a world that Katya had never heard of, the world not of the future but the past. She thought then of her grandmother's funeral, the dry grief of the state ceremony.

Katya sat like this for a long time, until the book from her childhood became heavy with memories.

The next day she returned to the church. There were other people there, standing at the wall of candles. Katya waited for them to leave before stepping under the arch and into the silence of the nave. The workmen were gone, she saw, though their vacant scaffolds still rose into the domed ceiling.

"You're back," came a voice lengthened by the emptiness. She turned around to see who had spoken, but saw only icons staring back at her.

Katya looked up, searching for the speaker. "Who's there?"

A hand gestured from the top of some scaffolding. "I wondered if I would see you again!"

She hesitated, then waved too.

"You can come up."

The great faces loomed, observing her hesitation.

Katya bit her lip. "Shall I?"

"Yes, of course."

The scaffold creaked as she stepped onto the ladder, the ropes and their pulleys rattling as she climbed. Dust and incense hung in the air, and her lungs filled with the dry sweet odour. At each landing she paused to stare at the murals, their surfaces painted with primeval stories of hellfire and goodness, secession and faith, wrath and supplication.

Katya's hands were white with dust as she

reached the landing, where she found the workman she had spoken to on her first visit. He stood before her in a long grey coat that hung almost to his feet. From the pockets there protruded folded papers, paint brushes and pencils. As she stepped onto the top landing, he came forward quite formally to shake her hand. His beard was unkempt and too thick for his face, which was gaunt and angular as a bird's. And there was about him the unmistakable smell of over-ripe fruit.

His name, he told her by way of welcome, was Boris Olegovich Spacinov. He was restoring the church's murals. He appeared shy, but also pleased by her presence, Katya saw, and he seemed eager to hide his awkwardness from her.

"I have never been close to such murals," she said, her words echoing, suspended like smoke in the great dome. The air was heavy, and the stillness seemed to rest on her. From here the murals loomed with fantastic proportions. There was something striking about them up close, as though she could feel their breath on your skin. You could walk the worn planking of the scaffold and move along the ceiling's curvature from one figure to the next, noting the different brush strokes on an angel's wing, tracing the tear on a saint's cheek, marvelling at the proportions of an arm, the elegant eccentricity of saints' postures. And, everywhere you went, the weight of their gaze. Storytelling on a grand scale.

"I've been looking at St. Michael..." She followed the painter's gaze to a large crimson horse stretching across the opposite side of the dome. The rider held a horn between his lips, a black spear in the other hand, gold wings drawn out at his sides, his feet bloody with flame. Beneath the horse, buildings lay on fire and people cowered. Their heads turned away, shielding their eyes.

"It is the Archangel bringing God's wrath. That tall one beside the window is St. George looking to the stars. On the other side, St. Florus..."

Katya's mind wandered off with her gaze across the horizon of figures. She examined the rows of impassive faces. 'I wonder what they are saying,' she thought. 'I should like to know who they are.' And yet, even so close to them as she was, she knew the sheer distance of time between her life and theirs was too great. In the end they were just faces, she decided, like those in a child's story.

From the corner of her eye she could see he was still looking at her. "It always bothers me," she said, "the way the faces stare at you."

"An icon is rarely painted in profile," he explained, leaning back over the railing to pass his hand tenderly across the horizon of faces. "Its message is communicated face to face."

She raised her eyebrows. "Is the message always the same?"

"Each of these murals is a tableau, a single image recalling an entire story. Together, they weave the fabric of a narrative that runs through a thousand years of our people's memory, deep into our identity."

Katya leaned over the railing. "What are these stories?"

Spacinov drew his fingers slowly through his beard. "Over there you will see the Nativity, the Raising of Lazarus, the entry into Jerusalem, the Ascension," and he turned to see if she was following him.

He scanned the ceiling, searching for something she might recognize. "There must be a story here which you have heard..."

Katya looked at him blankly.

"What about that?" she said, pointing to one at the cusp of the dome.

"The Annunciation." He adjusted his glasses before going on. "See how her hand is angled? Everyone notices the bowed head, her humility. But for me the real marvel is in the way the painter chose to part the small finger on her hand as a way of suggesting the girl's hesitation, the fearful delicacy with which she touches the future within her. With this gesture she tells us that the entire world is about to change."

Katya stared until at last it came to her. "She's pregnant."

The man grinned. "That's right."

She smiled. In the months to come, Katya would grow to appreciate Spacinov's quiet unpredictability and loud passions. She would be drawn to the way he accomplished small things. How the old man oiled the fold-out knife he used to peel apples, or the delicacy with which he rubbed each of his fingers before he began to work, and the way he measured the wick of candles with the nail of his thumb, insisting this was the length for the best light. And most of all, she appreciated the way

Spacinov sat for hours cross-legged before a mural, oblivious to everything except his work.

But all of this would come later. That day on the scaffold, Katya was not aware of the seed planted in her, the beginning of a future for which she had never planned, and for which no one could have prepared her.

She stirred next to the man, looking to break the tension starting inside her.

"Everyone is talking about the country's future, and yet you spend all your energy here on the past..." She blushed immediately at what she had said, half expecting him to take it badly.

Instead he smiled, the taut muscles around his eyes softening as his gaze looked past her.

ADAM'S CLASSES that morning passed like a long groan, and at the lunch break he fled the voices outside his office for the quiet of a small courtyard in the Arts building. There he found Andrew with several Russians, who left peremptorily as Adam approached.

"Sorry," he said. "I didn't mean to break things up."

Andrew gestured at him to sit.

Adam drew some food from his backpack. "Want an apple?"

He took up the fruit. "You mean, *yablaca*."

"Pardon?"

"That's how an apple is called here. You should be learning how to say things in Russian."

Adam sighed, staring at his hands. "I still can't believe I am here. I don't know anything about this country or how to live in it." Then Adam frowned in a way that made Andrew laugh.

"We're going out tonight. There's a party."

Adam glanced at his watch. "I need to get back to my office."

Andrew took a final drag on his cigarette. "You should come."

"Let me see." Adam watched leaves shift about the courtyard. He wouldn't go with the others to the party. He had become used to being alone since Clare left. He'd come to find a security in the cavity where she had once existed. His thoughts were chained to a circuit of memories that refused to relinquish her image. Even his body would not release her. His hand reached out to her at night, searching for where she would have been. Sometimes he looked up to tell her something only to see the empty space where he thought she'd been standing. Each time he rediscovered the absence of her existence he found the limit of his own. Yet even without her, he could still feel her. Absence, he knew, was itself a kind of presence. Only in isolation, that state Adam now both feared and craved, could he be together with her, with the companionship of memory.

But he had also begun to sense new dangers. In this foreign place, surrounded by people he did not understand, being alone and not knowing the language were treacherous. Social exclusion is a form of exposure, like losing a glove in winter, and here in this new wilderness he sensed the peril he was in. His father used to talk about people who died this way each winter near the town where he had grown up. When the bodies were found the only cause of death was a missing hat, a boot lost in the snow. A piece of the whole gone missing.

He looked up and found Andrew still there. "Okay," he said quickly. "I'll come."

The street they were on ran east-west through the city, and if you stayed on it, the cab driver told them, it would take you all the way to Moscow.

The route was an artery of history. On this same street the city had turned out to watch Napoleon's troops. The following winter the same soldiers had littered the road with their corpses during the retreat. In 1941, citizens looked on from burnt-out doorways and strafed windows at the passing columns of soldiers, only to watch them two years later as they fled west toward a winter sun already setting over Berlin.

As Adam looked out the taxi window, the street was again lined with people.

"New eating place," said the driver, glancing at them in the mirror. "McDonald's. You like, yes?"

Ford grunted from the back seat. "You have no idea."

Ignoring the question, Andrew asked instead, "Are we nearly there? I was told it wasn't far."

The driver waved his hand reassuringly. "There almost."

Adam checked the meter on the dashboard, then looked at his watch. They had been driving for nearly half an hour, seemingly without aim. They had stopped once already to ask directions, and appeared no closer to getting there – *there* being a party thrown by someone Andrew had met from the American consulate.

"It's not this guy's fault," Andrew explained, nodding at the driver. "Most streets have new names. Nobody knows them all, and the maps haven't been changed yet."

When the city was being rebuilt after the War, most streets were hastily named after various figureheads of the Party, poets or generals, ballet dancers and cabinet ministers. Since the communists had fallen from power, the old names had been painted over and new ones put in their place until most of the streets were renamed. Almost overnight the city forgot who it was.

As if to prove Andrew's point, the driver pulled over again to consult a map which took up most of the front seat. Adam watched street vendors accosting passersby.

After a moment the driver looked up from the map, scratching his head apologetically. "Street not here."

"Great map," Ford observed.

The driver looked over at him, feigning incomprehension to be polite. "You say what?"

"Keep driving."

The Lada shuddered to life and they swung out again into traffic, whizzing past the nascent rash of fast food places and clothing stores that had begun springing up next to the shells of blank, state-owned buildings.

Adam leaned back in the car's seat, careful not to press against Ford who was getting punchy. Andrew tried to cross his legs but they got caught up in the bed sheet he was wearing.

Ford scowled. "I told you we shouldn't wear these things."

He paused to straighten his laurels in the driver's mirror. "It's a toga party, what the hell else were we supposed to wear?"

Adam joined in sensibly. "You could have changed there."

A gap appeared in traffic and he jerked back in the seat as the Lada roared forward, transforming the street into a smear of signs and storefronts. The cab turned abruptly at a corner with an antiquarian bookstore, where Andrew told them there was a woman who would read your palm while her husband wrapped your purchase with issues of *Pravda* from the 1960s and 70s. Traffic was thinner on the side streets, and the driver made good time, weaving through alleys overshadowed by tenements with balconies cluttered with lines of drying laundry.

"This is not the right neighbourhood," Ford insisted, pointing out the window. "Nobody from the consulate flats here."

Andrew leaned over the seat and said something to the driver in Russian. Adam turned to stare out the window.

Leaning against the door, he felt a jab from the envelope he was still carrying in his pocket. That morning a letter had arrived from his father letting Adam know that he'd sold the house and was moving to Florida. He found it easy to picture his father in what must be one of the most nostalgic places on Earth. What he couldn't imagine, though, was his parents' house being owned by someone else. When he finally went home, Adam realized, he would be a stranger there too.

Ford closed his eyes and drew the toga under his chin. "Wake me when we get there."

Andrew was talking with the driver over the front seat. He sat back and turned to Adam. "We're lost."

The car stopped at the end of the block. The driver got out with Andrew who was holding the map now, and they stood at the corner trying to make out the street's old name beneath the new one.

Ford leaned out of the window. "Why don't you ask one of the *rodnoi?*" he called.

Andrew nodded at their driver. "He is a *rodnoi*."

"I mean one who isn't lost!"

To Adam, sitting in the back of the idling Lada, the situation alternated between absurdity and something sad. It seemed incongruous to him, these alien symbols on the new signs, some code splitting a place between two existences: then and now. He stared at the accretion of lettering on the building – words striking out one another, both splintered into orphaned letters, names blotted – sensing their aggression, the marking of territory. Like dogs pissing.

In high school he had collected moths for a biology class, using pins to hold them to sheets of styrofoam. Then he labelled each of their bodies in Latin, that language of the dead. But there had been a moth for which he could find no Latin name in the encyclopaedias, and in frustration Adam had thrown the insect away. The names of the other moths Adam had long ago forgotten, but the memory of that nameless, discarded one remained with him.

It was a lie to believe that you could uncreate what you could not name. It is that empty, indiscernible distance between a thing and its miscarried name which is the womb of language. This was the last thing Clare had taught him. There are words for everything, even if you don't know them yet.

The driver leaned against the building to consult the map again. Andrew, his toga wrapped about him against the cold, looked back at the car and shook his head.

Ford opened one eye to survey the situation.

Andrew and the driver returned and they drove until they emerged onto the street with the new McDonald's. The driver looked dismayed.

"Where go now?"

Andrew tapped him on the shoulder and said something in Russian. The driver pulled over in front of a bar down the street and they all went inside. It was a small place, only a few tables and a kiosk in the corner where a woman sold cigarettes. The place was busy with people who had come to watch the soccer match on the television.

Andrew ordered at the counter, and Adam was handed a glass with some black liquid which he drank without asking questions.

The driver was feeling badly about getting lost, and he stood a little apart from them. "You like soccer?" Andrew asked him in Russian.

The driver nodded, and to be polite asked in English, "Who favourite player?"

Andrew studied the contents of his glass as though the answer was somewhere in the dark liquid. "Baggio."

The driver nodded. "This Baggio's year."

After the first drink Andrew spread out the map, and the bartender helped them to look for the street. The driver seemed relieved at the turn in Andrew's mood and even offered to spot the next round, but Andrew refused and said Ford would pay instead.

"The hell I will," he snorted. "This guy's had us lost for an hour."

"Shut up," Andrew said. Not knowing what else to do, Ford ordered.

"I'll get the next one," Adam offered, trying to smooth things over.

Sometime later he followed Andrew and Ford from the bar. As they were leaving, Ford, who had improved greatly by then, insisted on hugging their driver, who had decided to stay and watch the end of the match.

"What a great *rodnoi*, that guy was," he blubbered. "I love the *rodnois* in that place. Best *rodnois* in the whole country..."

Adam flagged down a taxi.

Andrew stood next to him. "Are you sober?"

"No way."

"Well, shit," Ford sputtered as a taxi appeared at the curb. "Here we go again."

In the car Ford fell asleep, and Adam listened while Andrew explained the directions to the new driver. It was almost dark now, and as they drove Adam stared at the passing lights and people.

"That guy, the driver, he was a good guy."

Andrew nodded, his face growing oddly composed, the way it did when he had been drinking. "He knows a lot about history."

"I thought you were talking about soccer."

"We had to get to know each other first." He smiled into the darkness.

"Don't they talk about anything ordinary in this place?"

Andrew laughed softly. "Russians are incredibly bad at small talk. Just try it. Strike a conversation with a total stranger and in ten minutes you will have gone from the weather to hearing his theory about the moral progress of humanity, or about Shakespeare's early influence on Chekhov, or the codependent relationship between tyranny and liberty. They can't talk about anything small. My mother was the same way. It's their intensity."

"Their intensity," Adam echoed, and he stopped listening and looked out the window, remembering Clare and suddenly glad for the darkness.

Andrew paused what he was saying. "You all right?"

"What were you saying?"

Andrew became a little aloof when he was drinking, a hint of the Boston patrician leaking into his tone. His voice now drifted boozily about the half-dark of the taxi, absorbing the frayed edges of Adam's attention. "After my mother died," he was saying, "I did a lot of thinking. At one point it struck me like a knife in the back that I had seen every day for the rest of my life, set out for me and completely secured, with nothing left to chance. What I saw was not particularly bad. Really, it was everything I could have hoped for. But I could see it already, how everything would turn out. I understood that for most of us our lives back home have already happened. Sure there are a few undecided footnotes, but basically if you come from a half-decent gene pool and wear a seatbelt and don't smoke, things look after themselves. The thought of it just depresses me now." Andrew looked apologetically at his reflection in the rear view mirror.

Ford stirred in his bed sheet. "You are so full of it."

Adam stared into the window, hand over his mouth.

"This all sounds like posturing, doesn't it? I know it does, but I can't help thinking these things." He leaned back carelessly and lighted a cigarette. "Anyway, it's why I dropped everything to come to this place. That and the chance to see my father."

"You think you'll find him?"

"I don't know." Andrew was looking out the window now. "I had an address from when I was a kid. I used it to find the flat where he lived, but no one had heard of him."

"So now what?"

"Katya's father used to be some big shot in the Communist Party, and she thinks he might know someone who can help..." but then his voice trailed off and he ran a hand over his face.

Ford had a cynical grin. "That's right. Katya..."

Andrew smiled distantly though he didn't take up the topic. "I can't seem to care about the things that used to matter. At least here I feel like there's a chance of making a different life."

Adam rolled down the window, letting the air rush over him. When he spoke it was half to himself. "Teaching English has become what the military was for all those second sons of rich Victorians, forced to find their fortune in the colonies."

Ford stared. "You can be profound when you're drunk."

"I was quoting someone," his voice falling flat.

"Who?"

"Clare."

"Clare?"

He rolled up the window. "Nobody."

Adam sometimes wondered at his students' desire to learn a language which belonged in a far-off place. Learning English, he knew, was a way of preparing to meet the invaders. Their motivation, he saw, anticipated wrenching upheaval, a tectonic separation of places and peoples. Very soon things which had always been would end.

He wondered who would be moving into his father's house.

"What you said is true," Andrew muttered. "That's what we're doing here. We're the second sons. And we have found our fortunes, haven't we? Maybe not the sort of fortune we expected, but still a kind of wealth. History has ebbs and tides, but we are living at a moment of significance. How many people can say that? Just think how many guys spend their lives stuck in a frozen age, their potential choked by the inertia of their time. We should be relieved that we've cut ties with our parents' generation, with their ransomed safety. Think of those people back home kissing the feet of some old fart until they can fill his shoes. But here we are needed. There is opportunity in this place…"

Ford groaned, a deep, primitive sound that seemed to shake the tiny car. "Shut up!" He plugged his ears. "This place is two missed meals away from a revolution, for fucksake.

Besides which there are more pressing matters, like three guys I know lost behind the Iron Curtain wearing togas..." but just then his voice trailed away as the car came to a stop in front of a brightly lit building.

"Here you are," the driver said.

Ford opened the door and fell onto the sidewalk, where he was met by the shrill voices of Alice and Candace.

"Where were you guys? We've been waiting for I don't know how long."

Andrew appeared on the curb, flushed with himself. "Just a bout of identity crisis."

"It was much worse than that," said Ford who was still on the ground. "Another minute of his righteousness and I would have vomited."

Andrew adjusted his laurels and surveyed the others. "He'll vomit anyway."

With a flourish of inebriated bravado Andrew lifted Alice onto his shoulder, her toga nearly covering his head. She shrieked, feet kicking so that one of her plastic sandals soared into the bushes as they entered the building. Candace came behind dragging Ford, pausing so he could hug the doorman, who glanced at them as if he had seen all of this before.

KATYA MET Andrew at the flat on Granatny Street. He had brought a bottle of wine, and even though the days were getting cold they'd taken chairs onto the balcony and watched the city as they drank. She sighed as the wine moved along her shoulders, settling like heat upon the tightness in her chest. She had been to the hotel again and she still felt unclean and despairing.

Andrew was bundled in his coat. He leaned back in his chair to consider her. "What'd you do today?" he asked in Russian.

She ran a hand through his hair with false roughness, like you might with a child. "I was working."

He smiled uncertainly, recognizing this mood. Katya had long spells of silence when Andrew would find her lost in thought. He felt uneasy around her melancholy, sensing that it somehow threatened him. "How is the translation going?"

She looked into the street. "It's slow."

Below them a tram lumbered noisily up the street which was busy with people coming home from work.

"You're cold," he said, pressing her fingers to his mouth. "Come inside..."

She felt the warmth of his hand around hers, and at that moment she felt a desire to tell him everything about her family, the bleeding away of hope that left her afraid. She wanted to tell Andrew these things, to tell him the things she had said to Adam at the *dacha*. But in the same instant she knew that she could not articulate her fears in a way Andrew would understand. He had no reference. He would see only what she lacked, the objects themselves, not the emotions which attended their absence. Katya did not want assurances from him. She wanted him to know the strength it took to stare back at disaster. But Andrew could not understand, she knew. And this kept her silent.

Despite his ignorance of these things she did find consolation in Andrew, and she drew on that comfort, finding if not understanding then at least a temporary release. Words were not everything, in the end. And so she let him lead her now to that place they had stolen from the world.

His mouth tasted of wine, and she licked at it. He pulled her shirt from her shoulders. She felt his embrace tighten and he lifted her onto him. She bit into his arm until he cried out. As they moved to the bed she could see their shadow on the wall.

Andrew fell asleep as he often did after sex. But never her. She savoured this time, was looking forward to it even as he entered her. It came as its own release from the intensity of the union, this chance to be pleased with the after sensations of her body. She would lay listening to the sounds of the city, the refrigerator's hum, the thump and scrape of lives in the flat above them. She could see into the building across the road during the day, see children in windows, flags of laundry waving from balconies. When he woke, Andrew might move his face against her hair, his finger tracing the lines of shadow that ran like cracks across her skin.

"What is it?" Lydia asked.

Ivan looked up from his wife's writing desk.

"I have lost my pen."

"Your good one?"

"Have you seen it?"

Lydia's voice sounded hopeful. "Perhaps you left it at the Party office?"

"I will check tonight."

"You're going back?"

"Yes," he started, instantly forgetting the pen. "We are raising support for the protest."

"What sort of support?"

"They are calling for the army to step in, but it's not budging. So we are sending a delegation, but of course what is slowing us down is that no one wants to lose his head. It is all very delicate."

Lydia looked out the window, sighing as her husband's voice returned to its old earnestness. Ivan had grown increasingly agitated, going on at meals about what might come of the situation.

He straightened, his face lightening. "What is that smell?"

"Katya bought sausage this afternoon."

"They did not rob her, I hope."

Lydia made an effort to smile, and after this they spoke of other things until he became restless again and returned to his study.

On his desk were newspapers and reports of the situations in the capital, which had consumed his attention since problems at the parliament began. There had been a debate that same afternoon which had turned the local Party office into a hive of union leaders, municipal apparatchiks, veterans' groups and other sympathizers of the old cause. People spilled outside the meeting room and into the hallways, clutching sheaves of notes while waiting their turn to be heard.

Despite the crisis they were debating, Ivan secretly relished this time. As he sat in his office, he could not help letting his thoughts return to the meeting, reviewing the emotion and energy of the debate.

"What do the deputies stand for?" one man had bellowed, punctuating each sentence with his fist. "Is this why we voted for them? Have they said anything about basic services? What about heat? What about bread? On the television they talk of liberty and brotherhood, and wave rifles, while the country can't feed itself. We must first consider social order and the rule of law," he stammered. "The same law that these deputies disrupt!"

"Who is being served by the law now?" someone shouted from the gallery. "Our people or the foreigners?"

Uproar from the incensed crowd. "Sit down grandfather!"

The man left the tribune shaking his head. From behind him a woman took his spot, her face flushed as she faced the crowd.

"Comrades, I come to you on behalf of your fellow workers at…"

Many of those in the assembly stood rapt in the debates, breaking their attention to light a cigarette or mutter heatedly to the person next to them. Others huddled with their backs turned to the meeting, whispering among themselves. In the gallery sat a dozen soldiers with their grey coats, all of them arguing in loud voices until they were shouted down by those around them. At one of the doors steelworkers loitered just off their shift. Silent throughout the speeches, they responded only with glances and nods among themselves. At the front of the room a woman nursed her child, while with her free hand she took notes in the margin of a newspaper.

Throughout the day people continued to arrive and by midafternoon the windows bled with condensation. As the crowd grew uncomfortable they began interrupting whoever was speaking. Periodically the room boiled over and disputes started between individuals. At one point two members of the press appeared at the back of the room but a handful of men threw them out, only to be sent looking for them five minutes later when the council learned they were from a paper with Party sympathies.

At the front of the room, Ivan had listened euphorically through it all with the other members of the executive. He was elated by this infusion of energy, this hope of resurrecting what only a few weeks ago had seemed dead. At the end of each debate committees were formed, delegates nominated, resolutions made, ratified and passed, declarations sent off by courier to the local media, followed by cheering and applause. One member of the executive concluded each decision with a few words from Marx or Lenin, the familiar catechisms sending tears stumbling over the aged faces in the crowd. Above them the old flag hung like a gash on the wall. The tribal fraternity had been renewed, drawing them all together with that fragile confederacy of nostalgia.

Yet for all the hope he felt amid the organs of the Party, Ivan envied those behind the barricades in Moscow. At these times his boyhood memories came back to him, and he glowed with a feeling of destiny's thread sewing his life into a tapestry of great names and events. The thunder of insurrection in Moscow seemed to him now an echo of shells rumbling across the rooftops of Leningrad, and again he felt there was a reality, a certainty, in the triumph of those events. Between speakers Ivan stared out one of the great windows in the hall to look upon the giant obelisk at the end of Victory Square, feeling himself mirrored in the monument's granite faces, their gaze hovering over this moment.

Ivan finally took his turn at the podium late in the afternoon. He paused there to remove his coat. A murmur went through the hall at the sight of his loose sleeve as people remembered the stories of him. Ivan heard his name whispered among the faces now watching him, and a rush of his old pride returned and in an instant he was no longer a humbled apparatchik, but instead he was again a rising star of the People's Party. Looking out over the surrounding faces, Ivan felt that all was not lost, that the Party could still protect them from the nightmare of chaos that had come upon them again out of the west.

"Comrades," he started, his brow quilting with concentration. "I am moved to respond to earlier remarks made here regarding order and law. Such concerns only consider the surface of our troubles. Look below this surface, and you will find that cold and hunger are a cause of the present state of things, not the reverse." A murmur fluttered through the hall as he paused to wipe his cheek with a handkerchief. "Negotiation and compromise have their place, but this crisis would not be upon us if such recourses had not already proven impotent." Applause from the crowd. "In recent days I have often wondered what warms our Communist deputies still loyal to the People, who alone face the unnumbered forces of our oppressors. I can only think that it must be a larger idea to which they have dedicated themselves, to which they have attached their lives. What will there be for these men if they fail? Imprisonment? The firing squad? Will they be remembered for their struggle? What will happen to your lives if these men fail? Will the breadlines become shorter? Will our wants ease? Do any of us understand the implications of this moment?"

A fretful mutter of assent gathered in the hall's ceiling, coaxing even the chandeliers into faint applause.

Ivan stepped back and opened his hand to the assembly. "Our nation must choose between cultural and economic slavery to the Western imperialists, and the determined interest in the common good which led our people out of serfdom, that built schools and universities, that gave women rights decades before the West. That dream has been resurrected for us by the Party's deputies in Moscow – will we not answer it? Is the cold that bad, comrades? Can we not be hungry a little longer?" He looked around the assembly and the hall stared back, their faces taut and inspired. "I think I know the answer, comrades. And so there is only one question remaining to be decided here today..." And he paused again, the rapid fire of invectives abruptly slowing as he pounded out the final syllables with his fist. "When do we take back history for the People? When do we leave for Moscow?"

Those in the gallery began stamping their feet, sending a shudder of thunder through the hall. As it began to die down members of the council looked at one another. The chairman – a pale man wearing only his shirt in the room's heat – went to the podium. "Comrades, you have spoken – now let the President listen! Let the world listen! The voice of the People whose resolve gave birth to our Party will now rise to save it!"

A roar of haggard passion engulfed the room. Ivan shook the hands thrust at him. People in the crowd embraced. Hats and bits of paper leapt in the air.

When the assembly calmed down, a resolution was passed to support the insurgents. A delegation of Party members was elected to travel to Moscow and join those on the barricades. "Citizens from every corner are rushing to save Russia," the chairman declared. "We, too, will answer the call with our voices, with our conviction, with our blood if it is needed!"

When the resolution was completed, a boy carried it to the printing press in the basement. Even as the assembly began to disperse, there came from the floor beneath them the rhythmic thud of the press's gears and hydraulics, and Ivan could not help but grin at the familiar sound of the old Party voice.

AS THEY entered the museum each felt dwarfed by the great lobby. They stood looking about, voices lowering instinctively to the hushed tones of a funeral home.

Ford stared at the empty hall. "At least we got here before the tourists."

The expats left their things at the coat check with grey-haired men who sold tickets and handed out pamphlets printed in different languages. The group passed in ones and twos through a columned gallery made bright by a wall of high windows looking onto a courtyard. The palace had once been the home of the nobility before the Revolution, after which the building had been saved by the Soviets. The new government now used such places as means of collecting hard currency from tourists.

They moved alone or in pairs, gaping with vapid appreciation at a suite of staterooms – gilded portals, painted ceilings, Kashmiri screens, Rococo commodes, mosaics, and, in one room, a stuffed alligator next to the fireplace. Connecting these rooms was a long passage smelling faintly of disinfectant, the walls lined with portraits of nineteenth-century nobility in all their doomed postures of entitlement. From room to room Adam and the others connected the numbered dots in their pamphlets, moving almost wordlessly through the cold palace.

At the end of the corridor was a receiving hall decorated with ornamental panels and a series of mounted busts. This wing of the palace concluded with a library, which featured a collection of muskets and scimitars on walls of crimson damask. The adjacent reading room was crowned with a low dome descending upon shelves over which ran Classical scenes: Socrates drinking hemlock; Titus killing his sons; the Roman goddess of wisdom and her owl with the moon rising behind them.

For most of the morning they moved through the palace's relentless affluence, coming finally to a ballroom, which, like the last moments of sunset, seemed the brightest of all. It was a rectangular chamber. The ceiling was painted with a panorama of subjects, and lit with three great chandeliers. Along the north side stood a series of arches, supported by ornamental columns painted with leaves and long-beaked birds.

Adam let out a low whistle.

Ford shook his head. "Shee-it."

"Everything's so romantic," said Hillary, gazing at the ballroom. "Like something out of *Cinderella*."

Troy made a sound at the back of his throat. "Are you kidding – haven't you read any Tolstoy? These places were shark pools."

She gazed wistfully at the room. "It must have seemed impossible back then that all of this would disappear."

"We should have kept our coats," Alice shivered.

Adam crossed his arms. "They don't heat these places very well."

When they were tired they returned to the lobby. They waited at the coat check among a busload of tourists whose guide called in vain over the general turmoil. "*Hierher, bitte...bitte!*"

After gathering their things they moved through the crowd and into the relative quiet of the street. At the curb Andrew turned to go.

"It's been fun..."

The others looked at one another uncertainly. "What are you doing?"

"Meeting some people."

Alice bit her lip. "I thought we were going to the art gallery next?"

"It's quite good," Andrew remarked absently. "There's even a small Repin collection."

Emil crossed his arms. "You've already been there?"

During their first weeks at the university, Andrew had become the centre of their group of teachers and academics, who clung to his confidence and ease in this country. As September wore on they grew more comfortable here, though the group still kept largely to themselves, the alien world around them entrenching their reliance on one another. This preoccupation with themselves was fed by a series of brief romances and unlikely friendships, which put off the uncomfortable idea of venturing forth on their own among the locals. Gradually they evolved into an incestuous clique, their anxious self-love constructed around shared nostalgia. The distractions of their youth now took on immediate importance. They discussed in earnest the details of old movies or the origins of the grunge movement. Together they laughed over remembered episodes of *The Simpsons*. They alone had knowledge of these things, which became a kind of border that kept outsiders out.

But as Andrew began spending more time with Ilyin and Katya, the group's confidence waned. His growing absence was an affront to the expats' faith in their own self-sufficiency.

Adam watched with the others as Andrew crossed the road. At the other side, he turned and waved to them before disappearing, blending easily into the crowds of strangers surrounding them.

Later that afternoon Adam sat with the others at Monsieur Wong's. It was busy, so instead of talking they sat watching the activity around them with satisfaction. Waiters in berets and striped shirts hustled people to tables where they were served by waitresses with chopsticks in their hair and wearing dragon-patterned frocks. The place still had that new smell of plastic and glue, and as customers sat they looked appreciatively at the decor. Most of those who came in were young, sporting leather jackets, jewellery and that conspicuous atmosphere of the city's *nouveau riche* – software specialists and money changers, local nabobs and managers.

People reclined self-consciously in oversized rattan chairs, staring at the vases of faux bamboo and the usual smudgy Monet portraits of distant women and ponds.

"Cool," Ford pronounced, stamping the place with single-syllable approval. Several others nodded assent.

Once or twice a week the expats inspected the new restaurants opening throughout the city. These places were among the first wave of foreign investment to appear in the former Soviet bloc, the missionary outposts of large American and European chains eager to convert native tastes. At night a person's gaze was drawn to their storefronts, glinting like pyrite on the otherwise dull asphalt of the city's streets. For foreigners such places offered brief moments of repatriation, from which they looked out, like kittens from a sack, on the dark river which had swept them up.

Wherever these places appeared, the group of expats from the dormitory would queue beneath the familiar signs with genuine anticipation, nudging each other into the cramped harbours of bright plastic and hard currency. The menus were usually printed in Russian, and they would laugh uncomfortably at the new sound of familiar things. They sighed and cooed over the cardboard cradles of fries or pizza or burger combos. And when they were fully satisfied, when every detail, from the straw dispensers to the pastel prints screwed to the walls, had been inspected and commented on, they would leave oddly contented with themselves, satisfied that it was just like home.

Adam saw how these expeditions resuscitated the spirits of the other teachers, and he joined them that night hoping he too would find some reprieve from the culture shock he faced. Instead he felt disappointed in himself, sensing that he was not properly appreciating the experience. Rather than remind him of what he missed, these forays only blurred their familiarity for him. The fabric of his loyalties had begun to tear, and behind it he found something missing, some quality without taste or colour or texture, but which, when absent, altered these things. Coke now tasted the same as Pepsi, and he had almost forgotten why Gap was cool and Levis wasn't, whose hamburgers were grilled and whose weren't, or what brand whitened better than whatever. Not that he had previously cared about these things, only that their distinctions, however bland, had once been entrenched textures in his life. But subtleties like these were not real here. Where you bought your jeans meant nothing when their real value now lay in the fact that you could trade ten pairs of them for a car. A pack of Marlboros or Camels could still buy a cab ride. Hamburgers and colas and gum were fragments of a faraway place. For the expats at the university, these were not only items to be purchased, but a currency with which to buy back a piece of themselves.

But for Adam, this part of himself was gone. Going to a new restaurant was like seeing someone you knew without clothes on. Things he had never really looked at now glared at him, so that the more he discovered the less he felt he knew. The more layers of familiarity he found in these places, the more naked they actually appeared. The other expats were often irritated with his lack of enthusiasm on these outings, his despondency acting as a slow leak in their bubble.

"Don't let it depress you," Alice counselled. "Lighten up and enjoy yourself."

The first thing Adam noticed when they sat was all the seams he had never been aware of – the kitschy uniforms of the staff, the aggressive blandness.

"It's not how I remember it," he observed, though Alice wasn't listening.

Hillary was staring at the menu. "I never thought I would be eating Chinese food in this country."

"Chinese and French," some people reminded her.

"Just look at the menu," Troy cut in. "'Dim sum, giant fortune cookies, and even Mongolian meatballs.'"

Alice glanced at the door. "I thought Andrew was coming?"

"He's just late."

The food appeared, and for a while they were busy eating.

During the meal Adam caught glimpses of his reflection in the glass tabletop. He was aware of himself eating and smiling like the others. There was a sense of anxious contradiction about them, he saw, as if each was clutching in one hand what they had let go of with the other. At one moment they were praising each other for getting out of the demoralizing routine of short-term teaching contracts and dead-end work back home, and the next they were discussing how international experience would enhance their résumés in the West. They blamed their parents' generation for the poor job prospects, while running down the Russian university that had hired them all.

"Damn it," Ford said, sulkily jabbing a wonton. "It wasn't supposed to happen this way. We're the ones who did our homework..."

Ford had studied sociology at Michigan. After graduation he discovered that the only job he could find was selling futons for a family friend. In desperation he had gone to graduate school for a couple of years before giving up and taking a teaching job overseas.

In 1993 it was still possible to live pretty well in the former Soviet bloc if you had some foreign currency. This was one of the few positive surprises for those who had gone east to find work. In their own countries they had foregone material extravagances for years, learning to get by on grant money, student loans, and the skeletal salary of part-time work. By their late twenties, most of them already held doctorates yet still lived in student ghettos, or downtown above sub shops; most, too, had never owned a car, unless a parent had donated one. Their apartments were crammed with books and marking, a few plants, furniture from the Sally Ann, the walls decorated with old posters, or watercolours done by someone's aunt. By thirty, they had quietly begun enrolling in community colleges, taking night classes in software development or something useful.

But here, in their new country, even a modest amount of hard currency allowed them to live in relative excess. To see a movie cost pennies, and a first-class train ticket was a few bucks. Clothes, alcohol, books – these things were available at a fraction of their cost in the West. Good seats at the opera ran for twenty-five cents. A Lada could be purchased for what, back home, would amount to the price of a few tanks of gas. A few hundred bucks from your parents went a lot farther than meeting last month's rent. There might not be heat in your dormitory, but you could literally sip champagne each night while you froze. Though they complained about their new country, there were few among the expatriate teachers who did not appreciate this change in their fortunes. If Adam and the others were insolvent in their own countries, here they found themselves with an astonishingly austere sort of prosperity.

Adam stood and went to the restroom at the back of the restaurant, where he splashed water on his face. Glancing at himself in the mirror, he noted that his hair was getting long, making him appear unfamiliar, even to himself. He watched the retreating water suck one of his hairs into the drain, thoughts of Clare coming back to him.

The week they moved in together, Adam had borrowed the old man's car and taken Clare driving in the country. She brought a tape of Puccini and hummed along. They rolled down the windows. It was September, and in the city behind them they had left a calendar of assignments and deadlines.

"We have to get out of here," she'd insisted. "In a couple of weeks there will be exams, and then the leaves will start changing. This is the last good month." He had always remembered her saying that.

"I should probably be planting bulbs," she went on. When she had seen the yard behind their apartment, Clare announced she was going to plant tulips. "If I wait too long we won't have any flowers in the spring."

"No, this is better," he said, smiling at her.

They were driving in the country, and everything was warm and golden. There was a dirt road she knew of that went down by the river. Between singing and giving directions, she paused to stare at her hand in the light of that nearly faultless day. They stopped at a place below some rapids where the water was calm and there was a spot to stretch out.

On a log they ate the chicken and bread she had packed. Later they went swimming, drifting and talking together in the river's easy current, afterward making love on the clay bank.

For a long time they lay at the water's edge, their voices mingling with the breeze and the sounds of the river. They spoke of classes and lack of money and graduation, of their apartment and the future.

She ran a hand playfully over his head. "Look," she said, holding open her palm. It was streaked with a tangle of wet hair.

He scowled at her hand. "What's going on?"

"You're balding."

"Are you sure?"

"Have you looked in the tub lately?"

Adam stared at her palm. He was propped on his elbow, his own hand on her belly. Next to them trees shivered on the surface of the water, the reflection so deep you might climb the branches all the way to the bottom. He glanced at her. "Why are you with me?"

"Don't get serious."

"I am serious. Really."

Her face became still, and she sat up to look at him. "Think of all the countries I've travelled to, where I've worked – Indonesia, South Africa, Nepal..."

"So you have a lousy travel agent."

Clare shrugged and lay back. "I like troubled places."

Rolling over, Adam gazed at the branches of a tree leaning over them. Somewhere a frog trilled, and all around them the breeze whispered in the tall grass. He began to feel better. "I guess I don't scare you."

"Only sometimes."

"Yeah?"

Clare was watching him. "Sometimes I think you're the most afraid person I've ever met."

He looked incredulous. "What am I afraid of?"

"Failure, your father, me..."

"I guess I just hate judgement," he replied, in a self-mocking tone. But he saw she was frowning.

"I don't care if you hate the rest of the world," she said, "as long as I'm not a part of that. I am your home now, and you are mine."

"You make it sound like it's us against the world."

"This is me being serious."

He drew a hand over his face. "You're right."

"You're ready for this, aren't you?"

He looked into the grass. "I don't want to be anywhere else."

Through the leaves slivers of sunlight fell on him, running like fault lines across his skin. She found his hand. He felt the ring, still cool from the river.

"It's the truth," he said.

Standing over the sink in that restaurant, Adam understood that this was the moment he began lying to her. All of these thoughts of Clare came back to him in the washroom not as a memory, but as one moment of feeling, with the smells and sounds of the restaurant. When he returned to the others Adam resisted his reflection in the glass table.

Not long after dinner they gave up waiting for Andrew, and decided to leave for the club without him.

"He'll show up," Ford assured them, but from the way his jaw was set you could tell he was unsure. "He's the one who told us about this club."

The club was located in an area of the city constructed after the war, the neighbourhood built with a square, mean architecture that aged as badly as the ideology which inspired it. The crumbing facades of buildings looked onto the street, alleys and courtyards congested with trash. But on some blocks the dilapidated structures had been taken over by cellar cafés with their clientele of students and intellectuals, or made into punk squats that attracted crowds of aggressive-looking teenagers wearing long coats and t-shirts with the names of obscure rock groups.

Without explanation Ford directed the group into an alley, where they passed around a bottle he produced from his coat. Then Troy lighted something and handed it to Adam, who took a drag self-consciously.

"Leave some for the rest of us," said Alice, and she winked at him as he passed it to her.

Voices from the street skittered among them, and the group drew close to one another in the darkness. When the joint came to her Hillary giggled before taking a drag, saying, "I haven't done this for a long time." The others smiled at one another. As they got stoned their anxiety over Andrew's absence turned into a kind of nervous excitement. The bottle made another round, and Adam noted the faintly sweet taste left by Alice's mouth.

Ford had been drinking hard all night, and the pot had put him in a good place. "This is great," he breathed, staring at the last of the joint. "I realize how uptight I was before coming here. But with you guys, it's like I can finally be free from all that shit." As they finished the bottle, another joint appeared. "Andrew doesn't know what he's missing."

Candace said something in reply, but Adam wasn't listening any more. The cold had disappeared, and he felt a warm and unfamiliar security.

"You okay?"

"I'm not used to this," he grinned, his voice coming to him from a distance.

"Shit man," Ford said. "You're too quiet. It scares me sometimes how quiet you are. You gotta live out loud, dude. Gotta just let yourself go…"

Adam laughed for no distinct reason, and when the second joint was handed to him he held its warmth in his chest for a long moment before letting it go, forgetting to exhale when he spoke so that he ended up gagging.

A hand thumped him on the back. "Dude, that's the way…"

They left the alley and followed Ford for another block to a warehouse that looked abandoned except for a sign over the door which said PANDAEMONIUM in jagged strokes of neon lettering.

Candace stared with open approval at the surrounding dilapidation. "How *off-piste*," she cooed.

Ford leaned into Adam. "Do you know what she's saying?"

Drums throbbed from inside, and as the bouncers let them pass the group was caught up instantly by the intensity of the music. They were led down a stairwell reeking with damp and smoke to a room in the basement. A hole had been knocked in one wall, and through it they saw limbs and bodies moving on the other side.

Ford crossed the room and motioned to them before disappearing into the narrow passage. One by one they squeezed through to the other side where they were met by a charge of sound. Adam halted as soon as he came through the opening. The heat formed a thickness in the air which seemed to stick in his lungs. Next to him the wall was beaded with condensation. A murky mass of bodies moved to the drums' pulsing, and it was a moment before he could locate Alice and the others among them. Looking around he saw they were in a large open area that stretched beyond his sight into shadow. Against one wall were the lost, writhing forms of the band which seemed to be in a struggle with themselves. Pink and green lights bled through rafters onto the crowd, and from each corner spotlights swung out over their heads in jerking arcs. Behind the band Adam could see stacks of black speakers looming like dark totems through the smoke and shadow.

He found the others next to the bar. Ford was yelling over the music. "...and it's German!"

Adam caught Alice's eye. "What's he saying?"

She pressed her mouth into his ear. "The band – *Kostuemhaus* – they're German," she screamed, pointing over the crowd toward the band. "They're very big in Munich!"

Ford appeared, offering beer to each of them. "See," he cried holding up one of the bottles, "I told you – Rothaus in this place!" Alice moved away to talk with someone else. Ford nodded at the stage, and said something Adam couldn't hear.

"Sure," he agreed as loudly as he could. "Like, totally."

Ford frowned at him, and then left in search of more beer.

Waitresses in black leather and studded collars moved through the crowd with trays. If you wanted to order a drink you had to pull a chain attached to their collars.

Alice returned, and she pointed as Hillary tried to catch one of the waitresses. Adam watched her lips moving, straining to make out what she was saying.

They stood at the bar, drinking and watching the band. Candace danced with herself oblivious of the others, the strobe lights breaking up her motions. She swung a glass as she danced so that beads of liquid appeared in flashes of pink and amber over her head. The others picked up her mood and began dancing in their own circle. Soon Ford and Hillary disappeared into the crowd, and now and then Adam caught sight of their faces. When they grew tired the group paused and Troy bought the next round and then Adam followed.

Songs melted into each other, the deepening pulse of drums overlaid with the singer's hoarse chant, the amplified syllables pressing on the crowd until the words seemed to come from their own mouths.

The pot reappeared, this time handed about by Candace who had bought some from one of the bartenders. Ford and Hillary surfaced, and for a minute they all stood about perspiring and stoned and grinning. Then someone began dancing again and the others followed. The joint left Adam feeling shaky and he hesitated by the bar, but then Alice had his hand and was pulling him away, clutching him as they began to dance. Light blinked in rapid bursts, now purple and blue, keeping time with the drums. His head swam as they moved, and to steady himself he tried focussing on the spot where Alice's hand pressed on him. She smiled and Adam knew she did not understand how close he was to atomizing before her, his flesh becoming like sand between her fingers.

He broke away from her and pushed into the self-embrace of the crowd which pulsed with the music. The dancers' faces were contorted by the shuddering light, their lips moving uselessly.

302

He found a washroom and retreated into one of the stalls, hiding there for several minutes. His head spun and he let it come to rest against the door, centring his attention on the circle of cold pressure between his eyes. It was a long time since he had been so stoned, and he'd forgotten this part. Darkened images danced behind his eyes. The music like a bruise inside his head.

The walls were scarred with ulcers of rust which leaked like open sores from the paint. He clenched his teeth, tried to steady himself by counting the cigarette burns in the floor. He listened to the sounds in the washroom. There were rough noises and shuffling about. Feet appeared below the door. There was a knock and a hoarse demand.

His fingers shook on the latch. The door swung open and he faced a guy who leered at him in a blur of piercings and leather, his mouth a silhouette of black lipstick.

The voice was flat and severe. "*Pashli.*"

Adam winced, bracing for some sort of assault.

The man laughed. "Tourist, yes?"

Adam paused with his mouth open, unsure of the answer.

"You come to see the band?"

"No. Not at all."

Outside the washroom he found Alice waiting for him amid the drums and shadows and trembling light. She said something, but he couldn't hear so she grabbed his hand and pulled him along. She was hot from dancing, and her shirt felt damp against his hand. As they approached the bar, the others were standing about looking sober. Andrew was there with his Russian friends.

Alice leaned into Adam, shaking her head with disappointed gravity. "He hasn't even introduced us."

"What's the use?" he said. "It's too hard with this music..."

This annoyed her, and she left in search of better allies.

Andrew appeared next to him. "Sorry we're late," he shouted. "Isn't this place awesome?"

He made an effort to grin. "I was just going."

Andrew was looking at him. "Are you okay to get back? You'll need a key. They lock everything up at midnight."

"Of course," Adam said, but after a brief search he was unable to find his keys, so Andrew gave him his own.

He shouted something, but by then Andrew was talking to Katya.

Adam left the club, feeling stoned and self-conscious as he fumbled out of the warehouse in search of a way home. An hour later he was still feeling groggy as he crossed the street in front of the dormitory.

At the corner he heard a child's cry from an open window, and he stopped for a moment. The cry hung in the air about him, following him to the dormitory.

In his room he undressed and tried to sleep, though later he was woken by a knock on the door and then the rattle of the knob. Through the wood he heard a woman call his name. Framing his existence in her voice, a question.

"Adam?"

It was Alice.

He was quiet, uncertain of what to do. There was, he saw, nothing to say.

A truck was passing under his window and he turned away from the door, looking instead into the window. Light from the truck fell on him, discovering his nakedness, and as the vehicle moved up the street, the dark covered him again.

THEY CAUGHT a tram which took them out to the Uzbek neighbourhood in the city's east end, then walked the rest of the distance behind a turnip truck. The streets were narrow and busy with people on their way to the market. As they turned the corner they met a wind which funnelled between the grey, brooding buildings. Katya pulled her black *shapka* down over her ears. "You do not need to be here," she said, returning to her former complaint.

"It should not all fall to you," her mother muttered, glancing uneasily about. Lydia had insisted they begin going to the city's large weekend market where prices were said to be good.

As they walked Katya examined her mother again, frowning at the woman's coat. "You shouldn't have worn that."

"What is wrong with it?"

"It is too nice for the market."

"I am tired of looking poor," she said, becoming angry. "Anyway, aren't we all supposed to want to be rich now?"

"You can't give people here a reason to think you have money."

Lydia stopped and shook her fist. "We are only going to this place because we do not have money!"

Held in a stadium built for the 1980 Olympics, the weekend market eclipsed the weekday trade done in Krasnya Square. Three streets converged at the stadium's main gates, and before dawn on weekends each road was clotted with vehicles from the surrounding farms and villages. At the corner Katya and her mother paused as a line of trucks rolled past, flecked with black mud from the country. In some of the vehicles farm boys sat on crates or burlap bags pointing curiously at people. As Katya and her mother crossed the street, a truck passed with children looking out from the dirty windows.

The stadium's rotunda was circled with immense mosaics of athletes, while over the main entrance hung a ragged motif celebrating Soviet

Sport. Inside there was no order to the place. Merchants set up their goods wherever there was room, and by midmorning the market had bled into a maze of meandering aisles and congested warrens where vendors bickered and swore down to the last kopek, closing deals with a show of teeth. Clothing lay in mismatched piles, old apple crates sat heaped with bootlegged CDs, while Japanese radios blasted American country and western music. There were cheese and fish mongers, a pair of women at a table of false teeth, tanned farmers selling vegetables, men hawking everything from pornography to yarn, a tubercular-looking guy with bolts of velour, rows of Sony televisions each animated with the same episode of *The Simpsons*, and a truck of butchered cattle. Sheet roofing, copper piping, rugs, electric guitars, fruit and vegetables – all stood next to one another in the arena.

Katya saw right away that her mother misunderstood the adamant attention of vendors. Even as Lydia brushed them aside, her vanity drew them closer. In this place her mother became a liability, incapable of distinguishing between appearances and intent, while the brazen vulgarity of merchants made her skittish.

"Now stay here," Katya insisted. "Keep out of the way while I haggle."

"What kind of word is that?" she frowned, but stood back all the same while her daughter searched among the vendors for the things they needed.

Between purchases Katya explained to the old woman what she was doing. "Watch over here," she said, pointing to two women at a stall. "If the short one does not respond with encouragement then the transaction will die..."

Lydia listened to her daughter as she pointed out how customers faced a merchant. As the arguing closed on a price their eyes tightened, shoulders slightly raised. Katya tried to read each trader's body, looking for cracks in his resolve. Sometimes one of them would spit, leer, or otherwise attempt to intimidate customers, some of whom flinched or cowered.

"There it is," Katya whispered. "Do you see how he sighed? He appears to capitulate only after he has his price. You are okay with these people," she counselled, "as long as you can read them."

It took almost an hour to buy most of what they needed. Lydia had too little money, and

Katya was often forced to try several vendors before finding one willing to meet her price. "I did not think that woman would go lower," she confided. "But as I was losing hope she began to stutter, and I knew she would go down."

"How do you know so much about these things?"

Katya walked on, as if she had not heard.

"I'm sorry. We will not speak of this." Lydia reached for her daughter's hand as they left the stadium. "I am no help to you in this place. Why can't I just buy something, or sell something? Why must we always be tricking each other?"

Katya looked back at the stalls, her voice resigned. "These days everyone must be someone else."

Then, as she turned to leave, they both started. Across the road had stood a statue of the great leader, which now stood missing its head and one hand.

"Who did this?" Lydia said.

The torso and limbs remained undamaged, but the left shoulder was badly scarred where someone had struck at the base of the neck. It made you uneasy to look upon it – both legs braced defiantly, one arm lifted in triumph over a head that was nowhere to be found. Fragments of stone lay around, and crows walked about them as if searching for flesh.

Katya grabbed her mother's arm. "Let's go home."

The following afternoon Katya met Andrew at Café Rusak, which sat over one of the shops near their flat on Granatny Street. The Rusak was an intense, idiosyncratic place that drew its atmosphere from the customers who entered it. There was always a mismatched clientele at the café. Silent chess games and loud debates frequently went on side by side. Professors met students here for impromptu discussions. Young men sipping from the small cups of coffee congregated here to talk about politics or the past, while close by pensioners sat reading copies of *Pravda* or *Trood*.

That day Andrew showed up wearing a heavy military coat.

"Do you like it?"

She looked him over.

"You don't like it."

"Why would you want a soldier's coat?"

"It's kitsch."

"What is *kitsch*?"

"You'll get the humour if you think about it."

Katya frowned. "I have thought about it."

"Okay, then." He smiled tentatively. "Let's get something to drink."

Several of her friends from the university were also at the café, so they joined them, though Katya would have preferred to be alone. Ilyin was there, and as soon as they sat he began questioning his cousin.

"Where have you been lately? Mom has been missing you."

Andrew blushed. "I'm sorry," he started. "I'll come around tonight, or perhaps tomorrow afternoon?"

Ilyin smiled. "Whenever you like, you know. Whenever is fine. We're there." He glanced at Katya. "You're really busy now, I guess. I can understand, but my mom, you know she..."

"I'll be by tonight. Really."

"Of course you will," he said, smiling now to show him everything was all right. "Truly, though, Mom would like it."

"We're going to order," said Katya. "Stay here and we'll join you."

Then Andrew and Katya made their way through the café. There were a dozen or so tables along the walls and several more cluttering the middle of the room. At the back was a wooden counter with a charcoal grill, where a man made your coffee with a Turkish *cezve*. The door stood open regardless of the weather, and in the winter snow sometimes blew in and gathered around your chair. Andrew drew his coat around himself. "I need a coffee," he said.

There was a queue waiting to order, and as they waited Katya felt his fingers touch her hand. She looked over her shoulder.

"Do you think they know?"

"My cousin does."

"You've told him."

"Only a little."

"Has he told the others?"

"Ilyin? No, he'll keep it quiet." Andrew leaned into her so that her hair touched his face. "Does it matter?"

She drew back just enough.

He was staring at her mouth. "We'll keep quiet then."

Katya coloured, the fresh warmth of this attraction rising in her chest. She kissed him.

"You're terrible at secrets," he murmured.

Andrew went to join the others after they ordered, while Katya waited as the coffee was made. Each ladle had a long handle, which allowed the man to stand back from the fire while he worked. His face was warm and flushed. As the man ran a hand through his thinning hair, Katya recognized him as a former colleague of her father. The warmth and attraction she had been feeling vanished, and her stomach contracted.

He smiled at her over the grill, wiping his hands on his apron before speaking.

"Yekaterina Ivanovna! How good to see you again. How is your father?"

"He is well. And you?"

The man glanced around meaningfully. "I cannot complain," and he began wiping down the counter with the edge of his apron. "You have met a nice boy," he observed, nodding to where Andrew and the others were sitting.

Katya flushed but did not know how to reply. For a moment she was silent, not having any words to answer him.

"I see he is in the military. Where is he stationed?"

"He's very far away."

"Tch, tch," he said. "That's always the way."

Several people pressed behind her impatiently, and he emptied a ladle into saucers. The odour of coffee pressed on her. "Say hello for me to your father," he called as she moved out of the way.

'What am I doing?' she thought. From across the room she watched Andrew huddled in his soldier's coat and talking with her friends. A bad taste formed in her mouth. Her eyes hardened and she tried to shake the doubt from her head. 'No,' she thought. 'No, no…'

Andrew and the others were already deep in their old discussion as she sat down.

"Why should we worry about what the Europeans think?" someone was saying. "Is theirs the only game left to play?"

Ilyin nodded. "Read Tiutchev, read Khomiakov. We have always had a different path from Europe. No, we cannot make partners with those who do not understand us. We must find our own way."

"I disagree," Andrew rejoined, straightening the collar of his coat. "This country cannot go on watching everything crumble. You must move toward the West. The future is there."

Katya sat a little back on her stool, feeling awkward. Andrew's zeal reminded her uncomfortably of her father.

"What?" retorted a woman with a green scarf. "Do you think you can just ask them for help and then afterward expect them to leave? Look at Prague or Warsaw – there are foreign companies buying up entire streets. They come with dollars and pay with roubles. We're being devoured by our own currency."

Ilyin set down his cup. "No one thinks we could go back to communism," he said, glancing apologetically at Katya. "Too much has happened. The question now is what is best for the country. But the answer is not to jump into bed with the West."

Katya shifted.

One of the others nodded. "It would be national adultery."

"That's just putting your head in the sand," Andrew said, throwing up his hands. "Right now your progress is choked by corruption, which is a kind of civil war. You need to make alliances. Russia should join Europe, because it is the best thing for Russians. There could be a single economic bloc stretching from Lisbon to

317

Vladivostok: half a billion people with access to technology, education, and natural resources. It would make Russia a real power again. You can no longer look to your military to make you strong. The new conquerors are equipped with MBAs, not tanks."

Across the table people were shaking their heads. "This is not going to happen. You do not understand the desperation of our politics right now. We need our armies. If you really want to change things you will pick up a gun, or else sooner or later you will have one pointed at you. Look at things in Moscow."

"There is another way," one of the women said, her voice lowering. "We must look to the past for our future. That is where we left it. We must fulfil Russia's destiny as the Motherland of all Slavs."

"That policy only leads to suspicion and xenophobia." Andrew stared into his cup. "Russia is still psychologically a ghetto. You were locked in the past while the world moved on. If you are to catch up, you will need to understand what it is you are catching."

The woman with the green scarf kicked the table. "You would make this country a store front. If we keep on this way, we will all be clerks for someone else's ambition."

Katya stood. "I need to go," she said abruptly. "Goodbye…"

Andrew stopped her on the street. Instead of going to the flat as they had planned, Katya insisted on returning to school. "There are things I need to do."

He looked confused. "What's the matter?"

She turned on him. "How much did you pay for that coat?"

Andrew coloured as he told her.

Her father's friend waved through the café window.

"You were cheated," she hissed, waving back at the window. "Did you even haggle?"

That afternoon he returned to the university dissatisfied and confused. At the department office one of the secretaries gave him a fax that had come in from England, and he swore after he read it. Later he bawled out some of his students, then berated a librarian for some oversight that was probably his own and immediately apologized in a gushy, unsightly way.

When Katya arrived at the library she was flushed with anger and exertion. She was upset and confused by Andrew, and everything was unclear in her head. As she set out her papers and pencils she felt her breathing slow, and her thoughts turned to the translation she was working on. She sat for a long time, going over the passage before her, turning the words in her mind. Motes drifted in the light. A man with a blue sweater passed near the table, his shadow momentarily severing the light. Her eyes traced the words on the page, decoded their meaning, as she took it all into herself. Andrew gradually faded to the back of her thoughts. When she had memorized the poem Katya began to repeat the words, whispering them over and over to herself.

The clock ticked at the far end of the room. The man with the blue sweater reappeared, now laden with books. She did not know how long she had been repeating the poem until suddenly its parts began to metamorphose into Russian: words exchanging their outward selves, like a person changing clothes. Soon the rhythm of her incantation found its own energy, and she was no longer concentrating on the words as they transformed on her tongue, and instead she was writing them on the page, letting them unfold and open into Russian from a momentum and interpretation that came instinctually from within her. The light had shifted by then, and fell now through a window at the far end of the reading room. Katya's whispering slowed and then faded, but by then she was concentrating on the written words, instinctively measuring their meaning and cadence, weight and counterweight, bringing to them that balance and beauty so distinctive of her own language.

When she could do no more that day, Katya set down her pencil and leaned back in the chair to survey what she had accomplished. And she smiled.

Andrew sulked around the campus that afternoon until Katya came out of the library.

They walked together. A breeze drew them along, pulling at the handbills on trees and lampposts.

"I have something to tell you."

They came to the bridge below the park. It was almost dark by then, and they stood over the river and watched the city's lights come on.

Andrew spoke for a long time, whispering out of habit. He told her he had fallen in love.

"You do not even know me."

"That is what you're supposed to say."

"It's true all the same."

"How do you feel about me?"

"What am I supposed to say to that?"

He shrugged.

This made her angry. "You act like I should be comforted by what I feel, that it is some consolation for everything that is happening."

"You know that it is."

"Nobody knows anything. Nobody knows what is happening. Things are going on that I do not understand, that are taking me away from myself, from my family. And you want me to care about what I am feeling for you."

"I know it's scary right now, but it won't always be. You have to trust –"

She laughed at him. "How can I trust what you say, when you can't possibly know how things will turn out?"

"You can't be afraid to live."

Katya started. "That is just like you! Righteous statements and needless recklessness. Well, the stakes are very much higher for some of us."

He took the fax that had come from London and let it drop into the river. "There."

"What was that?"

"My life raft."

"I don't understand."

"It was a job offer. A good one. From England."

"Why did you *do* that?"

"I have nothing to go home to. I am staying here. With you. I'm evening the stakes."

Katya looked into the river. "They are not even. Not even now."

He watched her in the fading light.

When she spoke her voice was sad. "You should not have done that. We do not know each other, not really."

He touched her. "It feels as though we do."

The next day they met at the flat, and for a long while she tried to believe that Andrew was right.

After his recklessness on the bridge, Katya released herself, allowing the feelings they talked about to take her up and carry her away from her life. Most afternoons when classes ended, she would walk quickly through the bright afternoon light to the flat where Andrew would be waiting. If she saw him at the window, she forced herself to slow her ascent on the stairs, to count each one, drawing out the anticipation she felt. By the top step her chest would be tight with expectation, and as she came to the door she made her hand pause on the knob until she regained herself. But as she opened the door he would be there in the half light of the hall and she would take his hand and let him lead her inside.

She would rest on the old bed watching his hand on the slope of her stomach, his mouth on her breast, fingers tracing the length of her. If it were late, she would light candles and set them around the room so that they might find one another in the shiver of light. Here she reclaimed that autonomy now lost to everyone in her family, her country. Here she forgot the price of food, the almost-empty box of medals and jewellery. Those evenings were like fine clothes that did not belong to her. The time in the flat was a chance to savour something that came both from and for her, a chance to live in a way she knew could end any day.

It was here, in the after light of those afternoons, that Andrew began to share himself as he had not done with anyone before. He spoke at great length about his parents: his mother's exile, her disappointed marriage, his own childhood in America. And his father. He told her again and again things she already knew, repeating episodes and facts as if to make sure she truly knew, that she did not misremember, that she understood what had brought him to this place, even to this flat they now shared. He told her of how he had come to Russia to meet his father, of finding the flat where he had lived, and the pictures at the theatre. He told her about wanting a face for this man he had never seen, to see his father, only to see him. "I don't know what he looks like. Can you imagine not knowing what your own father looks like? I have shown you the photograph my mother tore in half. It's all I have of him. An ear and the color of his hair – that's what I have. All I want is to see him, to see what colour his eyes are, how tall he his, the way he holds a cup of coffee. Everyone knows something about their parents. You don't know what it is to have only a piece. A piece! That is why I have come here: to meet my father. I cannot see what comes after that," Andrew said. "I often imagine going someplace to meet him – usually it is at a flat or a restaurant – but when I open the door there is only an empty room. He has not come. No matter how often I imagine meeting him, I can't see farther than that moment when I arrive and he is not there, which of course is precisely what has happened since I got here."

On these afternoons Andrew often found her watching him, her eyes tracing his expression as though trying to find the lost thread of his thoughts, and immediately he would drop whatever it was he had been thinking to rekindle that story which was the root of him. "My mother always wanted me to speak Russian so someone else would understand that part of her. What she never knew was that I only learned Russian so that I would be able to speak with my father when I finally met him." Here Andrew's voice thinned to a whisper, and he found Katya's eyes still on him. "All that time she thought I was speaking those words for her...I knew it, too. I knew she thought I was doing it to be closer to her, but I wasn't." As he spoke the sunlight had faded into the west, drawing shadow after it until it covered them both in their nakedness. Soon Katya was left with only his voice in the darkness. "I lied to her. I know I did. My whole life I have wanted to meet my father, but even as a child I understood that I could not hope to know him if I didn't know his language. She gave me that."

They were silent for a moment, with only the heavy sound of his breathing between them. And then, in the darkness, Katya found his face and kissed it, pressing her mouth against each of his eyes so that she could taste the grief she knew would be there.

That same night when she got home Katya surprised herself by telling her father about Andrew's father. The family was in the living room. Katya was pretending to read at the table, while Petya marked exams next to the balcony doors which rattled with the wind. Lydia and Ivan sat together on the couch. The radio was on in the kitchen, and music drifted among them.

Ivan read from a newspaper. He half listened as Katya began speaking about Andrew. "What would you like me to do?"

Petya was looking at her from over his work. "How do you know this American?" he asked in English.

Katya ignored her brother and instead leaned toward Ivan, one hand coming to rest on the vacant sleeve of his shirt. "Can you still find out things the way you used to?" she asked doubtfully. "Can you help my friend?"

Ivan was irked by her insinuation of his fallen influence, but, savouring as he was the potential revival in the Party's prospects, he assented to her request.

"Write down the name," he said. "I'll find out what there is to know."

ANDREW MET Adam in the hall outside his room.

He stood with his coat over his shoulders, an unlit cigarette in his mouth. "I have an errand," he said slyly. "There might be some lifting. Want to come?"

Adam looked at him suspiciously. "We're not going to do anything illegal are we?"

"Perhaps a little."

Adam frowned. "I'll be staying in the car."

A look of relief came over Andrew. "Great. Let's go."

After turning down the job offer from England, Andrew now found himself feeling increasingly insecure, a sensation he responded to with almost morbid recklessness. He would go out drinking with Emil or the others, and they would have to drag him home. He became a loud drunk. He took risks he wouldn't have thought of before, dumb things that could land you in real trouble here: standing on a police car, or swimming in a public fountain. More than once the night had ended with them running from the police. It was as though Andrew was trying to confirm that life was in his control, that the influence over destiny he had felt back home was still there, that his sense of power existed here, too. He was still bulletproof.

Adam almost always came along when Andrew was like this, feeling both leery and protective of his friend's rash excesses. Adam sensed a confused rage behind Andrew's recklessness, and more and more it seemed as though Andrew was lashing out at something, as though trying to hit a ghost. For his part, Andrew became aware of this concern, and he felt an unexpected assurance in the quiet man's presence.

Outside they waved down a cab, and as the car pulled away Andrew took two bottles from his coat pockets. "Thirsty?"

"Are you already drunk?"

He waved at the question, and Adam, feeling a sudden thrill at the carelessness of it all, opened a bottle.

Settling into the back seat, Andrew smiled blandly. "Are your classes getting better?"

Adam ran a hand through his hair. "They would be better with another teacher."

"You'll find the hang of it. When things start getting to you, just make sure you blow off some steam."

"Is that what we're doing?"

"It's important to loosen up. Helps you adjust to the place."

"You seem pretty well-adjusted."

He grinned. "I like it here."

"You are drunk."

"Maybe," he admitted, but then the grin faded, replaced by another thought. "On the way to the toga party you mentioned someone you've never talked about before."

Adam looked out the window.

"Is she your sister?"

"No."

"Mother?"

"No."

"Girlfriend?"

"No."

"Wife?"

He was quiet.

"Complicated, was it?"

"We were together. Now we aren't."

"Is that what happened to you?"

"What?"

"Something's happened to you, that's plain."

"I don't understand."

"We both know that's crap. We're all here for a reason. Though I suspect yours is different than most. You can't tell me it's because you've become disillusioned with your career. There's more to it for you."

"Why are you so interested in me?"

"I could ask you the same thing."

Adam flushed. "I accepted my failure. Maybe I keep wondering why you're seeking your own."

"I thought I explained all that." Andrew was looking out the window at the passing city. When he spoke again his voice was quiet. "I've been thinking about what you said that night."

"I didn't say much."

"You talked about coming here for the opportunity. You're right. The world has shifted, has begun to turn a different way, and this is the new axis point. Right here, at this moment. Who wants to watch the world change on the television?"

"I would. There's no practical reason for me to be here other than financial necessity."

"Neither of us are here for practical reasons."

"At least you have family here. That counts for something."

"That only made it easier to bail out of my life back home."

Adam took a drink. "I can't believe you gave up a job for this place."

He shrugged.

"You're an idiot. Worse, you're a cliché."

Another shrug. "Probably."

"You don't think you'll regret it?"

"That wouldn't mean it was a mistake. If I decide to go back I'll find something."

"When you're like forty."

"What the hell."

Adam set down the bottle and stared at him. "Do you know what you're doing right now?"

"No. But I feel young here, and I like that. Don't you?"

He turned away so that Andrew couldn't see his face. "You haven't said any of this to Katya, have you?"

"Of course not. Why would I?"

He turned back and faced Andrew. "I don't think I will ever feel what you do here."

"Are you kidding me? Where else in the world is your passport a fashion accessory? I use it to get past the lines at clubs. What else can you want?"

"How about some hot water? How about not lining up for food? How about fixing the elevators?"

"Details."

"Important ones."

"So why did you come?"

Adam frowned.

"Oh, right. The person named Clare..."

"I don't like this topic."

"Let's talk about something else then."

Adam took a long drink. "Right."

"How about women?"

"What did I just say?"

"I mean other women."

"Oh, much better."

"What do you think of Katya?"

He stared into the bottle, as if estimating its depth. "She's quite something."

"Yes, she is."

"It's pretty serious then."

"I'm probably being an idiot."

"Probably."

"Well, shit. I've done worse things with my life."

"We've already covered that."

"Open the other bottle, will you."

"Why are we drinking again?"

"Homesickness." He handed the bottle to Adam as the cab pulled up next to one of the big hotels. Andrew opened the door. "Wait here," he told the driver.

On the street they were met by a large man in a leather coat. Andrew shook his hand. "Alex," he said, "this is my friend..."

The moneychanger only nodded and turned back to his client. "Tell cab go behind," he ordered in his halting English, pointing to a green truck at the corner.

The cab pulled up to the truck, and Alex opened the back.

Adam gaped. "What's this for?"

Andrew winked. There were cardboard boxes of food, a wedge of cheese, vegetables, a coil of sausage, vacuum-sealed pasta, wine, and, last, a tall cage.

"You bought a bird?"

"It's a parrot."

"A parrot's a bird."

"Katya's going to like it."

Adam looked at him. "What are you doing?"

"What do you mean?"

"You know what I mean. Look at all this stuff."

Andrew grew red and he slapped the car's roof. "Will you shut up!"

Adam froze, eyes widening.

"I just tore up my old life. I didn't ask you to come here so you could critique the way I start a new one. Besides, what do you care if I bought a parrot?"

"It's not the parrot," Adam said, looking at the things loaded into the trunk of the cab. "It's just that it's not that easy to start over."

"How do you suggest I go about starting over? Should I sulk around and whine, and when someone asks me what the fuck is wrong I can say nothing and then remain mysterious and sad and all alone with my self-pity."

Adam pushed his hands in his pockets. "You don't know anything about me."

"If I don't know anything it's because you've chosen not to tell me. You want to suffer alone? Fine. But I'm getting on with things."

"With a parrot?"

A tour bus groaned along the street and pulled up in front of the hotel. From among the kiosks and shop fronts there was stirring as the moneychangers moved into position. People emerged from the bus with cameras and bright plastic bags from one of the galleries.

They both stared as the tourists stretched and looked about.

Andrew frowned as he met Adam's eyes. "I am in love with Katya, and she's going to like the bird. It isn't important if you don't understand. She will."

Adam's voice lowered, and he squinted at Andrew over the roof of the car. "It's not easy to start over."

"Okay, then it will be hard." Andrew ran a hand over his face. "Just shut up about the bird, will you?"

After that they were quiet for a moment as the moneychanger finished loading things into the idling cab. Adam glanced at Andrew and lowered his voice.

"How does he get this stuff?"

Andrew opened the car door. "He knows somebody, who knows somebody, whom you and I do not want to know."

When he was done the moneychanger addressed Adam for the first time. "You teach English, yes?"

"Yes."

"My kid five," he said, holding up an open hand. "He at school in English."

"That's young."

"When older he will learn German, French maybe. I tell him if he don't learn languages he end up with job waiting tables."

Sticking his head out of the cab, Andrew handed Alex a roll of bills. "In my country the waiters speak more languages than the professors."

The moneychanger grinned, counting the bills. "This crazy fucking world."

"You said it," Adam grinned, and then the cab pulled away, disappearing a moment later into the afternoon traffic.

KATYA MET Spacinov the next day as he was leaving the church.

"What are you doing?" she greeted.

He was wrapped in his long coat and carrying a basket. "Come along and see."

She walked with him through the winding streets, past the clusters of people going about their day, the laughter of children on the way to school, university students running to catch the tram. Spacinov seemed oblivious to it all, and plodded along at his own erratic pace until at last they came to a small shop. Inside they were met by a man behind the wooden counter who gripped Spacinov's hand and kissed him three times with the traditional greeting.

"You are well?"

"Well enough."

The man glanced at Katya.

"My assistant."

"I see."

"You have eggs?"

The storekeeper gestured over his shoulder. "Come."

They were led past the counter and into the back of the store where they went through a doorway that opened on a yard. At the far end was a low shed, and inside they were met with that warm, putrid odour of straw and manure. There was a stir as they entered and the birds shuffled fretfully among themselves. The man poked about the nests for eggs which he handed with much ceremony to Katya.

She held the eggs self-consciously, smiling at their warmth in her fingers.

"That is enough for now," said Spacinov.

In the yard, he paid the man and this time they went through a gate that led back to the street. They took a circuitous route to the church, pausing at the stall of a fruit vendor where Spacinov purchased enough apples to fill his basket.

When they'd returned to the church, he showed her a small table set up next to some of the scaffolding. They spread out his purchases.

"This is quite a lot of food," Katya observed. "Though it will make you an odd meal."

"It is not for eating." The old man grinned at her. "The eggs I need to make paint."

She raised her eyebrows. "And the apples?"

He shoved several apples into the pockets of his coat. "Come and see."

They climbed the scaffold until they reached the place where Spacinov had been working.

"Before I can repaint the broken portions of a mural," he explained, "the layers of soot and dirt must be removed…" Spacinov opened his pocket knife and began to peel one of the apples. The shavings of red skin dropped into his lap. When he was done he cut the fruit into quarters, removing the core from each section before setting them in a row next to his foot.

When he was done, Spacinov held one of the pieces between his fingers, pressing it delicately against the mural as he drew the sliver of apple over the surface. The fruit was soon dark with soot and grime. He sliced away the outer layer and again pressed its damp flesh to the wall, repeating the small careful strokes. She stared as he held the fruit between his fingers, the way he used it to stroke the cheek of a saint. With each pass he steadily drew away the veil of neglect and filth, uncovering the story beneath. Spacinov worked always on one mural at a time, beginning at the head and working downward from one level of scaffold to another until it was complete. It was weeks before St. George seemed to awaken from darkness, another before his horse appeared. Standing there on the scaffold, the faces of the murals revealed themselves in gradations, their expressions a lurking glimmer, awakening steadily and almost imperceptibly. In this way, Katya watched a mural be reborn into its immense brilliance beneath the measured caress of the old man's fingertips.

Most mornings now she went to see Spacinov and watch his progress. Striding the boards of scaffolding, she held a candle close to the figures he had already cleaned, gazing upon the radiance around her. Here she could trace the crescent of St. Sergius's earlobe, could press her fingertips to the eye of the Baptist. Spacinov said that to anyone looking up at the murals, she might appear to be a lock of the Virgin's hair.

She found Spacinov one day cleaning a badly damaged portion of the church. Paint had come away along cracks in the wall, veins of age tracing over the surface of the mural. The image clung to the wall like flakes of bark.

"Its splendour feels incongruous," she murmured, looking around. "It has a kind of fragile resilience."

The old man stepped back to consider the mural with her. "When we love, beauty is often deepened by injury," he murmured. "Whatever harm an icon has survived will only enhance its affect to the believer." He turned imperceptibly so that his stare rested on her. "For me, the most damaged ones are the most powerful."

As weeks passed, Katya began to know Spacinov in pieces. His mind was laid bare to her, like a book fallen open, so that the knowledge and thoughts he had been hording for fifty years whispered to her from the shadows.

During these mornings the old man often forgot Katya was there, his thoughts emerging from the guarded places of his mind. For decades, Spacinov had had to conceal that ember of passion inside him, always afraid that its heretical light would attract the suspicion of the government's dark men, who knew him for different reasons. When at last the state's censure thawed to indifference, he carried on his work more openly, seeking out the old artefacts of faith in belfries and basements of ruined churches, once picking up a dozen icons for a few kopeks from a man selling scrap wood. But only now, after the communists' collapse, did Spacinov find himself free to restore the old images without fear. Katya sat wherever she found him, making herself comfortable on an empty apple basket or a stack of lumber, listening to the artist's rambling voice. He spoke to her absently while he worked, lulling his mind until it loosened and flexed like an animal waking. He explained to Katya the rift which began during the seventeenth century between a priest, Avvakum, who championed the rigid forms of the old icons, and the new generation of artists who painted the saints in more life-like poses.

"Avvakum understood that an icon is not viewed, but read. Almost everything about an icon in the Old Style was regulated by tradition. The position of the body, the restriction of its

posture, and the absence of colour on the lips –
these things are part of an unspoken grammar.
We refer to an icon as *perevod*. A translation.
For each one is really a re-articulation, a
rediscovery, of that ancient language."

Katya sat up, considering what he had said
for a moment, clutching this thought close to
her.

"The beard of each saint, for instance, is
always rendered the same, allowing one to
identify them individually from icon to icon
through the ages. The same is true of their
clothing, which signifies the religious order to
which each belongs. Only the eyes of a figure
are liberated from the precept of tradition. The
painter, who composed his subjects with utmost
discipline to that tradition, is allowed to distil
his whole soul into the icon's gaze. It is the eye,
that navel of the human soul, into which all of
the artist's creativity is concentrated. This is
why the icons are so striking. As we read the
icon, we feel a gaze that is as alive as our own.
An icon is a kind of mirror into one's self." He
smiled distantly, his voice becoming delicate
with emotion. "The goal of the icons is to deliver
us to that point where sorrow and joy intersect,

that paradoxical intimacy of opposites in which transcendence becomes, even if momentarily, possible."

"What of that one?" Katya said, pointing to a mural on the far wall. "That one disturbs me more than all the others." And as she spoke, she turned and looked now on the winged élan of angels, domed churches, clusters of gaunt saints and awkward-looking people. Lower down, a lone figure sat lashed to a tree with a snake suspended above him from the branches. A ladder, disproportionately large, rose diagonally to a door in the sky where haloed faces looked. On the other side of the tree flew creatures with black wings and hair of fire above a pit, into which people were being flung. Along the bottom, a devil rode a crimson dragon through darkness and flame.

"What is that?"

The candle shivered with the old man's breath. In the faint light motes scattered at his voice. "That is the Apocalypse."

Katya frowned at the mural's intense compression of color and activity.

"It means 'the unveiling'. When all that was hidden is at last revealed, and all people meet their fate."

"What is happening to those people in the fire?"

"They're condemned."

"Condemned for what?"

"They're condemned for their transgressions. We know about that in this country, don't we?"

Katya's voice was defensive. "Every society punishes those who break its laws."

He turned to her, a scowl appearing beneath his beard. "There are different kinds of laws, Yekaterina. To break the laws of people brings the judgement of people. But there are other laws which are a deeper part of us. They form the essence of who we are. To break one of these laws brings a deeper vengeance."

Katya looked at him, but did not speak. Spacinov appeared shaken, but then after a moment seemed to regain himself.

She watched him gently dab at the soot and grime, as though taking slivers from the palm of a child. The mural was busy with figures, and Katya caught the old man staring at the damned as they sank into fire.

"It's terrible," she said.

Spacinov's voice was hoarse, barely a whisper. "Yes, it was."

"Was?"

The old man straightened his legs. The motion sent a gentle shudder through the scaffold, and a trail of dust fell slowly to the floor. "The first mural which ever truly moved me was of the Apocalypse. Much like this one."

They were silent for a moment, each taking in the great mural opposite them. Katya stared at the lone figure at the edge of the scene.

"That man – why is he tied up?"

Spacinov became still. "He watches as those he knows are taken up to Heaven or sent into Hell, while he alone remains. Neither realm will claim him. You see how the painter depicts the torment of being lost between two worlds..."

"Yes," she whispered, feeling suddenly the press of the old man's gaze upon her. "Yes, I do see."

THE SITE of the test had been chosen both for its isolation and the geography of the surrounding terrain. The initial test zone was located far out in the country, away from the cities, and free of woodlots or elevated formations which might distort the uniformity of the results. Specialists from the army had been sent to take soil and water samples from the neighbouring fields and wells, while others selected plants and insects for analysis after the test.

There were few inhabitants in the area, though at some distance from the test site there was a village which the team planned to use for an observation post. Here Boris and the others billeted in a number of buildings throughout the village. The place was made up of a collection of houses, with wooden shingles and neat fenced-off gardens, some stores in the village square, and behind these a rail line with a derelict station.

Boris was posted in a church, which, like so many other buildings in the village, had been taken over by the Project. He arrived by truck with a variety of personnel and gear.

As he stepped out of the truck, Boris walked about in the bright sunlight and surveyed the outside of the building. A unit of soldiers unloaded equipment from the vehicle, and Boris went into the church with them to see to its unpacking.

The building had been emptied of furniture. Boris paused briefly as he entered to stare at the elongated bodies on the church walls. He chose a cot along the far wall, dropping his bag of clothes at the feet of St. John the Almsgiver.

The soldiers stacked the crates in the centre of the floor, and sounds of their work began to reverberate within the dome overhead.

"I'm going to look about," he said to the officer in charge. "Send for me when you're done."

Boris passed through the iron gate of the church and stepped into the road.

The streets were wide and tree lined. Birds had gathered in the road to bathe in the dust. A man came along pushing a wheelbarrow of potatoes, next to him skipped a child in a blue sweater. Sunlight filled the far end of the square, where men from the collective farm gathered in the evening to play dominos and drink. Across the road sat the school, and from its windows now drifted voices reciting the names of continents. At the corner four babushkas with bright-coloured kerchiefs sat together on a bench, behind them goldenrod and high grass swayed heavily in the breeze.

Boris walked out on the road and stared about him. The air was heavy with stillness and the sounds of the village.

'They do not know,' he thought. "History is being made in their front yards, and they do not know it."

As the days passed, other scientists settled quickly into the empty church. More cots had been set out for them in the openness of the sanctuary, and here they spent almost all of their time, working, assembling equipment, eating and sleeping. Planks were set on chairs as makeshift desks. Surfaces became layered with books and chess boards; English copies of *Physical Review* lay about, dog-eared with use. On tables or chairs sat half-eaten biscuits, broken cigarettes, empty sardine cans, teabags, a penknife, heaping ashtrays. There were dozens of over-familiar books sitting about. Mandelshtam's *Essays*, the novels of Steinbeck, Shteingauz's *Mathematical Kaleidoscope*, or Heitler's *Quantum Mechanics*.

A stove had been placed against the wall, and at night they sat around it reading and playing cards. Years later Boris would not remember any of his colleagues discussing the Project except during the day. They did not speak of their work in the dark.

Candles were carried about in empty sardine cans, and their light sometimes revealed the wary faces that watched them from the darkness like characters in a child's tale. At night Boris would stretch out on his cot and try to sleep. But instead he found himself drawn away from rest and into the world of the murals, and long into the night he would try to decipher the grand neglected stories. As their preparations progressed, the men grew quiet in the evenings, drawing into themselves where each man tried to escape the stress of his work and the importance of that moment they now hurried toward. Some turned to reading, others played cards or chess. Boris found no solace in these distractions, though, and instead wandered through the church with a candle, examining its walls.

One evening he stepped out into the cold to enjoy the solitude. Wood smoke drifted against the night sky. He stared at the stars, wondering as the Ancients had, at its garden of destinies. From somewhere in the dark came the sound of a truck, and, farther away, distant laughter. Next to him something scurried over the pavement.

He shivered.

Along the wall he found the woodpile and gathered a number of boards in his arm. Inside he found the others still arguing, their voices echoing through the church. As Boris lifted the iron lid on the stove, the light of the fire appeared on the wall. He selected a number of boards from his load, and one at a time pushed each of them among the coals. But as he was replacing the lid, Boris called out.

"What is it?" asked one of the men. "What do you have there?"

Boris picked up the scorched board and held it to the paraffin light to show them.

It was the face of a child.

"My God," he said to the man. "Do you know what we're burning?"

Boris went with a lantern that night and collected all the painted wood. He took these inside and spread them on the floor. The other scientists from the Program watched him with amusement. "What is this, Boris? Have you decided to decorate?"

He stood back and surveyed what he had salvaged. From out of the wood peered the same elongated faces as those staring down on them from the ceiling – their eyes gazing into faraway thoughts.

Squinting, Boris bent his neck closer to the wall and raised the lamp so that it shone above his head. With his other hand he reached out, the index and middle fingers hovering over the surface of an icon. "Extraordinary, aren't they?"

There was a shifting of bodies, and he could feel his colleagues' eyes on him.

"It's like we are meant to look at them," he said. "But the moment you make contact, you realize that we do not exist for them. It is a strange feeling. It's as if it is we who are not really here."

Someone cleared his throat. "You're not going to leave them there, are you?"

Each morning Boris set his men to unpacking the equipment from the crates. The contents were spread out on the church floor and inspected. Porridge and tea were brought to them from the canteen in the village, and he and his colleagues ate in silence on empty crates and packing straw. When they were done, two of the technicians hoisted their equipment into the bell tower, where it was assembled and tested. The work was tense and precise. There was very little conversation except the most necessary. When his men did pause, Boris often caught them looking at the sky.

He went about checking and rechecking equipment, assessing the sample readings, cross referencing calculations. Sometimes his mind wandered to the church cellar where he had stacked the wooden icons, and in the evening he descended into the smells of stone and damp so that he could look upon them again. From behind the weak light of his candle, Boris gazed at the traces of color that bled through grime and misuse. The long faces stared at him from the ancient wood, from another time, unsettling him and haunting his thoughts so that he could still see their expressions while sleeping in his cot or while working with his equipment. As the days passed, his interest centred on a picture of a man riding a horse with flame for wings. Beneath its hooves, Boris traced the outline of a ladder with almost a dozen bent figures climbing it toward a bank of white cloud. Beneath the ladder, he noticed that a series of blots were actually black demons flying about the ladder, plucking at the figures that climbed it, sending them falling into pits of flame at the bottom of the icon where other faces and arms strained against fire and smoke.

Within a week most of the men at work on the Project had been evacuated with the villagers. Those who remained now waited at their assigned posts with the darkened glasses they'd been given. There were military people here, too, and their staff shifted about, checking their watches and consulting the maps that placed them reassuringly in the margins.

From his station in the church tower Boris could survey the preparations being made in the deserted village. Dozens of cattle, horses and pigs had been tethered at strategic spots around the perimeter of the village, each of them painted with a number identifying their location. Cages of cats, chickens, ducks and rats were stacked in long rows at similar spots, and through the day you could hear their particular calls as each group was fed. Soldiers at the outskirts of the village had stationed two hundred prisoners brought in from one of the mines.

Through his binoculars, Boris thought he could see the grey bunkers of the outer station, where the generals, chief scientists and Party representatives were observing the test. A single road connected the village to this location, a brown thread strung for kilometres across fields which waved at him in the breeze.

A communication post was set up in one of the barns at the south end of the village, and the time remaining was announced every five minutes during the last hour, and every thirty seconds during the last ten minutes. The effect of these updates was a steady increase in the agitation among those in the village.

Boris looked over the ledge of the tower so that the sun rested upon his face. He closed his eyes, trying to will away the tension. The engineers next to him were poised beside their equipment. As a voice announced the final minutes, an almost physical stillness settled upon the village. People no longer appeared in the streets, and the engines of trucks fell silent. Pigeons sat like flakes of silver on the wooden roofs of homes. From chimneys leaked blue trails of smoke which drifted into the fields.

An officer handed around a flask, offering a lengthy toast while everyone took a drink. People found a place for themselves in the tower. No one chose to speak after this. Sometime in the last minutes, Boris ceased to hear the metallic voice of the speaker. A great anticipation came over him, and he clutched the stone ledge to keep his hands from shaking. The officer observed this and Boris thought he saw the man sneer.

Boris gazed out at the fields. The place where he leaned was warm from the sun, and he opened his palm on the stone and his flesh took in its heat. Birds shuffled and stirred along the roof.

There was a stirring of bodies behind him, and Boris straightened. The final countdown had started and the men in the tower looked in the direction of the detonation site. A hush fell over the town and it seemed as though even the flies stopped moving.

"Here we go," someone muttered.

On the horizon there appeared a white bulb. It rose with beautiful ferocity, and in unison the men in the tower raised their hands as if to ward off the sight. One of the men held up an instrument for measuring the plume and began calling out numbers to another fellow who sat recording them with a stopwatch. As he watched the rising bulb, Boris heard a change in the man's voice, and almost immediately the recorder interrupted.

"You've got it wrong," he whispered. "That can't be."

"I'm using it properly," the other said.

The officer stepped forward, concerned. "What's the matter?"

The recorder glanced at Boris. "There's something wrong. It can't be."

He looked over the officer's shoulder. "What are you talking about?"

"This is all wrong," the man said holding out the chart. "It's all wrong..." The recorder stood, shoving the officer out of his way as he lunged for the rope ladder. The officer tried to stop him, pivoting backwards as he caught at the man's arm. The recorder pulled away and stumbled into Boris, knocking him off balance.

Boris's head struck the side of the shaft, and it was another instant before he realized what had happened. Then all at once the tower's narrowing tunnel of light opened and he was falling through the great space of the dome. Around him passed the enormous faces of the murals — sainthood and damnation, heaven and hell — so close he could touch them. As he fell Boris took in all of the faces as if seeing them in an extended moment, watching the approach of what he thought was his own death with a strangely calm curiosity.

And then at that moment there was a terrible roaring and the faces painted on the ceiling suddenly broke away, like a puzzle thrown in the air, and the entire roof was replaced by a sky of fire.

Boris landed among the crates and packing straw, breaking ribs and both of his arms and almost blacking out from shock. Laying there his lungs shuddered, choking on burning straw. Above him the sky had turned to flame, rolling in waves that licked the shattered arches of the church. He stumbled among the burning crates, fell down and again got up. He staggered this time to a stone doorway where, with a backward glance at the sky, he threw himself down the stairs to the church cellar, his hair on fire.

Boris felt the ground tremble. Debris fell on him, and from the passageway the fire shrieked like an animal that had cornered its prey. Bricks came loose from the ceiling and broke upon the floor. He crawled to a corner, holding up his broken arms against the wrath and roar from above. Bits of cinder and burning straw blew into the basement where they seethed in drifts about his body. Through his fingers Boris gaped at the silhouette of someone's face, jaw line and forehead growing out of the shadows, and then he saw the icons' eyes.

When Boris emerged from the basement, he was a remnant of himself – his face swollen and black, clothes all but gone. His hair was reduced to stubble, the scalp raw and blistered. The church was filled with ash and wreckage – fragments of stone and men and equipment twisted together – the high walls scorched, the great faces now barely discernible. All trace of the roof and tower had disappeared, and the sky was black with churning smoke. Looking up he found one of the murals still stared down at him from a remnant of wall. The left side of the face was black and charred, so that the figure's head seemed to be emerging from the dark, half hidden. But from the remaining portions, he could make out the expression of the face, the gaze of the remaining eye heavy with judgement.

For a moment he met the eye. He felt its gaze sink beneath his chest, searching him, and he covered his face. His chest contracted until he could not breathe and he ground his teeth.

When Boris looked up again, he was surrounded by ash. The pain from his burnt hands brought him back to himself. The mural's face stared at him and he fled the church, passing beneath the smashed archway and into the yard.

But here Boris suddenly stopped and all thought of himself disappeared. His mouth fell open and even the pain in his hands faded as he looked out at the transformed world.

"What have we done?" he whispered.

The blast had melted the silicon in the soil so that the ground now resembled a crust of black glass. The area about the church was littered with charred pigeons. In the street, wraiths of smoke hovered about larger forms in postures of torment. Prisoners stumbled about, crying or groaning, chained to the scorched bodies of other prisoners whom they dragged through the streets. Soldiers lay twisting and shrieking on the ground. Some of the animals had escaped after the blast and now raged madly about the streets, howling in blindness and terror. Horses, their backs streaked with flame, trampled down bodies and wreckage until they too collapsed.

Boris stumbled wide-eyed through the pandemonium. As he reached the edge of the village he turned and saw behind him a rising pillar of flame and smoke which clove the horizon. He covered his face, trying to block from his sight what the world had become.

He began to walk. Groans and parched cries called to him. Behind him the eye stared from the ruins of the church, the gaze following him until he disappeared into the smouldering fields.

Spacinov began to peel a fresh apple. The old man set down his brush, staring at the back of his hands as if noticing the scar tissue for the first time. He laughed softly, making a scolding sound at the back of his throat. "You asked me," he said at last, and pointed to the mural on the far wall, "about the mural with the Archangel delivering God's wrath."

The old man's eyes traced the long brush strokes of red and ochre, the coiling flame that enveloped the naked huddle of the damned. Spacinov slipped his gloves back over his hands. "I have stood inside that mural." The scaffold creaked as he leaned over the railing.

"They sent soldiers first, followed by fire crews who put out the smouldering debris and cooled the burnt earth. Finally, the security men came. A list of names was recorded as corpses were identified. After this list a second was prepared, recording those whose bodies had vanished." Spacinov cleared his throat before looking at her.

"On that list is my name."

PART III

Our stories are the link across the gulfs
of time and individuality. Indeed, human
trauma may be defined as the blow which
interrupts the story, whether personal or
collective, breaking the continuity of time
and human relations, and thus blocking the
ongoing formation of a meaningful whole.

Gordon Wheeler, "Translator's
Introduction"

KATYA LIKED to arrive at the library a few minutes before it opened. It allowed her to sit on one of the concrete benches which ringed the courtyard of the building and review in her mind a particular poem or passage she was translating. Other people would already be there, as well. Students and professors, visiting academics from abroad, most of them bleary eyed and silent, smoking or eating something they'd bought at a kiosk. There was a quiet recognition between them, and they would stop and exchange a word or two while waiting for the library to open.

Once inside, though, individuals immediately dispersed, each disappearing into the rows of bookshelves in search of a familiar carrel or quiet table. Katya moved with a sense of purpose, climbing to the fourth floor and spreading out her papers and books as she liked to, before settling into her familiar chair at the end of the table.

And almost immediately she began to drift away. The delicate sound of a page being turned, the scratching of a pencil across paper – like whispers, these noises led her deeper into the forest of thought, creating that most necessary of conditions for concentration, the respect for silence. Then, at last, she would feel the familiar joy as her mind began to open, her ideas speaking to one another independent of her will so that at times it seemed she was observing her thoughts and instincts from a distance. Looking back on that autumn, it would later strike Katya as an irony of her work that the deeper she went into her mind the closer she drew to the poems.

She weighed words, mouthing them silently to herself, syllable-by-syllable so that they hung on her mouth like beads, her mind's ear tracing the hard tones of their consonants, the sharp burst of energy stored in the long vowels, until she felt their cadences in her own breathing, made their rhythms her own. In this way, she sought out the unseen edges of words' meaning, their nuances, until she knew them.

But on one of the poems Katya found that she made almost no progress. The poem itself was not overly difficult on the surface, but as she worked through it she stumbled on a word used several times in the poem. The English word would not rest in her mouth. She had known the word in English for years, but never before had she been tasked with articulating it in her own language. It was like a shape that could not be described, did not fit with any taxonomy, which persisted in eluding her attempt to transfix it, to give it a Russian name. Like a child who refused to be dressed, it kept kicking off the left sock even as she wrestled with the right.

Gradually the poem began to disturb the peace she felt in the library, and Katya began searching for help. Her professor only smiled at her when she came to him. Yes, this was indeed a large problem, he admitted. "It is true that this is an unusual poem, written by someone long ago. And yet the poet is still speaking to us, isn't he? Your task is to determine if he has something to tell us, even now." And at this he touched her arm reassuringly. "History is most valuable to those with uncertain futures," he murmured. "Do not give up so easily. Remember you are not alone.

You may of course speak with other academics," he reminded her. "There are several professors in the English Department you might consult."

Katya searched his face. "I have already consulted someone about my project," she said. "I will speak to him again, if it is necessary."

But instead of talking again to Adam, she went to her brother, trying to explain to him the root of the poem's difficulties. "How can I translate a word that does not adequately exist in the language into which the work is being translated? How can I do this?"

Petya rubbed his chin as he stared at the open pages of her work. "I'm telling you the truth, Katya," he said, "I do not know that there is an answer. But it is a most interesting dilemma to be solved."

"Dilemma? This is a disaster! How can I solve what is by definition – and I mean literally by definition – unsolvable?"

"Surely you have other options – there are phrases you can draw on. Foreign references."

"You do not understand me. It is not merely that there are words that don't translate, but the poem is about, and repeatedly alludes to, a concept that evades our language. How can I do this? It is as if I am trying to describe sunlight to someone who is blind. We do not even know we don't have this word as it is meant in English. We have words were think are equivalent, but they're not. What can I do? I cannot invent a new word!"

Petya smiled at his sister. "You are right. This is a difficult task. But your professors have assigned this work for a reason. You are always speaking about being true to both the work you are translating and those who will read it. In this case, it would seem that you cannot be true both. You are being forced to choose allegiances." This explanation only further irritated his sister and Petya, sensing he could do no more for his sister, went to check the mail, leaving her no closer to a resolution.

That night when he came home, Ivan found Katya studying in her room. He handed her a piece of paper, though when she reached out for it he abruptly pulled it back.

"You asked me to find out about a man..."

She straightened. "You found him?"

Ivan considered the paper in his hand. "Who is looking for this man?"

Katya moved from her desk to sit on the bed. "What did you find?"

"He was a musician."

She searched her father's face. "You've found something?" she asked again.

"I've been told there's not much to see. A small marker in the cemetery."

Katya exhaled. "Then he is dead."

"Did you know about the woman? The one who betrayed him? What she did?"

"She left him in America."

"So you know the circumstances?" He paused, staring at the paper. "The person who is looking for this man..."

Katya glanced at her hands. "He teaches at the university."

"What did he think he would discover?"

She nodded at the paper. "Not this."

Katya looked at her father but he seemed to be struggling with his thoughts. "There are many difficult things in our past," Ivan began. "Things that are better left unknown."

When she spoke her voice was firm. "He wants to know. I think this is why he is here. His father is someone he never even met. There can be nothing wrong with knowing now. Even the truth."

"How will you tell him?"

She stared at the paper. "I will have to find the right words."

Ivan paused, as though he might say something else, but instead he handed Katya the paper. "Tell your friend that there have been worse ends for men like his father."

Then he left her alone with what she had asked for.

Katya went with Andrew to the cemetery. The place was located at the east end of Galinsk. They found a tram which took them to the edge of the city, and they walked the rest of the way beneath a wind-driven sky, clouds rushing onward, broken and scattered by invisible momentum. Andrew stopped when they came to the gates of the cemetery.

"How do you feel?" she asked.

He didn't answer.

As they moved beneath the naked birch trees, they were met by a stillness that seemed to look down on them from the branches. Leaves lay yellow and rotting at their feet. Everywhere they were surrounded by that languishing, pungent odour which is fall. Katya felt for Andrew's hand.

It took them an hour of searching among the monuments and fenced-off tombs before they located a small stone with his family's name. There was no other information or ornament on the grave except for the profile of a man's face, no larger than an apple.

Andrew knelt hesitantly for a closer look. Water dripped on him from the branches. He stared at the face in the stone, his finger tracing the letters of his father's name. "There is nothing more?"

They cleared away the leaves around the grave. The cemetery was empty except for their voices. For a long time they hovered in silence over the cleared spot of ground. When Andrew spoke at last, he lowered his voice as though afraid of being overheard.

"He lost his position with the orchestra." Andrew was looking at his hands. "Because of my mother?"

Katya stirred. "Yes."

"And after that?"

She scanned the page helplessly, though by now she knew every word. "It doesn't say…"

"Was he punished, like in prison or something?"

"It doesn't say."

"Did they send him to Siberia?"

Katya looked at him, frustrated but patient. "It doesn't say."

"What does it say?"

Katya sighed, folding the paper in her lap. "It says that your mother betrayed her country. It says in that same year your father was removed from his position with the orchestra. It says that later he took his own life." She held her breath, watching Andrew. "It says that he was buried here."

Andrew stood, biting at his lip. "That's all?"

Katya held out the paper to him. "It is all the words say."

He hesitated an instant before taking it. She moved to one of the benches along the path, while he stood reading and rereading the page, searching it for something she might have missed.

After a while he came and sat next to her.

"Where did your father get this?"

She shrugged. "He is still an influential person."

"He wouldn't know who – ?"

Katya pointed to the page. "This is what he knows."

For a long time they stood without speaking, both of them staring at the carved face in the stone.

"Why would he kill himself?"

"You know why."

Andrew looked at her. "This is all there is, then?"

"I'm sorry." She placed a hand on his arm. "There is nothing more."

After the visit to the cemetery, Andrew did not talk anymore of his father. Katya held her breath through this time, waiting for him to return to England or America. But as the days passed Andrew began to talk instead about Russia as if it were his home, referring more often to his teaching friends as "the foreigners."

Andrew now went more often to their flat, and Katya knew that he sometimes stayed overnight without her. She found his clothes hanging in the closet, books that she had never read on the shelf, dishes she had not eaten from in the sink. These items were like flags on previously neutral ground, claiming it as his. He stopped meeting her at the door when she arrived, and instead she would find him reading in a chair or asleep in the bedroom. More and more the small flat seemed to Katya like a place occupied by someone else's life.

One evening she was on the balcony looking down the street into the square with its statue and the benches used in good weather by chess players. Figures moved along the sidewalk, and from windows came light that warmed the darkness. The balcony's iron railing felt strong, so she leaned farther into the cool air. Through the glass door came the sound of Andrew in the kitchen talking to Chaika. Wind carried the hard smell of frost. A car moved along the street, the complaint of its engine softened by the distance. Below her, wires stretched in various directions between buildings, lacing together the different buildings and lives of the street. She leaned back into the shelter of the balcony, drawing her arms around herself.

Coming inside, she looked about the kitchen where Andrew was still cleaning up from the meal. Since learning of his father's death,

Andrew had been spending most of his time here when he was not at the university. He compulsively added new items to the flat, returning each day with more things he had found at the markets or in kiosks, or for sale in the street: a tablecloth, tea, an electric kettle, plants, someone's family dishes, a set of silver *stakhans.* All these things began to accumulate on the shelves and surfaces around the parrot, Chaika.

Despite her initial protests, Katya had grown fond of their new pet.

Andrew looked up when she came in. "How do you say cracker in Russian?"

"Why?"

"She's a parrot."

"So?"

"It's something they're supposed to say."

Andrew had taken to teaching the bird words in Russian, though so far Chaika showed no signs of comprehension. All they had been able to extract from the bird was a bad rendering of *Read my lips*, which always made Katya laugh. "Great," she had observed. "Even the bird is American."

Andrew began moving restlessly about the kitchen – opening and shutting cupboards, wiping down the counter – knowing she had to leave.

"If we were in my country," he mused, looking into an empty teapot, "I would have brought you flowers. As it was, I had to settle for sausage."

Katya grinned. "That's the best you could do?"

"These are unromantic times."

"At least dinner was good."

"The first time I had this meal was at a place I used to go to in Piccadilly called Quag's."

"Good restaurant?"

"I saw Hugh Grant there."

"That's something."

"Would you like to see England?"

"Hugh Grant is England enough for me."

"You make me feel Russian."

Her smile stumbled. "And yet, you're not."

"You wish I was."

"It would be simpler."

"And more complicated."

He passed a hand over her thigh, seeking reassurance. "Will we finish the wine?"

She shook her head. "I will have to go soon."

"Why don't you stay the night?"

Katya made a face.

"I mean it. Why not?"

"I do not want to lie about all of this."

"You don't think people know?"

"They do not know."

Andrew was quiet. "Your family."

"Of course."

She was growing tense. To change the subject she said, "Do you ever wish you were back in America?"

"There were better movies," he said, taking her hand.

"You are homesick for movies?"

"And *Star Trek*."

"What is this?"

"You'll find out."

"Is that all? Is there a woman you like where you live?"

He frowned. "I live here."

"Yes, for now."

He withdrew his hand. "What are you doing?"

"Nothing."

"It sounded as though you were – "

"But I wasn't."

She felt the warmth of his hand against her face, his eyes touching her. He found her hand and raised it to his mouth. Her other palm she drew slowly over his temple, his neck. "Why did you do that?" he murmured.

"What?"

"You know what."

She blushed. "I'm sorry. I meant nothing."

For a moment he was quiet, next to her.

"You're shivering," she whispered.

USUALLY THE letters came with just a card or a brief note. Each envelope was found by Petya, who had been making an effort lately to get the mail. Though they were addressed to Katya, their stamps made him suspicious and so he read them. At first he dismissed the contents, told himself they were nothing. But by the end of the week he had read five more of them.

Petya came into Katya's room and shut the door. Opening his briefcase he took out the letters and placed them on her bed.

"What is it?" she asked.

"You know a lot of foreigners," he said flatly, his eyes never leaving her.

Katya coloured. "What are you talking about?"

He pointed to the letters. "Do you know these people?"

"What is this about?" She sat up.

Petya explained about the letters, the whole time searching his sister's face. "You do not know?"

"You're the one who has read them!"

Petya looked again at the envelopes, and when he spoke his voice was almost intimate. "I will destroy them for you."

"Why?"

"These are not – these are proposals."

She stared blankly.

"These men," his voice darkening as he tried to explain. "They want to bring you to the West. They are willing to pay if you will marry them."

"What?"

Petya looked away.

Katya took the letters from his hand. "You're not making sense. Petya?" But he would not look at her.

"Petya?"

"It is a type of business," he said finally, almost blurting the rest. "Men in the West, they – it is all quite obscene."

Katya paled as the idea dawned on her. "How do you know about this?"

"It has happened before," he said, shrugging. "You probably gave personal information for something entirely innocent – a free magazine subscription, or a contest."

Katya looked down at her hands, noting how strange they seemed. *What beautiful hair!* Petya's lips were moving, but she struggled to understand what he was saying.

"Then they sell your information to men looking for a wife."

Katya stumbled through the thoughts pressing on her. It came to her then from a distance, a thin ribbon of odour. She wrapped one finger with hair and brought it to her nose, eyes widening as an idea opened behind them.

"...sometimes they ask personal questions or take a picture. I have heard they put it all in a terrible kind of catalogue..."

"A catalogue?" Petya's words settled like cold breath along her neck. *A girl like you should be noticed...* Katya glanced at the envelopes, sealed with the saliva of desperation, her name spelled out in alien markings. She went to her closet and ripped back the pocket of her bathrobe.

"What are you doing?" said Petya, startled out of what he was saying.

Katya went to the bathroom and emptied a bottle of shampoo into the sink, watching it coil about the drain.

Petya called to her from behind the door.

Her hands shook as she worked the tap, cupping the water to her face where the skin felt numb. Each cheek grew red as she scrubbed. *We would love to know more about those who enjoy our product...* A woman with nails like fish hooks asked Katya twice to spell her patronymic. *So many letters!* She could see herself with the giftwrapped bottle, smiling as the camera lens tightened around her, cutting her off at the neck. The cameraman grinned, a faultless picket of teeth.

Cheese, he said. And Katya had thought he looked hungry.

She decided not to tell Andrew about the letters. She did this partly because they embarrassed her, but also because she sensed that he would not see their real significance. He would get caught up with the affront and be blind to the larger danger. Pride, and that comforting ability to distinguish himself from his own culture, allowed Andrew to see those men as something unrelated to where he was from, who he was. As if a limb could be a part of anything other than the body it grew from.

But without knowing how, Katya understood that the letters from those men intruded into her relationship with Andrew, had slipped behind the fragile wall she had built to keep out the world. Katya sensed for the first time how much could be lost to the foreigners, the extent of their naïve ability to take, which had grown to become almost a kind of moral blindness in them. And, like the sudden stillness which precedes a blizzard, she understood that these letters were, like Andrew, proof of a coming storm.

And for the first time Katya saw the same pattern in her translation work, where again and again the origin of an English word could be traced to a conquered language. English, that tongue she loved next only to her own, was a mongrel creature, stealing unscrupulously from other languages, even their idiom and argot. Her dictionary was magnificent and corpulent with pillaged wealth, like the tomb of a khan or emperor. The Complete Oxford English Dictionary was a conqueror's purse.

The signs of invasion were everywhere. In the last year foreign words had appeared like flags on street corners, cigarette packages, and clothing. Words had already been replaced, even the *gostronome* near their flat had become a 'grocery,' the new name spelled phonetically in Cyrillic.

Even Andrew's name, she recalled, was anglicized from Andrei, and this shook her until she felt a tightening in her throat. She had not thought to call him by his Russian name.

This sense of foreboding, of being under siege by someone else's words, grew steadily on her until by chance one evening Katya mentioned to Andrew a difficulty she'd had in the market the day before, and he offered her money.

"I'm not asking you to help!" she retorted, feeling a sudden rush of the anger that had been building in her. "I only told you these things so that you will understand."

"What is it I don't understand?"

She frowned, fear and disgust rising up in her. "You should try to comprehend my family's difficulties before trying to solve them."

He looked at her. "I want to help."

"How can you be certain our problems will be solved so easily? What we're going through is not merely about money. Can you imagine how much our world has changed? Has it not occurred to you that our lives have not always been like this?" She shook her hands in disgust. "No wonder you don't understand my family."

"Understand them? You won't even let me meet them!"

"Yet you're certain they need your help." She looked at him fiercely, aware of the lunacy of her argument but also feeling that what she was saying had some deeper truth.

"You just said you wished things were easier."

"There are things we need, yes. But they are things you cannot give, but which you presume to have. You would only make the situation more complicated, maybe even worse. Think of your own mother. From everything you've told me, she was as unhappy as her husband was wealthy. Aren't you offering my family the same security that failed her?"

He threw up his hands. "So you don't need help. Fine. I won't offer again."

Katya looked at him, knowing that she had reached a decision without realizing it, without him realizing it. The problem, she suddenly saw, was that she could not think of him the same way, as exciting, an adventure. As innocent. The letters from those men had changed the way she looked at Andrew. He had transformed, was no longer just a person, but also a symbol of where he came from: he knew the language of fast food and Hollywood and brand names, he was a passport and an airplane. He could change his reality. He could choose her world, her life, even if she would not. A soldier's coat became *kitsch*, a flag was translated into a souvenir. A battlefield could become a theme park.

She suddenly wanted the fight to be over.

"If someone needs a new pair of shoes," she said, her voice soft now, as though speaking to herself, "you measure his feet before trying to make them."

"What?"

She made an effort to smile. "It is something my grandmother used to say."

"Really?" He grinned at her, misinterpreting her motive for diffusing the tension. He put his arm casually around her. "What would your grandmother say about me?"

As Andrew kissed her, Katya drew back inside herself, as if from a rattling window. "She would have had no words for you."

He laughed, his voice now loud and brash, thinking the storm had passed.

After their argument she twice cancelled seeing him, then failed altogether to appear at a third meeting. For a week she stayed away from the university, going only to attend classes before hurrying home to check the mail.

One afternoon at the end of the week Ivan came home early and went directly to his study and slammed the door. Silence rested on the flat, each member of the family becoming aware of a swelling tension. Katya sat at her desk before a blank page, unable to find the words she sought. Her attention kept straying from her work to the absent ticking of the clock she had sold the previous week. The memory of its sound measured her uneasy thoughts, nagging her with thoughts of Andrew. She leaned over the blank page, twisting her hair absently with one finger, and tried to push the clock's voice from her head. A chair ground against the floor somewhere in the flat. The heavy sound of feet. A door opened, then another. From the kitchen, Lydia's faint call to dinner.

They were all waiting to eat when Ivan entered the kitchen, but instead of joining them he remained standing.

"What is this?" he demanded, dropping a letter on the table.

Katya froze.

Petya glanced at the envelope. He looked at Katya and coloured.

"You opened it."

Ivan pressed his fist into the table. "I did."

She stared at her hands. "Then you know what it is already."

"How long have you been plotting this?"

Katya braced as her father raised his arm. But instead he struck her brother, knocking the fork from his hand.

Petya stared for a moment at the wooden table, his eyes narrowing with resolve before he looked up. "That was unnecessary."

"How could you, Peter! How could you?"

Katya shook her head. "What are you talking about?"

Petya pushed away his plate. "Don't make this into a personal insult."

Ivan withdrew instinctively to higher ground. "You have received the best education your country could provide, and this is what you do with it?"

Katya looked around the table. "What is happening?"

Petya bit at his lip. "The American school made me a good offer. The money is better than I could ever –"

Ivan picked up the letter again. "Can't you see you're being seduced? This reads like a love letter!"

"What is it?" Katya flushed brightly. "I don't understand what you're saying now. What is happening, Petya?"

Her brother turned to her, taking a breath before speaking. "It's a good job. And it's a good university," Petya explained. "You could visit. Could come and..."

"Are you out of your mind?" Ivan shrieked. "Me in California!"

"Why would we go to California?" Lydia looked from one to the other, completely lost now by their senseless words. "Ivan, dear, what is happening? What is this about?"

"It's no worse than anywhere else..." Petya said, still staring at his father.

For a moment everything was still. Katya took a long breath, holding it in as if afraid to let it go. 'I must keep this breath inside me,' she thought. 'I must hold it as long as I can. Every breath after will be taken in a different world.'

No one looked at Ivan, and when he finally spoke his voice was so soft that they leaned forward to hear him.

"If you leave," he said to his son, "then you are done with us. We will never be Americans. Even if you leave. This is what I want you to know."

Katya stared at her brother, aware that Petya was trying not to look at her. "I am not coming back, if that's what you are suggesting," he said, his jaw tightening. "I'll send money."

"You think I would touch it? You are not a scientist, Peter, you're a whore."

He flinched.

"The day you walk out on us, you become an orphan, lost forever on a map."

"No – " Lydia broke in, at last grasping what his words meant. "Stop talking!"

"I'm not walking out of this place – I'm fleeing!" Petya shrieked, ignoring his mother. "Along with everyone else who can."

"You would really go, then?"

Katya closed her eyes.

"I have to, don't you see? Something must be done. I have to go, for all of us. If you will not accept my money, then they will..." his voice now almost a sob, as if he was confessing something. He pointed to Katya and Lydia.

"What would you know?" Ivan stammered. "You've had everything your whole life. And who gave it to you? You think anyone else will lift a finger for you?"

"Can't you see – I'm only doing this to save the family!"

"By abandoning it?"

"I had to do something. Can't you see what is happening?"

"We are surviving."

"We are not surviving. We are bleeding to death. We are disappearing in pieces, a few things at a time. And it will go on like this until nothing remains. I don't think you realize what is at risk."

"If you think these are hard times, you should have seen what people survived during the War. In Leningrad, if it weren't for the Party, we would – "

"Our whole life is being sold around us and you go along with it gladly so long as you can cling to the Party. Is there nothing more important?" Petya pointed to his sister. "Even she does not know how much she is willing to give for that dream. But you do. Yes, you do, don't you?" Petya lunged suddenly across the table at his father. "I can see it in your face. You would sacrifice us all for that Party of yours..."

Ivan's eyes bulged with rage, and he gripped a chair to steady himself. "Without the Party we have nothing. And so, yes, in the final reckoning, the Party is everything. Why can't you see? It is the last thing standing between our country and everyone who would take it from us."

"What is the Party protecting if you have to sacrifice everything to keep it alive?" Petya raised his chin, his hands shaking now. "The ground is disappearing under your feet. But still all you can see are clouds. Haven't you wondered why things around here keep disappearing?" He pointed at Katya.

Lydia looked at her. "You told your brother?"

"No! I told no one!"

"She didn't have to – just look around!" He turned back on his father. "You don't know, do you? You don't know what she's had to do..."

Katya stood. "Shut up, Petya!"

Ivan stepped away from the table. "What are you talking about?"

"Can you not see?" he continued, yelling now at his father while holding Katya back with one hand. "How long can it go on? What happens when there is nothing left to sell, eh? Can't you see how this will end for her? Have you read *her* mail?"

Katya struck him, then again. "Shut your mouth! Shut it – shut it!"

No one moved. Katya looked around the table, taking in each of their faces. Blood formed beneath her brother's cheek, like a tear. Each of them clutched at the silence, holding back the words each knew came next.

Blood dropped, tapping onto the tablecloth.

It was Ivan who broke the silence at last, his voice sharp, cutting. "This is how it is, then?"

Petya straightened, his hands unclenching. "Yes."

Ivan looked around the table, his voice so soft now they almost did not hear him. "You do not know what I know." Then he turned his back and left the kitchen.

When Katya entered the church she found it deserted. Flame danced silently from candles along the walls. She was chilled and wet from the rain, and as she stood in the emptiness and silence she felt suddenly that there was nothing here for her. Feeling foolish she turned to go, but at the same moment something gave way inside her. Her knee buckled and she fell.

Clutching onto a crib of candles, she drew herself up. But instead of standing she took one of the candleholders and threw it at the wall. The glass broke upon a prophet's face.

She felt torn and frayed, her body and emotions detached from one another, her limbs almost unaware of the cold now seeping into them. She looked at her hands, wondering why they were shaking.

On the wall, a saint stared at her, holding her in a long silence. A sob ached in her chest, the pain struggling to be released.

Katya knelt and pushed each palm into the broken glass at her feet, crying out as the shards sank under her skin to the pain already there. Almost as suddenly, her cry died away and, like a flock of startled birds, the stillness settled again around her. She stared at the mural she had damaged. Something now in the prophet's expression seemed to become animate, drawing her out of herself, though only for an instant.

Katya looked down at the stone floor, watching her blood seep into the cracks. One of the candles sputtered and died out, a ribbon of smoke cleaving the darkness in two. From inside her came a stifled sound like the breaking of bone.

The saint trembled in the candlelight.

Spacinov found Katya there, as she knew he would, and brought her to his chamber at the back of the church. Here she sat wrapped in a blanket on the bed with him next to her, one hand resting on the old man's wrist as she told him everything that had happened. Her life, Katya saw, was quickly giving way. There had once been things you were certain of, things you could place your weight on without looking down. Now everything she knew was coming apart, broken by a force so large she could see neither where it began nor where it would end.

'In one week,' she thought, 'I have lost both my brother and Andrew.'

Spacinov stared, weighing his thoughts before speaking.

"Our country is awakening from our long sleep. But we are still like an animal after hibernation. This is our most vulnerable time, and the hunters are all about. I do not trust these people who come here to change us. They are as dangerous as those who want to keep things the same."

Katya was still for a long time after he finished. The church's silence rested on them. "It is true that things are changing," she said, at last. "None of us can stop it. I have accepted this. But I am afraid of what is to come."

The next morning Andrew caught up to her in front of the library. There was a new anxiety in the air between them, a collected breath held back against the cold. Students hurried over frozen puddles, ignoring the nervous scattering of pigeons at their feet.

Katya stared awkwardly at Andrew, and he saw by her expression that something had changed.

"Are we going to talk?" he asked, surprised at the resignation in his own voice.

Katya sighed, preparing herself. "Of course."

"Where are you going now?"

"Home."

"Right away?"

"As soon as this is finished."

Andrew stopped. "Have I done something wrong?"

Hearing the ironic edge in his voice, Katya understood for certain that Andrew did not comprehend this danger she felt. Thoughts and emotions rushed over her and she flushed with anger.

"You know nothing!" she lashed, almost lunging at him. "You have never hated the things you love. You are too selfish to let that happen…"

"You can't include me with them – I'm one of you."

"I had forgotten," she spat. "You play at being Russian. You are so quick to betray your country, to change where you are from. As if it was easy to do such a thing. You go on about how unhappy your mother was, how you *had* to come here for her. Then we met, and you thought you would redeem her life if you fixed mine."

"What are you talking about? I only offered you some money. It's not like there were strings attached…"

But she went on without listening to him, ignoring the people around them who stared. "You're enamoured with the future of this country, but ignore your complicity in the murder of its past. But I'm part of that. You can't kill it without killing something of me, too. Do you think my life was always this way? Has it not occurred to you that we were once as confident and righteous as you are? But you in the West, you can't stop pointing and ogling at what you've found here. We're like a bad car

403

accident to you. And all you can think to do is offer us driving lessons.

"There is no longer a place for people here who merely want a dignified life. People are leaving, Andrew, because they cannot survive here. Where do those people go when they leave? And what happens to those of us who must stay with only the pieces of who we were?"

"I wish you'd stop," he cut in, his voice coming now in gulps. He stepped back from her, drawing both hands through his hair. Andrew shut his eyes for a moment, thinking of something to say, searching for the words to fix this.

Katya looked across the road and started. Spacinov stood among the leaves in the gutter. From the look on his face, she knew he had been watching for some time. She almost forgot Andrew as Spacinov walked toward her, his long grey coat hanging unevenly on his shoulders, like a broken wing.

Katya felt her face color. It occurred to her only then that neither man knew of the other. She had kept these two sides of herself apart. 'How did I do this?' she thought. 'How is it possible that I never thought to speak to

Andrew of Spacinov, of the icons?' Katya stood dumbfounded and speechless before the two men. It was as though she was introducing her left hand to her right hand. How could these two parts of her not know each other?

Andrew nodded at the old man. "Who's this?"

Spacinov rubbed his nose. "Why is this foreigner arguing with you?"

"You do not know each other," she began, glancing from one to the other.

Andrew coloured. He wished the man would leave so that he could talk with her. He glared at Katya, embarrassment rising in him like a bruise. "Katya, we need to talk."

"This is Boris Olegovich. He restores icons. I have been going to see him work. He is teaching me about icons."

Spacinov watched as Katya spoke. "That is correct," he said, speaking now in English.

Andrew stared. "We need to talk."

Pain crept along her chest. She felt his eyes on her face, and she wanted to touch him. "We have talked, Andrew."

"You know what I mean..."

Spacinov shifted and crossed his arms. "What is going on? What is this about?"

The question brought her back to herself, and she stiffened. "Whatever we have not said, you already know."

The blood drained from his face, and he felt he might fall. "What does that mean? Katya? What happened? What has changed?"

She bit the side of her mouth. "Don't ask me to say it."

They stood like that, each waiting for something to force the moment.

Andrew excused himself at last, pausing for an instant to see if she would stop him. "I have a class," he said by way of explanation.

The old man raised an eyebrow. Katya only stared.

"Was he very drunk?" Spacinov asked after Andrew had left.

"I don't think so."

"He is an idiot?"

"Not usually."

"He loves you then."

She smiled tiredly.

"And you?"

Katya watched over the old man's shoulder as Andrew crossed the street. "That is not a question that matters anymore."

KATYA NOW divided her spare time between finishing her translation assignment and paying visits to Spacinov. This day she had chosen to visit the old man, walking the familiar route between the university and the neglected church. On the way she came upon Adam.

"Hello," he greeted her in Russian. "Where are you off to?"

"Errands," she said defensively.

"How is the translation going?" he asked, returning to English.

"It's all I do, I'm afraid."

"I suppose it's good to be busy."

"Are you more settled?"

"I'm getting used to things."

"You should go out more. Get involved with people."

"You sound like Andrew."

She glared, and then relaxed, seeing he meant nothing else by this.

After this they walked in silence, each taken in by the activity around them. It was still morning, and the streets were crowded with people going about their day: a woman waving to someone in a window, children in school uniforms, stores being opened, trucks and cars groaning from one gear to the next in a shuddering current of semi-urgency.

When they came to the church, she said a goodbye and left him on the street.

"Bye then," he called.

Katya entered the church, its sudden silence severing her from the street noise, and when the door had closed she stood for a moment to let the pliant tranquillity settle on her.

Outside Adam watched her climb the stairs, then turned to go as she disappeared inside. But as the door began to close he glimpsed two faces inside the church. Even from the street he could make out the gaunt strength of a woman's stare. Grace and anguish.

Then the unblinking gaze was severed by the closing door, suddenly so that Adam gasped as though he had been struck.

Katya found Spacinov working on the scaffold. She moved to the ladder, her own body eclipsed by the figures depicted in the great murals: the bulb-like heads of saints, the poised arc of an angel's wing, St. Vladimir's finger, the radiance of Archipp's piety. Next to the palm of St. Spiridion, her own hand became small and pale as an egg. The old man was sitting on some boards, his coat drawn about him as he dabbed at the wall with a slice.

She brushed away the dust on one of the boards and sat. "Still working on old Sergius?" she said, nodding at the ear of the saint.

Spacinov glanced at her. "Anything new in the world?"

"Will he mind that I am here?" she asked, nodding at the priest who had appeared below.

"You will be fine," he said. "I told him you are my apprentice."

"This is allowed? I mean, I do not even believe in your faith."

He put down his brush and smiled. "Coming here is a kind of belief, is it not?"

Light leaked upon them from the windows overhead. The church began to fill with the remote sounds of the devout, who shuffled across the floor below. Soon the air smelled of wax and smoke. As the morning drew on, Katya fell into her own thoughts. Her father's medals were all but gone, and out of necessity she had continued to sell the rest of her family's belongings, quietly ransacking their lives. It was a slow, gnawing process, in which the past was converted to money, to be exchanged for food and light and heat. Walking about the flat she would determine what would go next, assessing the value a radio, a blouse, a teapot.

She pushed these ideas away. Instead she concentrated on the morning light as it seeped through the church's narrow windows and into the dome. She thought of her work at the university. An image of Andrew appeared, and she frowned, trying to push him from her mind. Lying back, she stared at the murals through the gauze of these thoughts, unaware of the shadow drawing across her own face as time passed.

After a while Spacinov stood and stretched. Moving to the railing he opened a small satchel and withdrew bread, cheese and a thermos of coffee, which he shared with her.

"Some tourists came in the other day," he observed, talking through his meal, "to see what all the fuss was about in here."

"Were you friendly?"

He turned up his lip. "Am I a tour guide?"

"You might have been polite."

"Why? They knew nothing of politeness. They came in here with their cameras, taking pictures of the murals without even a '*hello*.'"

"They are impressive," she said, glancing at the walls.

"Well these tourists did not seem sufficiently impressed. One of the foreigners declared them to be '*naïve*,'" Spacinov scoffed, pronouncing the word with disdain. "Said it as though he was an authority."

"Perhaps he was interested."

"*Naïve*! You are the translator, what is that supposed to mean?"

She shrugged, a habit she had picked up from Andrew. "How should I know?"

"I have watched the foreigners, the way they look at us smugly, convinced that we are finally becoming like them." He shook his head. "As if without communism, being Russian counted for nothing. They have always confused politics and identity in the West. I watch them sometimes out front of the museum. They come here by the busload as if trying to find something they have mislaid. You can see it in their faces: always looking about as though they hope to find something...their grandmother's silverware, or Papa's favourite watch."

Katya was quiet. "They think we are innocent," she said finally, her voice listless, elsewhere. "That's why they come. They want to see what innocence looks like."

She looked at the encircling wall of the dome, its silent faces. From somewhere in the building a door opened and then closed. Motes hung in the shafts of light from the upper windows. From beneath Katya came the scrape of feet on stone.

"Now there's another one of them!" hissed Spacinov, drawing close to her now and clearly enjoying himself. "Probably just off one of those horrid buses they're always peering out of..."

Looking down, Katya saw the offending person next to one of the murals. She caught her breath.

"What if I were to drop something?" Spacinov snickered. "That would scare him off..." He turned to see if she was sharing his joke, but she was gone.

Katya descended the scaffold, then crossed to the far wall where Adam stood. Only when she was next to him did he notice her.

His face was stricken, eyes glazed, his mind turned upon something she could not see.

He looked down at a photograph in his hand. Clare holding the child, the blue hospital sheet almost covering its face. The nurse had taken the picture as Adam had walked into the room, capturing the moment when Clare's gaze met his own, that instant in which the only other person in the world who understood the magnitude of what had happened was there. It was at this instant they both saw the irrevocable rupture that had taken place in their lives. For the nurses and doctors, this moment was perhaps a sad story to tell over dinner. For Clare and Adam this was the end of all that was known and believed.

His eyes left the photograph and looked again upon the icon, seeing the way the mother instinctively supported the child's body, the small head turned toward her. But the mother's stare met Adam's instead, and he saw then in her gaze the terrible entrapment she endured. To be bound in love to the object of your deepest grief. Adam knew that a part of Clare had never left that instant in the photograph, that she would always be there, trapped in the moment of loss. He saw too that he was there with her and the child, and always would be no matter how far away he went.

Katya stood awkwardly, uncertain what to do. For an instant she thought she might speak. But when Adam looked at her his expression left her silent. Recognition and anguish passed across his face, and he coloured. The pain in his stare held her. She saw the silhouette of herself in his eyes. Katya did not speak, sensing the lengthening silence could only be broken by him. Somewhere above her, she was aware of the scaffold creaking and she knew Spacinov was watching them. Still the pain in Adam's eyes held her, and she was afraid now even of breathing, as if the smallest change would be like a violent blow, shattering him. After another moment, though, Adam hid his face and left the church.

"What did he want?" Spacinov called from the scaffold.

Katya stood unmoving, looking now at the mural he'd been staring at. "I don't know."

"You spoke to him?"

"He had nothing to say." Her voice faded into the church's shadows and stillness.

Spacinov shook his head. "Another tourist."

"No," Katya glanced at the place where he had stood. "I don't think so."

"Well never mind, come back up. Your things are here…"

"Yes," she said, her attention still on the mural. "I'm coming."

After this Katya sat with Spacinov, but her mind kept returning to the anguish on Adam's face and she couldn't collect her thoughts. In an effort to distract herself, she took out her notebooks and spread them open on the dusty planking of the scaffold. Spacinov paused and watched Katya as she began to work, smiling quietly as the expression along her brow faded and came to concentrate around her eyes.

The final poem she was translating had been very difficult, and she sat pondering the dilemma. Since her meeting with her advisor,

Katya had made little progress and she now felt herself at an impasse. She had consulted a number of sources, even located a previous translation, but none of these things helped to satisfy the problem of properly translating this last poem. The linguistic significance of the dilemma absorbed her, and soon she was aware of nothing else.

Spacinov had drifted back to himself by then, and when he spoke it was his own thoughts he was responding to. "How can foreigners understand? Most of us do not understand! Take that mural over there. The Decollation. People look on it and wonder why the prophet waits for the executioner's sword when below him is the salver with his head already on it. People look and it is incongruous to them. 'How can this be, to have a head and not have it at the same time?' They fail to see that the painter is attempting to collapse space and time into a single picture. Two instants in time captured simultaneously. The brief moment separating them has been erased, showing us the man and the martyr all in the same image..." Spacinov talked quickly now, and Katya was sure he had ceased to be aware of her.

"There is in this mural the reminder of death's horrible proximity to us all. That sliver of time which separates the now of our lives from oblivion. We are reminded that the spot where we stand, the very breath in our lungs, is just a thin border between two worlds. And so, you see, the mural becomes a comment not only on the story of the prophet, but of time and its delicate function as the buffer between our life and what lies after it."

He sighed, running a hand appreciatively though his beard. "But how to explain notions of time to a generation that hasn't the patience to listen?" He gestured around at the church walls, as if beckoning to them for an answer. "The icon's eye is also its tongue. You must wait for *it* to speak. The rigidity, the mortification of the icon – what that fool called *naïve* – is a kind of statement that speaks always of the responsibilities of existence, its potential hopes and its terrible assurances. The meaning of our lives becomes conspicuous during periods when both the vanity and anguish of this existence are laid bare. And so the icons and murals are a reply to Life's fatal revelation. Theirs is a language only the suffering may truly attend.

417

For people who suffer there are sometimes no words for what is inside them, only the gaze of the icon."

Katya stirred and looked abruptly at the old man, her face lightening. She muttered imperceptibly to herself, writing furiously in her notebook as Spacinov rambled on.

"What are you doing?" he said at last, noticing her activity.

But instead of replying she held out her finger to silence him until she had done writing. The sun fell across them. Motes of dust drifted past them in a slow sweep. Finally she set down her pencil and straightened. "There," she sighed, running a hand over her face with satisfaction. "Perhaps that's the answer..." she murmured.

"What's that?"

"Something I've been working on but hadn't solved until just now."

The old man blinked. "You weren't listening to me?"

"I am sorry," Katya closed her notebook and began to collect her things.

"You're going?"

"I need to get back."

Spacinov set down his brush.

Katya smiled and turned to go, but as she reached the ladder she paused and turned to the old man. "I hate to agree with that awful foreigner you mentioned, but that is the word," she said reluctantly, glancing now at the grand faces around them. "These icons are *naïve.*"

He stopped to look at her. "Really?"

"You feel sad for them," she went on, her face colouring. "It is their atmosphere of – forgive me, again – of failure. They are almost life-like, but not quite. You cannot help but sense that they have fallen short of their goal, that whatever they were intended to be is never quite realized."

He smiled and put aside what he was doing. "This is not why you feel sad."

She laughed at his tone. "No?"

Spacinov stood and drew closer to Katya with his candle. The old man's eyes softened as he looked on her. He touched her arm. "You have it backwards." When he spoke his voice was not without kindness. "The painters knew that what we seek is not a mirror of our world but a vision out of ourselves."

Here he paused, leaning back to stare into the great face he had been repairing, and for an instant it seemed to Katya that the icon and the man had both forgotten her.

"These figures do not aspire to emulate our world," whispered the old man. "It is we who yearn for theirs."

"WHAT ARE we seeing?" someone asked again.

"An opera," said Andrew.

They had met at a café near the dormitory. Drinks were cheap here and over the last few weeks the expats had taken to the place. Gathering at a table by the window, everyone sat waiting for the food they had ordered. The place was crowded with students and young couples, everyone talking above the music.

Ford sat at the other end of the table with Alice, one of his hands brushing against her wrist as he poured a drink. The waitress put a new disc in the stereo. As the music began, the voices of those talking rose with it, their words mingling with the song. To Adam, who remembered hearing the song in some far off place, the room seemed to grow still. A knot of regret formed in his chest, images of the past coaxed from the shadows.

When he looked up Andrew was sitting beside him.

"Missing home?"

He nodded, taking the glass Andrew handed to him. "You know, I saw this band in a little bar...."

"They call it culture shock, but I think that's wrong," Andrew interrupted. "Back home you never really see who you are because you blend in with everything. But here it's the opposite. You get to see yourself outside the place that made you. It's not just that you see who you are in a new way, but your home too. Like a fish washed up on the beach, you're stunned because you never realized until that moment that you've spent your whole life in water, and now you're not sure you can live out of it."

Adam looked blank, as though he hadn't been listening.

Andrew turned in his chair so that his back was to the others at the table. "I know you want to quit," his voice lowered. "You want to go home."

Adam stared at Andrew, almost pleading. They were quiet for a moment, each waiting in case there was more to say. He took a long drink.

Waiters came with their food, the plates landing with a hollow sound that shook the table. A fork skidded across the porcelain.

Andrew hesitated, his hand resting like a shadow on Adam's arm. "It's not like I've found it easy..." and Adam knew Andrew meant his breakup with Katya. "But the world is changing, and this is the centre of those changes. This chance won't come again for us."

"I wish things hadn't changed at all."

Andrew grinned. "So you have something in common with Russians, after all."

Adam sighed. The vodka had settled in him like a sunset. He let the glass rest on his lips, a fleeting kiss of light.

Alice was unhappy about her meal, and she tapped her finger impatiently on the table searching the restaurant for the waiter.

"I forgot to ask where you went today. I heard you cancelled your class."

Adam held his breath. "I went to see something."

People began eating. The waiter saw Alice and came over. She stopped the tapping and Adam exhaled.

Everywhere ghosts of the past rose about him like walls made from photographs and memories, voices he used to know. Beside him, in the window, he could see only the silhouette of his own face, features occluded, his eyes somewhere behind the cataract of it all, staring back.

Adam had returned to the church that day to see the mural a second time. He had awoken in the morning knowing he would go back to look on it. As he'd slept his dreams kept returning to the woman's face in the mural, and the woman's eyes had still been in his thoughts that afternoon as he stepped off the tram and turned in at the church's door.

He turned away from Andrew and the others at the restaurant, his hand trembling as he remembered the sound as the church door closed behind him, the low thud reverberating into the dome. Adam closed his eyes and he could hear the sound of his footsteps fading into the shadows, could smell again the faint traces of incense and dust.

Candles shivered against the draft which had come in with him. From somewhere came the steady drip of water dropping like pebbles into the church's silence. Faces seemed to squint at him from the half-light. But this disappeared as he felt that stare come to rest on him, a gaze of blue and gold. He stepped out from the archway into the openness of the sanctuary, the sound of his feet now like a whisper in the immensity of the dome. Her gaze enveloped him, and he became aware then only of the Mother and her Child. But just as he came within reach of the mural a figure stepped out from among the shadows and challenged him in Russian.

"What is it?" Adam blinked, half expecting to see Katya again. "What do you want?"

It was an old man. And when he spoke again his voice chafed along the English consonants. "What are you doing here?"

Adam glanced about for help, but found only the looming faces on the walls which looked on silently, waiting. "This picture," he began, suddenly embarrassed and angry at the same time. "You can see it from the street."

Spacinov scowled, and then his expression changed with a sudden realization. "You are the one who came here yesterday."

Adam flushed, his throat tightening. "I was here. I saw this picture from the street."

"This is not a *picture*! And who said you could come in here? This is no place for tourists."

Something in Spacinov's voice made Adam straighten, and he found the old man's eyes before he replied. "I'm not a tourist."

"Of course you are. Now leave. You do not know what you're looking at."

Adam's eyes flared, and he thrust out his hand so that Spacinov stepped back. "I do."

The echo of dripping water seemed to grow louder, its impatient tapping reverberating into the great dome. Candles beside Adam shivered from an invisible draught. Above, the afternoon light seemed to still the fraying threads of smoke.

Spacinov saw that the foreigner was holding out a picture. As his eyes focussed on it, he squinted and drew closer until the photo trembled with his breath.

The first thing he noticed was the pattern of creases fragmenting the figures on the worn celluloid, the way they traversed the woman in

426

the photograph. He stared at the woman, following her own stricken gaze to the child in her arms. Spacinov looked up at the mural, the air rushing from him as he understood.

He looked back at the foreigner.

Tears fell from Adam's face into the silence. He was staring at the Child in the mural. "I know why I'm here," he said.

It was already dark as Adam and the other expats made their way along the bridge. Below, the city was reflected back at them, lights wrinkled on the black water. Their conversations skipped between them like small stones: earnest nonsense, unsolicited opinions and other fragments of who-knows-what flung at the darkness. Adam walked a little behind.

"Hold on," Andrew said. "I'm going to buy cigarettes…"

The group paused at the corner to wait for him. It was cold and they instinctively stood together on the corner. There was a break in the evening traffic, and they were startled as a group of military trucks moved up the street. From behind the tailgates soldiers peered into the night, their faces grey and stiff as old news footage.

Candace waved at them. "Where are they going?"

Andrew reappeared and stood beside Adam, and together they watched the trucks' hurried progress up the street. In the last vehicle one of the soldiers stuck out his index finger like a pistol and pointed it at them.

Andrew lighted a cigarette. "Those looked like friendly chaps."

Alice grabbed Adam's arm. "Let's go, fellas. Or we'll be late."

When they reached the theatre the expats joined a queue standing around a massive stone fountain, its basin clogged with leaves, limp and bright colored like dead goldfish. Behind a row of columns the doors of the theatre stood open, spilling light and excitement into the street. Adam paused to take in the grandness of it all. A gallery ran around the front of the theatre, channelling the crowd toward staircases that led to specific seating areas. People climbing to the second and third balconies looked over the railing at those just arriving.

The expats checked their coats with one of the attendants at a counter near the main doors. "Okay," Troy announced. "Where's the bar?"

They found the bar at the far end of the lobby, where they leaned against the marble counter and watched the crowd while Andrew ordered two bottles of wine. Around them voices flowed, bits of conversation rising into the chandeliers. The expats grinned self-consciously over their glasses.

Ivan frowned at the playbill, where the usual credits and production details had also been printed in English and German for tourists. He turned to his daughter indignantly. "Did you see this?"

"Relax, Papa," she whispered. "We're here to enjoy ourselves. It's been so long since we've been to the theatre..." Katya sank deeper into her chair. She was still stunned by her mother's unexpected purchase of their tickets. It was an outrageous and trivial expenditure, considering what little they had, but the gesture nonetheless touched her.

It had been Lydia's idea to come to the theatre the way they had before the Party's fall from grace, and she hoped the effort would bring together the two remaining members of her family. Lydia had accepted her son was leaving with a sense of finality Katya found upsetting. Almost overnight her mother seemed to forget Petya and to focus instead on the two people who remained to her. Since Petya's announcement, neither Ivan nor Katya had spent much time in the other's company. So Lydia had sold the bedside lamps in her room all on her own, proudly using the money to purchase two tickets to the first play on the schedule. And so father and daughter found themselves sharing, if only for that evening, a small luxury from their still-remembered past.

Ivan frowned at his daughter, but said no more about the playbill, and folded it on his lap. A cloud passed over his expression. His thoughts moved to Petya. 'Ah, Petya. You fool. Petya, my child...'

If only the boy could understand the danger, if only he understood what was at stake. Why could the boy not see? The old ghost pain stirred in his lost arm, and Ivan instinctively comforted the invisible limb against his chest. He felt his face coloring, his breathing quicken. Petya!

Ivan turned away from his daughter so she did not witness the grief welling up in his eyes. Petya! Who could have predicted his betrayal?

Ivan shut his eyes as tears began to fall, feeling each one as it wetted his ghost arm.

He straightened abruptly, wiping back the tears. This would not do. Petya was a terrible loss, it was true. But hadn't he survived other losses before this? Worse even than the loss of a child? Yes, almost. He has survived the loss of his arm, of his own parents, of Subov and his wife. He had come through starvation and bombs. He had survived it all. As the Party had.

Ivan's brow calmed and his fingers relaxed their grip on the empty sleeve. 'And once again the Party is facing its enemy,' he thought. 'And once again it shall overcome.' Just as he would overcome. They would fight together – he and the Party. They would fight the enemy that had stolen his only son. The Party was fighting to end the chaos that had enveloped not just his family, but families throughout the country. The Party was even now organizing its defense against the President behind the barricades in the capital. "Moscow," he whispered. "That is where it will be decided…"

Ivan ran his hand over his face. The lights dimmed in the theatre and the audience hushed, his own gaze narrowed and he knew then what he would do.

Katya sighed to herself as the darkness and silence descended over her.

Walls and seats evaporated into shadow and she was surrounded by a hush that seemed to swallow her. With her mother's opera glasses, she searched the stage as a single voice was unsheathed in the dark, drawing a shivering blade of light after it. The curtain rose as the rest of the orchestra released a long collective note, and Katya closed her eyes to let the music press upon her.

During the intermission Adam joined Andrew and the others at the bar. The high they had been on earlier had started to wane, and most were now resuscitating it with a vengeance. Ford, who had been drinking beer all night, ordered a bottle of champagne and insisted they share it.

"What do you say?" Troy said, offering Adam a glass.

No one was thinking about the opera anymore and the conversation became an expectant mutter as the bottle went around.

"I believe in cooperation between nations," Ford declared when everyone had a glass. He held up his drink. "To group efforts...!" to which someone added a joke that made Alice blush and they all laughed. The bar was busier now. Tourists grouped together around tables, whispering over their programs. People stood at the bar, shifting from foot-to-foot or repeatedly checking watches as they waited for their drinks.

Adam left them as the second bottle arrived.

Moving through the crowd he spotted Andrew standing at the end of the hall.

"What are you doing?"

"I wanted to look around."

Adam stepped back to survey some of the photographs on the wall.

"See this one?" Andrew said, nodding to the frame directly in front of them.

"Yeah?"

"There are thirty-seven people in this photograph."

Adam glanced around at the other pictures. "So?"

He brought his finger down to the roster beneath the photograph. "There are only thirty-five names."

"Wow," Adam said vaguely. "I wonder who was left out."

"That one," he said quickly, as though he'd been waiting to be asked. He pointed out a woman in the front row.

"How do you know?"

"That's my mother."

His eyes widened. "Really?"

"Really."

He stared at the photograph. "So I guess the second one…"

"Is my father."

"Wow." Adam stared. "Why aren't their names on the list?"

"My mother defected. They cut her out of everything after that. Him, too, though he didn't leave. They used to do things like that."

Adam leaned closer to the frame, unsure of what to say. "Which one is he?"

"I don't know."

He glanced at his friend. "You've never seen his picture?"

"Nope."

"But you've seen this photograph."

"A while back," he nodded, "when I bought the tickets."

"You never told me about this."

"You're one to talk about secrets," and he managed to grin. "Besides, it doesn't matter anymore," he said, in a voice which told them both that it did.

"So this country is not just about Katya for you?"

Andrew shook his head. "She was a big part of it for a while."

"She's here tonight."

He sighed. "I know."

They were quiet for a moment, each with his thoughts. There was more commotion around them. People were finishing drinks, going back to their seats.

Adam looked again at the woman in the back row of the picture, and an idea began to dawn on him. "Look at the date."

"What?"

"On the photograph. Look at the date."

"So?"

"We're the same age, you and I. Look at the date. That's the year you were born. Chances are you're there, too."

Andrew stared at the photograph again, frowning all of a sudden. "Seeing her there makes me wonder if her life would have been better if I was never born."

He watched the way Andrew looked at the picture. "Would it really help if you saw your father?"

"I won't now."

"Why not?"

"He's dead."

Adam felt himself color.

"What's the matter with you?"

He didn't answer, but instead turned into the gathering crowd and disappeared.

In the washroom he was alone except for two men smoking at the urinals. Andrew appeared a moment later with a cigarette behind his ear, pausing to ask one of them for a match. When it was lit he stepped beside Adam, pursing his lips so he could smoke and talk.

"You're not going to talk about it, are you?"

Adam didn't look at him.

Andrew sighed. "I hope you're enjoying the opera, at least?"

He shrugged.

"That makes you an elitist, you know."

"Does it?"

"No wonder you never got tenure."

Adam made an effort to smile. Voices rose outside the door.

Andrew did up his fly. "They should make this show into a movie."

"I'm sure they have."

"That's the problem for us," he shrugged. "Everything has already been done." Andrew smiled distantly, his mind changing subjects. "I think the rest of us are going to take off."

"You're not staying?"

"Someone told me about a new place near the stadium. Why don't you come with us?"

Adam shook his head. "I'm going to stay."

"Come on," he cajoled. "It's supposed to be a great bar, kind of a post-Cold War thing. Lenin meets the Hard Rock."

He winced. "No thanks."

Andrew shrugged, but instead of leaving he turned at the door and faced him. "I shouldn't have mentioned anything before," he said. "About leaving. I know it's hard here, and it is clear you do not like it."

He bit the inside of his mouth. "I don't fit with the others." Adam knew he was embarrassing, his habit of plaintive self-pity, the drawn out mourning.

"Screw the others. Be whoever you want." Andrew shook his head. "Don't you get how free we are here?"

Adam squinted into the cigarette smoke. "I don't feel free anywhere."

"You think I'm thrilled with how things have turned out? My own mother left this place because her life was being strangled here. But the world has changed. In the West most of our generation is excluded – you said so yourself. But here things are different. You see that. This country is being reborn. Democracy, open markets, globalism – it's all coming at once. There is going to be a place here for everybody. It finally hit me the other day. This is the country my mother wanted to live in. This is the place to be. Here and now. Besides, what would we go home to? Marriage and a minivan? If you stay here, your life doesn't have to be a Brady Bunch rerun..." Andrew's voice trailed off.

"I would take the minivan, if I could," Adam said. "I'd go back in a second if it was there."

"So why don't you?"

"It's not what's there."

Andrew stared. "What the hell happened to you?"

Adam looked at his friend. "You told me once I didn't have to be who I was back home. You're wrong about that. There are things that don't go away, that stay with you. Each morning people wake up and for you and the others it's day, but for me there's a part of the dark that never leaves. There are things that happen that change you, and you can't unchange them. Look around. You pass people every day who know what I know. There are homeless people, addicts, prostitutes – people existing on the knife edge of obliteration, who got there because of a single fuck up, a chance mistake, a war, a drunk driver, a fight, a bad needle, and became completely lost in the wreckage it unleashed. The terms of their lives changed. Think about this. When that happens, you know that you will never be the same person. No matter where you are, the one place you can't go is back. I came here because I wanted to hide. To start over. I want to be around strangers…" and he waved toward the door. "To be unknown."

"You've done a good job."

Adam smiled in spite of himself. "It hasn't made any difference. If anything it's worse here." He let his hands fall at his side. "I can't escape. You can't escape. I might as well go back to what I know."

There was a long pause as Andrew seemed to weigh something in his head. "Go home," he said at last.

Adam stood alone at the sink when Andrew had gone. In the mirror, his eyes looked wild, not his own. He stared for a long time into the middle distance, the empty space between him and his reflection.

He was looking at Clare.

In the end it was not a global crisis or some humanitarian outrage that had divided their lives, but an everyday aberration. One of the casual cruelties, one of the small and intimate accidents that accompany love.

He was late picking her up, so she had decided to take the bus rather than wait. It was winter, and as she was getting on the bus she fell.

Adam arrived after the ambulance. He left the car on the street and found one of the paramedics who said he should ride with her. Clare was already in the back, and it was a moment before she noticed him. Always when he remembered that moment Adam saw himself, his reflection in the window of the ambulance, and behind it Clare looking at him.

He whispered to her on the way there, trying to comfort. "You are safe now," he said.

But when she looked at him the pain in her gaze cut him off. "Safe from what?"

If he had stayed in Toronto he would have a job now in advertising or something. He would own a car, a TV. Extended warranties. Later he would have a house with some sort of deck. Adam closed his eyes, but she was still there.

When Clare could push no more they put up a screen across her chest and went in for it themselves with instruments made for the purpose. Clare had cried out, covering her face as the operating light was turned on her. The penetrating brightness trapped her body within its round weight, her hair spilling over the table's edge like yolk. Adam stood by, determined to stay, though he faltered when he

441

saw it. The doctor was trying to conceal it from him, but then there was a sudden release of blood and things happened all at once, and what he saw first and would remember the rest of his life was the smallest arm he had ever seen.

Clare looked at him, desperate. "What is happening?"

He turned and pressed his face into the wall.

When it was over they cleaned the child and wrapped it in a blue blanket. He remembered that. Blue.

Someone told Clare, and when Adam looked again at her she was sitting up, holding it against her shoulder. Her head was angled awkwardly, face gaunt and pale. She seemed frozen, every expression hardened by the anguish behind her eyes.

One of the nurses took a picture. "This will be important for you," she said.

He placed his hand on Clare's arm. "I don't know what to say."

She stared at where his hand touched her. "There is nothing to say."

The room was still. Hushed sounds, the odour of disinfectant, squeak of rubber soles.

Looking at each other then, Adam understood that they would not return from this.

"It's over," she said, and he saw that she understood, too. He nodded.

This was how it ended. Silence falling like a blade between them. It discontinued them. Severed them from the future, a part of their lives forever trapped in the past tense.

That night the doctor came with a nurse who stood by the window with a wheelchair. They talked with Clare. When they were done everyone left so that she could dress. He helped her, and after called a taxi to take them home.

She stared at the snow outside, her eyes full of winter.

"I am sorry," he said, though this is not exactly what he meant.

The taxi took them home, where Adam made sandwiches that they did not eat.

"I feel tired," she said, and he helped her to the bedroom. As he tucked the sheet beneath her chin his face drew close to hers, and she looked him in the eye.

"It was a boy," she whispered.

He pulled back. "They told you that?"

"They told me everything," she said. Then after a moment, "The nurse asked if I wanted to name it."

The fridge cut on in the kitchen. Sounds in the street. Music. Engines. A door slammed.

"What did you say?"

"I named him after you."

Adam stared, the breath gone from him.

"The nurse said a name can help you with the grief."

"Grief," he muttered, the word momentarily tricking him into speaking. "Is that what this is?"

She covered her face. "This is so many things."

Adam closed his eyes. He moved to the door, resting his head against the wood. He heard her move, drawing the sheet over her head. She was crying. "Go away."

When she was asleep he locked himself in the washroom. It was very quiet there, and bright. White linoleum they had put down that fall.

Leaning over the sink, he ran the water and tried to concentrate on the sound. "Control," he whispered to himself. If he could just control himself, he could deal with it a bit at a time. In pieces. His hands trembled and he gripped them tightly into fists until the shaking stopped. Then he held his breath several times, refusing himself relief even as his body rebelled, dominating the ache that rose in his eyes and chest and only accepting release when he thought he might black out. By the third time he was panting, his face red with the exertion. When he thought it might be safe, he turned off the water and straightened. There he was in the mirror.

He struck the glass, driving his hand into the face which suddenly broke apart.

Adam looked down at the glass. Fragments of him stared back in the splinters. An earlobe, the edge of his jaw, piece of lip and tooth. His left eye.

Blood dropped steadily onto the tile. He stood listening for Clare beyond the door.

The small room filled with the sound of his breathing. The image of Clare and the child broke through the pain. He shook his head, trying to tear it from his mind. The small arm was still there on the blue sheet, a streak of blood along its finger. A sound rose in his chest, and Adam covered his mouth to hold it back.

'What has happened?' he thought. 'What happens now?'

Adam held his hands under the tap until the sound of the water gradually drew him back from his thoughts. The theatre lights flickered. People in the washroom hurried around him. He did not move, but watched the water disappear into the drain.

There are things you must look at a long time before you can see them as they are. Adam looked back to that moment when he had looked at the broken mirror and all those shards of himself, and he tried to grasp what had happened to him and Clare. It occurred to him then that what he had lost and gained may not yet have words.

A thread of smoke still coiled from Andrew's cigarette which hung over the sink like a finger of ash.

When Clare first told him that she was pregnant, Adam had been surprised at the feeling of rest which came over him. This child, he understood, would anchor them to something, not a university or a career, but a mental place, a single word, to which everything else in his life would be moored. A home. A place so intimate that it reflected, rather than imposed on, your identity. The idea of being a father brought him a feeling of unexpected solidity, the locating of something he had never thought to look for. But when the child died, Adam was cast adrift, his existence now defined by the knowledge of what might have been, that shattered reflection.

As the door closed behind him he was met by the rush of voices in the lobby, the unfinished conversations. He looked around, recognizing no one.

He walked by the picture Andrew had showed him, passing between the crowds of strangers. The lights flickered again.

In the theatre, it grew dark. Katya glanced toward the private balcony, and just as the lights went down she caught a glimpse of all the empty chairs.

When Adam arrived back at the dormitory, he found it empty. In the common room he filled the kettle at the sink and placed it on the stove. Flame leapt from the burner next to his hand and he flinched from the pain.

The fridge cut on.

The pain.

The image of Clare holding the child wouldn't leave him. He thrust at it with other thoughts – his loneliness, his career, his father, Andrew – but the memory haunted him and would not go away. He could not resist its insistence.

He became aware of the quickening throb of his pulse, like drums in the night.

The kettle rolled across the floor. Air clotted in his throat, and he felt unsteady. He realized, like the swimmer in an undertow, that he was in the grip of something he could not see, a swallowing current of absence. Clare and the child had gone. But their space in his life remained.

Adam leaned against the edge of the stove where the flame shivered. He saw Clare and the child watching him. He looked at where the flame had touched his hand and focussed on the ache beneath the damaged skin. His fingers flexed open and shut like wings on a moth. Air passed from his lungs. He clenched his eyes. His hand quivered above the burner, and the taste of blood filled his mouth. Blisters bloomed and a faint smile passed across the agony of his face as he recognized the rapid throbbing which echoed back from inside him. He cried out. It was a desperate animal sound, a prayer-cry for deliverance.

Adam wept, clutching his hand now to his chest. Words crumbled in his mouth, names and memories fell and shattered about him. And the word he kept repeating through the grief and pain was the one he had tried the hardest to forget, the word that had haunted him all the way to this place. The name he shared with the dead child.

His sobbing began to slow at last, and he became aware of a loosening inside him. With it a tremendous heaviness flowed through his limbs, bending him until he lay spent and finished on the floor.

'There,' he thought, just before passing out. 'I have named it too.'

As they stepped out into the cold night, Katya experienced the disorientation one has after being to the theatre.

"So, what did you think?" she asked tentatively. Her father had been silent through the show and she prodded him now to bring him back to himself.

Ivan pulled up his collar against the cold. "Did you see the way the tenor was dressed? Clearly a political message. The audience loved it."

The street was quiet except for the hushed sound of those going home from the theatre.

"Already they are missing what they threw away," he raised his voice. "All we have in this country is memory."

They walked among the thinning crowd, Katya wishing now that she had not spoken. As they approached the corner, she waited by the fountain while her father found a taxi. Leaves lay matted and rotting at her feet. The cold was hard against her face, and she wiped at the tears it brought. She knew Andrew had seen her, but he hadn't acknowledged this in the theatre. What had she expected, though? She pushed the sting of it back from her thoughts and tried instead to think of her brother and his departure.

How would she manage without Petya? He had promised to send her money, but that did not bring the relief or sense of security she might once have thought it would. She squinted into the headlights of hurrying traffic. She could not picture her family, their home without him in it. He had gone away for his education, but he had

450

never really left the heart of the family. He had always been with them in a way that she knew would not be true this time. Their father acted as though his son was already gone, and ignored Petya if they were in the same room. Their mother, too, spoke to her son only rarely and then in a whisper, as though afraid her husband might hear her even when he was not home. The tension grated on everyone, and each of them consciously looked now for reasons not to be in the flat. It was as though everyone in the family had emigrated too. Katya rose early to be at the library when it opened, staying late until it closed. Once, coming home, she had seen her brother across the street but Katya had not known what to do, and he had passed out of sight like any other stranger.

Her father waved his arm at the stream of traffic until a cab pulled up next to him.

Ivan opened the door for her, but then stopped abruptly.

"What is it?"

"Listen…" he whispered.

Above came a low pulsing. People on the street halted. Someone pointed into the trees.

They descended from the darkness in groups, like falling angels. The throbbing drum seemed to envelop Katya as they passed overhead.

"Helicopters?"

Ivan didn't answer, staring instead as they passed over the city.

Two women appeared next to him. "What's happening? Why would the army be out now?"

"Do you know where they're going?"

Ivan stared, disbelieving. "It is happening. It is happening…"

"Come on," Katya urged, gently pulling him into the taxi. But Ivan remained where he was, looking on in astonishment at the sky. "I don't believe it," he muttered. "It's happening."

"What do you mean? What's happening? This has nothing to do you with us."

"They are getting ready."

Katya's voice lowered, an idea dawning on her. "How can you know this?"

"I have to go." Ivan did not take his eyes from the sky.

"Go where?" She pulled at his arm. "We are going home. It is late."

He turned at last and looked at her, as if becoming aware of her again. "It is much later than you think, Katya."

SOMEONE WAS shaking him.

Adam was lying on the floor of his room. It was a moment before he could sit up. "What is it?"

There was some shuffling. Cigarette smoke. Someone grabbed him by the hand.

"Shit!"

Andrew was trying to pull him to his feet, but stopped short when he saw the cloth wrapped about Adam's hand. "What happened to you?"

It was cold in the room. As Adam's eyes focused he saw that he was still in his clothes from the night before. He groaned and cradled his hand against his stomach.

Andrew reached for his friend's hand. "Let me see it – " and he began to unwrap the bandage. "Seriously, what happened?"

"I was making tea. It was an accident."

He stared at Adam for a moment. "Stay here."

"Don't worry."

He came back with a cloth and a bottle. "We need to clean this..."

Adam winced and turned away, too tired to argue. He closed his eyes tight and held his breath. When the pain came he gasped and tried to pull away, but Andrew was ready. "Don't," and he poured a little more vodka.

The pain burned through his hand. His arms began to shake, and sweat beaded along his back.

When he was done, Andrew began to talk and the words drifted through the fog and pain in Adam's head. He spoke of the new rumour that soldiers might enter Moscow any day. "The Army may be getting ready to throw its hand in with the Kremlin," he explained. "Those guys in the parliament building are alone in this. Only the people can save them now. The citizens have to come out. They have to stand up for the elected officials. Fight, even."

Adam opened one eye. "Fight the army?"

"They're going to have to fight, that or walk away from everything they've gained since Perestroika."

"Maybe they won't have to fight."

Andrew's hands paused as he tied off the new bandage. "They are talking about sending in the army, man. It's in the papers this morning. What do you *think* that means?"

Adam's head had begun to clear, but he still had no energy to argue. "It sounds pretty bad."

Andrew took the pillow case from the bed and started to make a sling. "This'll keep your hand from getting bumped on the way."

"On the way?"

"You're coming to the train station."

There was a large backpack by the door. Adam's mind began to clear. "Train station?"

"I'm going to Moscow."

Adam scowled, suddenly confused again. "What?"

"We need to go," Andrew snapped, his voice stiffening. "Your jacket's on the floor."

The station sat in the centre of the city. Soot-stained granite and steel once intended to impress travellers. Inside the main entrance was a statue of Lenin, his hand pointing to a dusty

456

globe suspended at the far end of the station. The lobby was crowded. Men smoked on the wooden benches. People from the country pushed about with gunny sacks. At one line several women argued loudly with the ticket girl. An old man slept in the phone booth. From somewhere in the ceiling a voice called out departures and arrivals which everyone seemed to ignore. Luggage sat about the corners and doorways with children playing among it. The smell of diesel exhaust and creosote.

Andrew waited in line for his ticket while Adam went searching for something to eat from among the kiosks. He met him at the gate trying to read the schedule on a large board.

"There's a place with coffee," he reported.

They found the shop and a little table, but Andrew stood as soon as they had ordered. "I need a newspaper."

Adam watched through the window, trying to ignore the throbbing in his hand. Crows cluttered the platform, strutting around passengers. Litter lay about the tracks, blackened and flaccid. The temperature had dropped overnight, and those waiting for trains huddled along the platform.

Adam shivered each time someone opened the door. When the coffee came he began to feel warm again.

Andrew returned with four or five newspapers which he scanned for information.

"This could be it," he said. "Everyone said this was coming."

Outside, a line of sports cars went past on one of the outer tracks. A steel snake gliding east, pregnant with Bavarian luxury.

Andrew kept lighting cigarettes and then butting them. "You should put more vodka on that tonight," he said, nodding at the bandage.

Adam stuck his hand inside his coat. "Have you thought about what you're doing?"

Andrew stopped moving and considered his friend. "Shut up, and let me do this. I thought you would understand. I realized last night – Katya and I are over. My parents are dead. I am never going to meet my father. There's nothing holding me back. And things are going to happen in Moscow. Big things – history is being written. Why shouldn't I go?"

Adam pointed to a photograph in one of the papers. "Clare used to talk about situations like this. If they start shooting people…"

A voice called over the speaker, and Andrew began to collect his things. "What are you so worried about? You were going to leave anyway. Now you have an excuse."

Adam put his hands under the table. "I didn't come here for this."

"Why the hell did you come here? Because Clare left you – is that why?"

"It wasn't to get shot."

"We've come to an extraordinary place, at an extraordinary time. It's not enough here to be who we were."

Andrew looked out the window. People picked up their things and began to queue on the platform. The voice over the loudspeaker announced another train, and there was a metallic shriek from somewhere in the station. He turned to Adam with a sense of finality, but when his friend would not look up Andrew's expression softened.

"Go home, don't go home. It won't matter. You can't go back to who you were going to be any more than I can. That person is gone, my friend." Andrew leaned forward until their faces almost touched. "I am trying to figure out who I'm going to be. You should, too."

As the door opened there was a rush of cold that passed over him, and Andrew was gone. Adam thought of Clare and wondered where she was at that moment. He thought of all the places she had lived, and he realized she could be anywhere now, somewhere far away. His father, too, would be gone by the time he got back.

He stood to see Andrew as he joined the crowd on the platform. But as he rose, Adam's eye caught instead on his own reflection in the café's dirty window and he stood there unmoving for a long moment, with himself.

Her father had left, and nothing was the same.

The absent clock ticked along in Katya's head, measuring out the emptiness that had settled in the family's flat. Moving from one room to another, she felt the holes she had made – the small table where her mother used to set her teacup, the porcelain figurines from the bookshelf, matching vases given to her parents as a wedding gift, the silver cup Petya won as a boy, a lamp that had sat on the hall table, the silk scarves her mother had used in her hair, a rug that had hung on the wall in her own room, the set of good plates...

In each room and cupboard were the loose threads where Katya had removed items she thought she could sell. But since her father had left for Moscow the anxious purpose behind her slow auction of the family's belongings had seemed futile. Rather than alleviating the agitation and strain in the family, Ivan's absence now added a sense of grief that sank to the core of her. It was as if he wanted to leave them before Petya did. Her father's decision to join the coup leaders in Moscow made Katya realize what would be lost when her brother finally left for Los Angeles. Standing now in her parents' bedroom, she stared at the pillow where her father had slept almost every night of her life, and she wondered what it meant that he was no longer with them. The family she had been trying to keep together was disintegrating not from impending poverty, but from larger changes that pressed on them all. It was not just her family that was changing, but the whole world.

Katya took a deep breath, taking in the odours of her parents' room, and holding them as long as she could inside of her. She tried to see everything then: the way the grey morning

461

light rested on the carpet, the motionless posture of her mother's clothes in the closet, an unfinished book on the table, the creases stretching across the white bed sheet. And then, when she could not bear it any longer, Katya exhaled, and walked back the way she had come through the silent flat, cataloguing the items that would go next.

The following day Katya left the university and walked the now-familiar route through the Old Quarter of the city to their flat on Granatny Street. She glanced enviously at the other people on the street, longing for the lack of care they seemed to have. She had been like them once, and she scowled now to think how ignorant she'd been of her good fortune. Katya wondered if she would ever again be like these people. Would there be a time in her life when she could breathe without the weight that always lurked now in her mind?

When she came to their flat she collected the garbage and threw it out. There were two teacups in the sink. She washed these, and left them to dry on the small plastic rack. She cleaned the counters and swept the floor, folded the linen and returned it to the closet. Wiped each surface. The last thing she did was to take Chaika to the balcony. The bird seemed confused at first without its cage, and for a time it sat on Katya's arm, craning its neck in all directions.

Katya whispered to the bird while her fingers stroked the length of its neck. "Fly away," she said. "Far away."

Beneath the feathers she felt the delicate vertebrae, the quickening pulse. The bird's muscles shuddered. Before Chaika lay the street stretching into more streets, and beyond this the open sky of setting light.

At last Chaika tensed and with a single gesture it plunged forward, a flare of colour against the horizon of concrete and shadow. Katya cried out at the bird as it lifted into the air. "Go Chaika...!"

But then as her wings opened a second time, the bird seemed to trip over itself and it fell scratching at the air with its claws.

Katya stood for a moment and watched the bird as it waddled about at her feet. "Oh, Chaika," she whispered. "Why won't you fly?"

She bent down and put the bird back in its cage.

The next day Katya went to see Spacinov and she told him about the bird. The old man just shook his head. "What did you expect? The thing was probably born in captivity. It had never flown in its life."

Katya winced at this. She had been hoping for sympathy. She folded her arms. "That was hardly Chaika's fault."

"It wasn't the bird who wanted it to be out of the cage."

He was repairing a portion of St. Michael which had come away from the wall. He had finished plastering the broken section, and he was cleaning his tools now in a pail of water. "Anyway, enough of this bird. How are you? You look pale. Are you well?"

Katya looked away without speaking. Spacinov said nothing more, and as if to break the silence he stood and stretched. Setting his candle on the rail, he removed the fingerless gloves he wore. He unlatched the small box with his paints and began to mix colours. Katya watched his hands.

The old man squinted at her. "What is wrong?"

Her own thoughts did not make sense to her at that moment, but instead of trying to understand them she felt confusion and anger rise up abruptly like an unseen wave.

He felt the tension clench in her, and he sighed. "Ask me," he said.

"What?"

"Ask me."

She looked at her hands, her face growing hot. "I don't understand."

"You bring the question every time you come here. It was on your lips the first time we met, but you could not find the words. Ask me now."

"I don't know what you mean."

"You are lying. Find the words. Ask me."

"I come here because I like the icons. I like to talk with you – "

"You are not a coward, Yekaterina. Ask me."

Something inside her stirred, a flame, and she sneered. "I don't know what you're talking about!"

He met her eyes. "Find the words."

His stare held her, and she bit her lip. For a moment there was only the sound of their breathing.

"What if your God is not real?" she blurted. The words struck against something hard inside her, as if reaching out in the dark. Once she had begun, she found that words came in a sudden rush. "What if these are all pictures of made-up stories?" Katya threw her arm out at the dome of murals. "What if they're all wrong?" she demanded. "What if all this means nothing? That would make you a fool. Wouldn't it?"

The old man looked at her a long time, searching her face for something he sought. "That is better now, isn't it?"

"The possibility must have occurred to you."

Spacinov smiled softly. "Listen to me," he said, his voice patient. "Our people have turned to the icons for over a thousand years. Through wars, famine and tyranny. We have survived our own history. Many people have not. The icons return us to the source of that original language which was discovered in us by our past. It is as though the word on each saint's lips is the first one ever spoken, kept there for us to hear for the first time, again and again. Through all of our trials the icons have preserved us. They are symbols not only of faith, but of survival." He reached out and

466

touched Katya's hand. "It is through them that we discover what we have lost. The icons are like pieces of ourselves we barely recognize. You spend your time concerned about the future. This is fine. But you should see by now that our future will be an ancient one." His voice became suddenly thin, trailing off. It was a long time after this before Spacinov spoke, and Katya thought he had forgotten her, until at last he seemed to return to himself.

"I have lived longer than you. I know enough to understand the limits that exist on human knowledge. So let me tell you of what I am certain: after we are returned to dust, after all this is gone," and here he pinched the scarred skin on his forearm until his fingers went white. "There is still more."

(

PART IV

Whatever has come to be has already been named....

Ecclesiastes, 6:10

IVAN WOKE.

He caught his breath as his eyes flitted about in the night. Gradually, he became aware of odours and faint sounds.

Voices somewhere. Light suddenly flooded the darkness and he let out a small cry as it exposed bodies, bleaching faces, hands, limbs, open mouths, all cast for an instant in white by the sudden glare. And then just as suddenly, the light was gone and Ivan was again alone in the dark.

A tremor passed under his skin and he clutched at the ghost pain in his lost limb. The next instant he was overcome with a nauseous sense of aloneness and panic. He held his boy arm tight to himself, protecting it. His pulse throbbed in his ears. He took a series of short breaths to help control himself. The light returned then, again revealing the collection of limbs and faces and bodies all about him. When it was gone, he held his breath until he remembered where he was.

Down the corridor someone stirred, then resumed a low snore.

Ivan sat up to rub the phantom arm, cradling its memory to his chest. When the light appeared again it revealed only the empty sleeve of his coat. Slowly the pain eased, and the limb disappeared again, went back to where he had lost it. Ivan leaned his head against the wall and shut his eyes. Sweat chilled along his back, leaving him shivering. He'd had more episodes like this since coming to Moscow. It was always the same, the boy flesh crying out from within the man's body.

He struggled to stand. His hip ached where the pistol they had given him had pressed into his side as he's slept. They had looked at his one arm and decided against offering him a rifle. "Keep this close," he had been advised as they handed him the gun. "You will need it before we are done." Ivan leaned back and tried to stretch out the stiffness until he felt able to walk. When he was agitated his body demanded motion, and, as he had so many times since coming here, he paced the corridors. In one room he found students from the naval academy, boys in their early twenties wearing camouflage and smoking in leather chairs around a long table. Others leaned against windows, taking turns training their rifles on the street. No one noticed Ivan.

The general mood had taken a turn for the worse after the power was cut. Occasionally now there was a metallic crack behind the walls as pipes burst, and in some rooms the floor became sodden.

The order and obedience he had long become used to in the Party was not evident here. Instead he was confronted with brooding disorder, fear and belligerence among those he met. For days it had been the same everywhere he went in the building, indolence and disrespect reigned. People carved obscenities into furniture, pillaged desks and cabinets for valuables. Two men found a collection of silk ties in someone's office, and they handed them around to friends who used them as headbands. Filing cabinets had been disembowelled, their contents spread randomly across floors and hallways. State secrets were trod underfoot, rolled into makeshift pillows.

There was a feverish reality in the besieged building that disturbed Ivan, but there was nowhere else for him to go, nothing to do except to walk shiftless and hungry about the frozen corridors and abandoned offices.

On one floor he was stopped by some pensioners who inspected him before letting him pass. Old men and women stood wrapped in blankets, awkwardly holding their rifles. Stiff with cold, they huddled around flashlights, and smoked the old-style cigarettes with cardboard tips. Next to the windows they'd stacked bricks, odd pieces of metal, homemade bombs – even a urinal taken from one of the washrooms – to be thrown down on the attackers everyone expected. In one hallway slept members of a Stalinist group, and Ivan passed among the portraits and banners with the old inspirational mottos over doorframes. In another section of the building he found a group of monarchists who had cluttered the walls and elevator doors with pictures of the Romanovs. Farther along was a group of intellectuals, who debated into the night. When Ivan passed them, they were breaking up a fistfight to do with Italian socialism. No one had given this group guns.

This night Ivan was particularly restless, and as he trod the familiar floors he felt increasingly agitated. After some searching, he located a deputy he knew in the People's Hall, where at any time of day you could find politicians and officials working by candlelight beneath the enormous flag that hung on the curtained wall. Nearly everyone here wore track suits or mismatched items of camouflage or khaki fatigues. Ivan almost didn't recognize one of the protest's organizers, who brushed by with an Adidas jacket and a Kalashnikov. Earlier that week one of the deputies had brought out a guitar, and the entire auditorium had listened to old folk songs. But tonight the People's Hall echoed with only the sounds of paper and hushed voices as politicians and their staff pored over documents and decrees. Amid all of this activity, Ivan located a deputy he knew. The man had managed to get himself a large flashlight, which he shone on Ivan as he approached.

Ivan looked at the deputy hopefully. "Any news?"

The man spat into the darkness. "The same."

"What about the television stations?"

He sighed and changed the subject. "How are you tonight?"

"Something has to happen soon," Ivan said, struggling to lower his voice. "It's driving me mad, all this waiting."

"We are all feeling it."

"If there was some order in the place. Someone in charge…"

He bristled. "We have leaders."

"Well, I don't like the company they keep. Who are these people?"

The deputy shrugged. "How should I know?"

"Well then what are we fighting for? What do these people have to do with our cause?"

"There are many causes here."

"What is that to us? I just passed some people who want to reinstate the tsar! Does that mean we're helping them?"

"Look around you," he whispered. "We need all the allies we can find."

"If everyone is our ally," he said, feeling increasingly confused and disoriented. "Then who is it we're fighting?"

The deputy waved him off. "You'll know who you're fighting soon enough."

Ivan gestured angrily at the man and turned away. A group of people stood in the corridor, and he stumbled into one of them as he passed.

"You drinking, old man?"

Ivan pushed the man away and struggled to steady himself. In the stairwell, he paused and tried to rally. Above him the stairs disappeared into darkness. The air was cooler here, and he seemed to be alone. Though exhausted, his mind sought distraction so he started to climb. It was almost completely dark. 'What am I doing here?' he thought. 'Does anybody know what we're doing here?'

Gradually the rhythmic rasp of his feet on the stairs became something to focus him, like a distant drum. Since arriving at the parliament, Ivan had become increasingly doubtful about the protest's organizers. This doubt was part of a larger despair that had spread through his thoughts since the Party had collapsed. What if the Party was wrong? The question stirred a new terror in him. The Party's contest with history had been going on so long those playing it had come to see it as permanent as the sky.

Ivan's head hung on his chest as he climbed. His lungs burned with exertion, seeking relief in the stale, unrewarding air. The sound of his feet echoed upwards into the stairwell, returning to him like laughter through the darkness.

His breathing became harder and he stopped to look around in the blackness. Ivan felt panicked. Reaching out with his hand he guided himself to a stair and sat. Thoughts of fear and anger wracked him alternately.

He rubbed his missing arm. Ivan tried to concentrate on the ghost pain, hoping to fight back the terror closing about his chest. "Where am I?" he whispered. "Where will I go?"

His voice returned to him from two directions in the dark stairwell.

Trauma, that aftershock of great change, is the mind's inability to adjust to a new reality. By refusing to accept a new world order we press ourselves toward madness. At the level of the senses, this represents the denial of sight, the subordination of vision to the dream of memory. For Ivan, the Party had been like an island that defied the currents of fate, a raft of permanence in life's tragic sea. The War had forced him as a child to accept the impermanence of a family, even of his life. But the Party's triumph in the War, it's survival against an overwhelming enemy, led Ivan to believe that the Party was permanent. It had brought history to its knees. For those who followed the Party, there was reprieve from the armies of fate that otherwise crushed an unallied life.

"Is this all that I am – some old man lost in history's storm?" he wondered, still whispering in the dark. "What have I become?" Ivan rested his head on his knees.

He hadn't been able to look at his wife as he had packed.

"How can you leave us?" she had cried. "Petya is packing his things in the other room, even as I speak. How can you think of going, as well?"

Ivan did not look up. "I must go now. I am needed. Everyone who believes in the Party is needed now. In the capital. Not in California!" and he spat the last word.

There was a tap on the door before it opened. It was Katya. "Is everything – what are you doing?"

Lydia raised her hands in helplessness. "You will never believe what he is doing!"

"What is happening?" Katya paled, looking from one to the other. "Tell me?"

"Yes, tell her. I do not think I can find the words to explain you to our child."

Katya met his eyes. "Papa?"

Ivan closed his bag.

"Tell her. If you won't tell your own wife, then tell her at least. Maybe then she can explain to me why you are doing this!"

He faltered, his gaze still held by Katya.

"What are you doing?" she whispered. "We had a nice time at the theatre. Is this because of the helicopters? Is that it? Papa, stop. Don't think of them. They do not concern us."

Ivan tried to step toward the door. Their faces almost met, but she would not release him. "Let me pass, Yekaterina."

"No, Papa. Stay with us. Don't leave. Not now." Her hand touched the empty sleeve of his coat. He felt her fingers on his boy arm. He shivered, the ghost flesh trembling at her touch. On his arm.

He pulled his sleeve free. "I must go."

"Why are you doing this? Tell me and I will understand."

In the hall he nearly collided with Petya, and the two stepped back warily and surveyed each other. Petya glanced at the bag in his father's hand. "What are you doing?"

He moved quickly down the hall, but as he got to the door of their flat Petya called out to him. "Talk to me! What are you doing? Please, listen to me..."

Ivan paused for an instant, as though he might speak, but then opened the door and left.

And he was gone.

Ivan lifted his head from his knees. What had Petya wanted to say, what would he have said had he replied to his son? Ivan shook his head. No! The boy had made his choice.

Ivan pressed his face into his arm. Petya.

His son's betrayal – the thought of it haunted his thoughts. It was a personal catastrophe to have lost his son to the enemy. When did this happen? Why hadn't anyone seen it coming? Or had they? Petya! How could he? Grief and anger shook him.

For a time only one word could be heard in the stairwell. "Petya – Petya..."

It gradually occurred to Ivan that he'd lost track of how long he had been sitting, and, not knowing what else to do, he resumed his shaky ascent through the stairwell.

It was sometime after this that he came out on the roof of the parliament. He leaned heavily against a pole, bracing himself against the frigid wind which buffeted and blew at him. Ivan paused, momentarily awed by the sight. The parliament was the tallest building for some distance, and from here he could look out on the city in all directions. There were no stars, but the glow of ten thousand lights made the sky smoulder. Clouds hung low and Ivan felt he could touch them from the top of the building. At times stray pieces passed about him. He shivered with the cold and damp but his breathing calmed in the fresh air, and soon he was aware of the restored rhythm of his own pulse.

Cadets of some paramilitary group had been posted there in case of a helicopter landing. They had brought an armful of files to the roof from one of the offices, and some of the boys were using the pages to make airplanes, lighting them on fire before tossing them from the building. The rest of the group sat around, cleaning their weapons or trying to sleep.

"Who is in charge here?" Ivan demanded.

The boys looked at him blankly. "You don't know?"

Ivan left them and walked to the other end of the building. Below, there was almost no movement in the street. Most of the crowd had gone home for the night, leaving only small groups of protesters and police. From here you could see the Ukraine Hotel, Red Square, the Kremlin wall and other monuments. Further on, the skyline throbbed with the twenty-four-hour glow of neon. Moscow flickered with brand names. The triumphal banners of the invader. And he couldn't read a word of it.

Ivan stared out at the city's lights as the wind pushed at him in intermittent gusts. He rubbed at his empty sleeve.

A thread hung from the ledge where he stood, and Ivan watched as it fluttered gently, hanging upon the great expanse of emptiness that stretched over the city.

One of the boys left the group and walked over to where he stood. "Got a cigarette?"

Ivan turned to the cadet, looking at the hand stretched toward him. The boy's wrist emerged from his sleeve, and he saw the skin was tattooed with the right angles of a swastika.

"Even you…" he looked with disbelief. Ivan took a step backwards toward the ledge. "Your friends there – who are you?"

The boy showed him his armband. "Don't worry grandpa, we're all on the same side."

Ivan clenched his teeth.

The boy prodded Ivan's coat with his finger. "Hey, what happened to your arm?"

For a moment Ivan felt unsteady again. The wind picked up the limp sleeve and for a moment it began to move, as though animated. He stared at his ghost arm, suddenly terrified to see it move as though the old limb had returned.

"Are you hearing me, grandpa?"

But Ivan couldn't take his eyes from the sleeve as it moved spasmodically back and forth.

The boy shook his head, and his friends began to call for him.

"What has happened?" he whispered, speaking now to the boy. "We defeated you…"

A sudden rage lunged forward inside him, and Ivan yelled out at the group on the other side of the roof. "Damn you!" he spat. "Murderers. You murdered them! Mama. Papa. Larissa. Subov. You killed them! Get off of this roof! Murderers! Who let them in?" he said, turning on the boy.

"Have we forgotten what they did? When did we forget? When did we forget?"

He turned back abruptly and ran at the group of cadets. He shouted with rapid, halting syllables, the words vomited like some putrid thing inside him he could hold back no longer. "Why are you here? Eh? Why don't you talk? Who do you think you're fighting? You're no different from the capitalists. That's the real enemy. Even you fascists are afraid of them. You've seen what's happened, haven't you? Seen what they've done. But when did we lose to them? Someone tell me – when did we lose?"

He spun around and looked again at the young cadet, his body a silhouette against the skyline. How many nights had he watched with the others from his roof as Leningrad burned? People dying in their homes. Ivan heard again the explosions and screams, as if brought to him on the wind.

He spit, trying to expel a sickening taste from his mouth.

The wind hit him, fiercer now, dragging fragments of fog across the rooftop and for a moment the city disappeared from sight. He sank on his knees, the sleeve waving wildly about him. Exhausted, he didn't try to stand, but let his thoughts turn deeper. "And Petya. Petya. How did I lose him?"

The Party's explanation of history had been violated, its totem of promises toppled and wrecked, the fragments made into kindling for its own pyre. He had been loyal. Had done what was needed. He had suffered for the Party, and it had saved him.

But now? Why not now? He was about to speak as the answer came to him, but he swallowed his voice, unable to bear putting it into words. And it was then that he felt it – the chaos, the madness that had almost taken him as a boy. That madness had caught up with him at last, here on this tower. Ivan trembled. 'It is like a ghost dragging me to the grave,' he thought, 'pulling me into the darkness.'

The cadets' laughter drifted across the rooftop. A murmur of abuse.

He held up his arm as if to fight away the terror that crept toward him. He swung out at it and missed. He swore at it, swinging again. Finding his gun in his coat, he fired into the wraiths of cloud.

When the cartridge was empty, he slumped forward. Finished.

A boot appeared next to his face. "You all right, grandpa?"

"Go ahead, you dog," he hissed, and he turned away his head for the blow. But none came. "Go on, I said." He welcomed it. The sudden pain and then nothing. It would be a relief at last to feel something different. Even nothing. "Go on..."

For a long time he lay like that before the city, blind to everything except fragments of memory, returning always to his son. What Ivan believed of life had ceased to be true. It was like being in the wilderness with a broken compass – you no longer knew which way to turn.

In time a razor of light appeared along the top of the city, turning the low ceiling of cloud to red. Night's shadows bled away and faded, and the colour of the earth began to wake. Ivan was unaware of the light upon his face. He stared at the city's lights, which glowed and kindled even against the coming dawn.

THERE WAS a sense of absence in the days after Andrew left, and to fill this gap some of the expats had gone to the city's large weekend market to kill time and pick up souvenirs. At the market gate they came upon the smashed statue of the old leader Katya and her mother had seen. The damaged monument did not seem to bother those going into the market, and the expats stepped around it like they would a homeless man.

Alice pondered the ruined statue. "Now, do you suppose this classifies as pre- or post-revolutionary behaviour?"

"In college we used to toilet paper the Washington statue every September..."

"Definitely a post-revolutionary act."

Troy was staring thoughtfully at the vandalized statue. "You don't think Andrew is up to this sort of thing in Moscow?"

"More likely he's conquering the bars."

Behind them Adam stood nursing his bandaged hand. Someone suggested a group photograph in front of the statue, and he offered to take it.

Afterwards they joined the current of people entering the market. "Don't worry," Troy counselled. "If you see something you want, I'll do the talking. I've done this plenty of times."

Alice took the offer and they broke up, looking in twos and threes about the stalls. At the far end of the stadium they passed a woman selling *shapki* from a corner of the tarmac. Alice stopped to look at the hats. She tried one on and Troy laughed at her.

"I call it 'totalitarian *chic*.'"

Adam stared at her for a moment.

She ran her fingers through the dark fur. "How much are they?"

Troy asked the woman, turning away from her after they had spoken. "She wants fifty dollars, but we can do better," he said, winking.

Adam stepped forward. "I want one, as well."

He turned to the woman again, holding up two fingers. "*Dva?*"

"Two?" She stared at him dubiously. "Ate-e dollar."

"Fifty."

The woman glared as though he had slapped her. "Go away. Seventy-ate dollar. No less."

When he finished Troy seemed dissatisfied, though he had got the woman down to seventy dollars for the two of them. "I should have done better," he muttered. He looked around restlessly at the other stalls. "What now?"

"I need a coat," Adam suggested.

Troy rallied, glad for another chance to prove himself. "Let me see what I can do..." By the time they left the market Adam had an armful of things. The others scanned his purchases, sceptical but amused. "You're going to look like a *rodnoi* with all that on."

He smiled at the idea. "Why shouldn't I?"

After they returned to the dormitory, Adam tried on the things he had bought. From behind the costume of state fashion, he appeared a different person. 'It is like being able to disappear,' he thought, staring into the mirror. And the image of himself as a stranger gave him

490

the sudden impulse to go out, to be again with people.

Outside he followed the crowds through the weaving, narrow lanes that surrounded the dormitory. Here he passed unnoticed by others – a couple arguing on the corner, four friends chatting with some girls at a kiosk, a parent scolding her child, a pair of soldiers muttering in deep syllables, three old women on a bench – their voices neither rising nor abating as he approached. He became aware of a distant closeness in people's words. Pausing to listen in the arcades and the little parks of uncut grass, he felt for the first time an inclusion in these unintelligible utterances, breathing their voices into himself.

Approaching the subway station, he noticed a moneychanger eyeing him, and as he drew near the man stepped forward aggressively. "*Dengi? Dengi?*"

Adam did not flinch but instead walked into the man knowing the moneychanger would move off at the last instant.

He passed among a cluster of kiosks, the proprietors leaning out of the windows to haggle with customers. Behind them workmen yelled to each other as they put up one of the billboards which were turning running shoes and soft drinks into monuments all over the city. On the sidewalk a man sat with a guitar, wailing out a Dylan song in a mash of Russian and English. Adam caught the tune in his head and began humming it to himself as he joined the crowd descending the broken escalator to the subway, unconsciously adding his voice to the noise of the city.

The following day when he reached the university Adam found a note on his office door. He went directly to the same room in the library where they had met before. There was no electricity that day, and she had been forced to work by the window.

Katya stood when she saw him.

"Thank you for coming," she greeted. "After our last meeting I located several more problems in the translation I am working on."

He sat down and began to unbutton his coat.

She shook her head. "There is no heat today," she warned, and he saw the breath about her mouth when she spoke.

Adam's reflection glared back at him in the window behind her, and he adjusted his gaze to look beyond the pane. Clouds brooding over the city had begun to thin in places, so that fingers of light poked through. He looked back at Katya, voice apologetic. "What problems?"

Katya took out her notebook and opened it to a marked page. "You will see, with this poem in particular, there is a unique problem. The poet refers to a word that is untranslatable."

His gaze followed the length of her finger to a word Katya had footnoted at the bottom of the page. He looked up at her. "The word freedom? What is wrong with it?"

Katya leaned back in her chair, concentration forming over her brow. "It cannot be translated into my language."

"That's fascinating!" Adam leaned back in chair. "You're serious? You mean there is really no word in Russian for freedom?"

"Not as it is meant here. You can see that I have translated portions of the poem, but I am unsatisfied with my work. When I considered the problem further, it became clear that the issue lay in my inability to translate this word, which, as you would say, kept sticking in my teeth. Each time I tried to translate it, the poem did not feel right – you understand? So I did some further reading on its derivations."

Adam looked up from the poem. "I don't understand."

She consulted a second notebook from the table. "Our closest word – *svoboda* – at first appears very like the English term, though a closer look at the etymology suggests that these similarities are superficial. The two words are not equivalents. Both allow for negative collocations which initially make them appear interchangeable, particularly when translating common phrases..."

Adam stared at a vein in her hand as he listened. As she spoke, she turned pages in the notebook until she found the reference she wanted.

"On the one hand, the English term supposes a legal condition which both becomes the basis for and protects an individual's independence. On the other hand, the Russian word connotes what you would call privilege, something one is given. However, your English word stems from a legal history that lies at the foundation of your political system. Whereas, for us, *svoboda* is linked with the benefaction of the tsars.

Svoboda implies a level of humility in those who receive it. In contrast, your word is implicitly linked with a legalized individualism. It implies the individual already has an inherent legal right to do and not do what one wishes. It suggests that one has the right to be left alone."

Adam looked up, blinking. "Alone."

"That's what I said." She glanced up from her notes. "You understand the problem, yes?"

"I think so."

Katya smiled, continuing, "In contrast, *svoboda* refers to the loosening of some sort of bond or restraint, and the feeling which this release brings. To Russians, *svoboda* is in large part an emotion, a feeling. Because of this, our word is associated with a sense of the vastness, the unlimited emotional, even spiritual, spaces within a person. While in your language this term is linked with the liberties of a person's physical, outward space."

Katya looked up from her notes. "The English word constrains the Russian term by assuming an interpretation that is opposed to its actual meaning. This is our problem then. The poem is about the ideal of freedom, but for me, as a translator, the very word I am asked to translate is at once too liberal and too narrow. Do you understand?"

He shifted in the chair.

Katya smiled again, folding her hands in front of her.

Adam looked past her to his own reflection in the window. The cloud had opened in one spot, spilling light here and there on the grey city. The vein in her hand flexed now with her quickening pulse.

"Are there really no other words?"

Andrew arrived in Moscow with the first real cold snap of the year. Steam and smoke drifted between the engines idling in Belorussy Station which was congested with the trains' dark blue carriages and the unbroken flow of travellers and luggage. The white arches echoed with all of the commotion in the busy station – loudspeaker announcements, passengers' voices and activity, the deep impatient rumble of the engines. Andrew stopped and bought coffee from a kiosk beneath the immense ornamental window that looked down on the passengers. The coffee burnt his mouth, but he could feel his body stirring to life as the heat settled into him. Outside the station he paused beneath the large iron awning that stretched almost to the street. He looked around, hoping to find someone who could help him. He spotted a likely group of people next to the cylindrical message board and asked them for directions. Where was the standoff concentrated? Had there been any fighting? Where was the revolution?

Those in line only shrugged. They were queuing here, someone explained, for the opening of a new fashion outlet up the street.

A group of cabdrivers were gathered across the road waiting for fares, and among them Andrew found one who knew where things were happening. But even before the car started the driver was trying to sell Andrew vodka, cigarettes, condoms, toothpaste, even a roll of film.

"Might want pictures," he said, noting his passenger's camera. "Make good souvenirs."

Andrew dropped his backpack on the seat, one hand resting on the door handle. "Just take me to the action."

"*Tak*," said the driver, and the Lada's engine stuttered heavily then launched into the street. "Welcome to Moscow."

Tverskaya Avenue was eight lanes wide here, and the car joined the press of traffic that shoved its way toward the city's core. Andrew distracted himself with the steady flow of people and shops and buildings. The yellow Lada slipped among the red and white buses, the exhausted blue trams, the Volgas, and the sleek Mercedes that sped easily between them all. Above the street, the sky was veined with strings of electric wires for the trams, or the flashing banners and corporate logos of foreign companies which had flooded the former world capital of communism. Through the widow, Andrew stared at the shops and restaurants around the Tchaikovsky Concert Hall, watching the crowds who came and went from the flashy retailers on the street. From here the buildings became more posh, with flats of pink and white marble interspersed with the older stuccoed buildings with their white columns and neoclassical embellishment. The cab turned at the next corner and entered a tunnel which emerged along the embankment near the Moscow River. Here was the immense October Hotel, with its limousines, tour buses, even a Ferrari, and the familiar strata of yellow taxis queuing for business.

"There," shouted the driver, pointing across the river's embankment. "There is your action!"

And as Andrew turned in his seat he was aware that he was holding his breath, and this knowledge made him feel giddy and self-conscious but he found himself enjoying the moment all the same. His first impression was of being before some sort of modern castle. The main part of the building stood like a broad white keep with curving sides, topped by a perimeter of battlements encircling a great clock. The building sat among an outer curtain of marble atria, meeting rooms, galleries and offices, with the Moscow River running like a moat before it all. Andrew had seen pictures of the parliament – known in Russia as the White House – in the papers the morning he had left for Moscow, but seeing it before him now across the river, circled by the milling crowds of protestors and onlookers, the vans and trucks of the international media, the place seemed to him important, even prophetic, and he knew he had been right to come here.

Andrew paid the driver and almost ran the rest of the way. The cabbie watched for a moment from his car, staring after the foreigner until he disappeared among the protesters and became suddenly indistinguishable from the crowd.

Andrew's hands were sweating as he wound his way among the people standing about, his earlier confidence faltering as he felt himself swallowed by the havoc. In places the crowd had separated into distinct factions with large spaces between them, as though they did not want to be associated with one another. In other places, though, the crowd was tightly packed and he had to push his way through the press of irate conversations and arguments, the elbows and hostile stares adding to his sense of confusion.

Blockades had been set up to keep back the crowd of journalists and sympathizers who shivered in the shadow of the building and waited for something to happen. The insurgents called sporadically to the crowd from a window, rallying supporters with promises and reminders of past outrages. Rumours drifted like smoke among the groups of reporters, who wrote everything down with a worldly languor: the President and his

500

allies in the Kremlin promised amnesty if the deputies would concede; the Church's Patriarch was returning from a tour in America to mediate the standoff; the President was accusing the elected deputies of hijacking democracy while they called him a despot; the deputies were shocked the Kremlin had cut off the water and electricity in the parliament; both sides vowed never to give up.

In desperation, the deputies of the Supreme Soviet had formed their own government inside the barricaded building, making Rutskoy, a leader of the uprising, their new president. After this, different officials appeared on the front steps of the white marble building to announce further decrees in brotherly tones from the loudspeaker. People in the crowd had mixed responses to these announcements, some applauding or waving the old communist flags, others murmuring ascent for each new proclamation, while many openly ridiculed the deputies' powerlessness. The atmosphere was noncommittal and tense. Everyone was waiting.

That week Andrew fell in with a number of protesters, where his youth and idealism

501

attracted similarly young and idealistic people. This group was made up mostly of foreign students or academics who were in Moscow on one pretext or another and had been caught unexpectedly in the historical moment. They liked Andrew for his Russianness which leant an aura of authenticity to their zeal, and his grasp of the language was deemed similarly convenient. Unlike his friends in Galinsk, this new group of expats was bolder and well connected. There were Russians, too, in this group, though they were more like accidental acquaintances and saw these foreigners as loose or transient associations rather than co-mates in the larger cause that gripped the capital.

Most of the group were living in a flat rented by a German teacher who had decided to leave when the protest started. In the first week Andrew had joined the others in the flat, and within a few days he came and went with the same sense of ease and entitlement as the others. He spent most of his days at the barricade, mingling with the other protesters and talking with foreign journalists who wandered the crowds looking for something to report. At night Andrew hung out at the flat with the others, drinking and debating what might happen. There was a Turkish student who showed them how to make up bottles of milk and vinegar for tear gas victims. One night someone gave a lecture on eluding arrest, the next evening the topic was water cannons and how to spot the yellow hue in the water that meant it had been mixed with pepper spray.

As the days passed, Andrew felt his life in Galinsk fading from his mind, even thoughts of Katya becoming more distant. Instead when he was reflective, it was to recall his parents and the country they had wanted, and these thoughts seemed to him to validate his presence there in Moscow. The deputies who had taken over the Parliament were trying to create a different country, one his mother would never have wanted to leave.

But gradually the initial notoriety of what he was doing began to pale, and Andrew found himself becoming restless. Twice he and some others had tried to steal equipment from the police, and both times the constables chased them with a half-heartedness that had insulted and enraged Andrew.

"The police don't think we're a serious threat!"

This restlessness infected other protestors, as well, and as the days passed the mood along the barricades became dark and almost desperate for something to happen. Some of the expats began to talk of making Molotov cocktails or weapons, while others spoke of going home.

One afternoon Andrew wandered down to the Parliament on his own, feeling insolent and despondent. As he walked along the river, he sneered at the police who stood about in small groups, leaning against water trucks and smoking, or reporting on their radios to invisible commanders.

As he entered the crowd he could hear someone talking over a loudspeaker, and he pushed toward the voice through the people who stood about listening. He had difficulty making out the speaker's scratched and broken voice, and he was forced to ask those in the crowd about different statements. "What are they saying now?"

"They've doubled the minimum wage," someone observed.

A man beside Andrew spat. "A fine thing. But who's listening?"

"What else?"

He strained to hear the people calling to the crowd from the barricade.

"Better conditions for the army..."

Someone laughed. "He thinks he's Santa Claus. He's buying us all presents!"

The man turned on Andrew. "Tell him I want my son out of Grosny – tell him that!"

A man behind them tapped her on the shoulder. "Where is Grosny?"

"There's talk they'll send all the recruits there soon."

Andrew yelled out the man's demand.

"He can't hear me," he said at last. "Find a reporter. They want to talk to people," but the man moved off, and Andrew didn't see him again.

Andrew swore. "Something has to happen. It can't stay like this forever."

Next to him was a man about his age with a leather jacket and an eyebrow full of rings. "My father's been saying that his whole life," and he laughed in a way that made him look sad.

"That's just nihilism," retorted a woman listening behind him. "That is our government in there. We voted for those people, and no one should stop them."

"They took over the parliament!"

"It was theirs already! Why does everyone forget this? Wasn't that why we voted for the deputies – we put them there!"

"Well, I can't agree with their methods."

"What choice did they have? The President was dismissing them. Where did he get that power?"

"Power is not given, you fool."

The man with the rings gestured at the soldiers and the barricades. "Is this democracy, then? Is this what we have turned our world upside down for? Anyone can have this chaos!"

Andrew listened to the conversation for a while and then glanced in disappointment at the parliament building. He decided to go for a drink and get warm before coming back. He went several blocks along the river embankment until he came to one of the hotels used by tourists and foreign businessmen. There was a bar just off the lobby, and he went in and looked for a spot to sit. The place was crowded with reporters who all seemed to know one another. Everyone sat around the low tables in small, muted groups, or hunched at the bar. The sulky silence however was undermined by the restless energy of the reporters' hands, which fingered straws, ashtrays, toothpicks, pens, cutlery – whatever was close. The cameramen almost always chose to sit, their equipment stowed within reach. Their faces were tense with boredom and irritation. Some were plump, chain-smoking types who drank scotch, or gin and tonic, others were the hyper and wiry sort who ordered only Diet Coke or, when they could get it, espressos.

Andrew found a table with two journalists.

"Can I sit here?"

One of the men gestured at an empty chair. They were both journalists – Avery and Hugh – with English papers.

"Just getting here?"

"I came to see the coup."

The one named Hugh curled his lip with disgust. "You mean that staring competition?"

"I heard they're bringing in the army."

"A rumour."

"You don't think something could happen?"

"The only hope for the guys in that building is chaos and unrest," and he gestured around the bar of reporters. "Anyone here look unrested?"

"I don't know," Andrew passed a hand through his hair and leaned back. "I've been here for a while. They're calling for revolution."

"You think they're waiting for a revolution?" It was Hugh who spoke but a waiter appeared, and he ordered a drink before going on.

"Listen," he continued. "Revolution is about turning the world upside down. After things collapsed in '89, the status quo here was abandoned in favour of rock bands, the mafia, movie stars, good cigarettes and any car that wasn't a Lada. The People have shacked up with the American dream, and it's not a one-night stand. It is four years since the Wall came down and Mercedes is selling more cars here than in any other city on the planet. It's a little late to be calling for revolution. It's happened."

Andrew pushed his glass around on the table. "You think that's why there's a standoff now?"

Avery shrugged. "History is like an elastic. The further it's stretched in one direction the harder it snaps back in the other."

Hugh put one of his feet on a chair. "The only card that hasn't been played is the army's. They had their chance to support the communists two years ago and didn't."

"The stakes are high for the President," Avery added. "This is his Rubicon. If he crosses it history will dismiss him as just another dictator.

But if he holds back and compromises? Well then, the Kremlin may just have its first democrat."

It was hot in the bar, and Andrew used a cocktail napkin to wipe his face.

"If the rebels really want to win they should sell their weapons and start a bank. What they're doing now looks amateurish. Just listen to the politicians – not one of them understands what they've gotten into. They've fallen together off the same roof, and each is blaming the other one for gravity." Avery nodded in the direction of the parliament building. "Besides, the military is an obsolete instrument of conquest, and anyone who thinks differently is in for an ass kicking." The reporter paused to consider the plastic sword from his drink before pulling off the cherry with his teeth. "Nowadays you don't invade a country. You buy it. If you want to conquer someone you don't need to defeat his army. You buy up his resources, his energy, his banks, or his debt. If you're really smart, you devalue the fucker's currency and then buy him at whatever price you set."

Andrew looked at the crushed napkin in his hand. Around him slouched journalists at their tables, watching the television or scanning newspapers. Now and then someone stood to stretch or take off his jacket. A few of them loitered around the cigarette machine by the door. Irritation and restlessness drifted like odours in the room.

"Don't listen too hard to my friend there," said Hugh. "What this place needs is someone with authority, and fast. No one is talking about the real issue, which is that the stakes in this showdown are larger than the fate of a single country," he glanced around the room of bored reporters. "One day some kind of nuclear device will be detonated in a large metropolitan centre in the West. Remember what I am telling you. This will happen. When it does I promise..." and here the reporter leaned forward in his chair. "I promise you, they will trace the device back to this country which has a mountain of the fucking things and has stopped paying the people who guard them. Anyone who says civil rights are more important than incinerating Washington or London or Berlin is a fool, and a dangerous one. As for buying a country, well that's fine-sounding but utterly useless except in fat places where people lose their appetite at the sight of their own blood. So I won't be lamenting the precarious state of Russians' democratic privileges, because until they get their stockpile of weapon-grade plutonium under control I don't care if they can vote, and neither should you. For most of the world, the only way to hold onto a country is at gunpoint. Period. And right now no one's sure if there's live ammo in that gun."

He looked at Andrew as if he couldn't decide whether to laugh or not. "Why do you care so much, anyway? You don't look like you miss many meals. I'm guessing the stakes are more academic for you than some of the people here."

Andrew squinted at the two reporters, feeling unsettled and frustrated by their casual confidence. "It's more than that," he replied, feeling suddenly unsure and a poseur. "My parents, my aunt, Ilyin – I'm Russian."

"You don't sound Russian."

He shrugged. "I am."

Hugh shared a glance with the other reporter. "If that's the case, then you'd better hope the People want the same thing as the guys in that building."

Andrew coughed. "They do."

A stir passed through the room. The reporters straightened.

"What's going on?" Andrew asked, looking up from his glass.

People stood, reaching for coats and bags. Cigarettes were stubbed out. Several phones started to ring in the lobby. Someone swore. Chairs moved across the floor, bumping into tables. A glass shattered.

A cameraman rushed past the table and Hugh grabbed him. "What's going on?"

"Someone got a call from the highway." The man was almost breathless.

"What happened?"

"It's the Army," the cameraman blurted. "They're coming."

Katya found her mother in the kitchen. In the corner Chaika puttered restlessly in her cage. She stroked the bird through the wire bars, whispering softly in an effort to placate it. She sympathized with Chaika, she too felt unsettled here. From cupboards and shelves, the spaces and empty spots looked down at her – holes where familiar items used to sit – as if blaming her. It was the same in every room now. Wherever she went in the flat, it was there, the stare of emptiness. The pieces of their lives that had fallen away, the fragments sold to save the whole.

'How ironic,' thought Katya, looking around at the half empty flat. 'Papa gone to Moscow, and Petya will soon be in America. Everyone is leaving...' but she stopped herself here.

Lydia instinctually reached across the kitchen table to grasp her daughter's hand, gazing at her with an expression that alternated between hope and anguish. Katya saw the meaning in her mother's face.

She spoke quietly again of preparations, and afterwards she held her mother, letting the old woman cry into her shoulder. Katya had been spending more time with Lydia, gradually explaining the changes they would have to make. A few days before Katya had gone to the doctor with the old woman, to confirm what she suspected.

"Really," Katya said afterwards. "It all feels like an old story."

"That doesn't make it any less difficult," her mother began, but instead of finishing her thought she broke into that cough instead.

"Here," she said, taking the ring from her hand. "See if you can find someone who wants it."

Katya began to protest, but checked herself.

Her mother held her breath, though in the end she succumbed to her old ambivalence. "Only you know if you can."

After this Lydia stood and looked around the kitchen. "I think I will lie down," she said, more decisively.

"Yes, you look tired."

"Yekaterina," Lydia paused in the hall. "You know that I will not leave. I will be here with you…"

That night Adam was woken by someone pounding on the door. "You'll want to see this," came a voice through the door. It was Emil.

Adam shook the sleep from his head, becoming aware of something unsteady in Emil's tone. "What's happening?"

But Emil didn't reply, and Adam found himself following the sound of the television down the hall. He squinted in the dim light, ducking beneath the lines of wet laundry people had hung in the hallways, puddles of water on the floor. The heavy smell of wet cloth.

He found them around the television, concern etched on all their faces. Troy nodded to an empty chair. "We don't know anything yet."

After Andrew left for Moscow the foreign stations had begun providing updates from the barricaded parliament. Within a few days, though, even the reporters seemed bored with the apparent standstill in the situation, and many of those in the dorm had begun talking about other things again. Then, the day before, all of the country's newspapers had been shut down by the government.

Adam sat tentatively.

The television was filled with the face of a reporter. He spoke into the screen, trying to talk over the voices behind him. 'It happened quite suddenly this evening, just as officials had begun to hope for reconciliation between – ' There was a concussion of sound and the next moment the camera jerked about, and the screen switched to a field of green pixels.

"Night vision," Troy nodded, as if he approved.

The new camera angle looked on the parliament from a distance, its walls greenish yellow. A woman's voice broke in, narrating the scene in staccato syllables. 'We're looking from a hotel across from the standoff underway between parliamentary leaders in the Supreme Soviet and military units loyal to the President. Just – Wait now. The police are at our door here…it seems we're being…'

Adam looked around the room. Alice was in an old university sweatshirt, her knees tucked under her chin. Emil straddled a chair and smoked. The others sat on couches or the floor wrapped in blankets, speaking in low voices. Nothing like this had ever happened to any of them. Clare would have known what to do, he realized.

One woman left to see if she could phone her family, but a few minutes later she was back. "No international calls."

"They've done that before," Ford said over his shoulder, trying to reassure.

On the television the anchorman had returned to the screen, his face framed with headlines, and he began a live interview with a panel of diplomats and academics.

Someone groaned with frustration. Ford handed Adam a can, avoiding eye contact.

"Thanks." A feeble sensation welled up in him. He tried to focus on the label, and the oddest thought came to him. "My dad drinks this stuff."

Ford half grinned.

The interview dragged on for several minutes. 'In my opinion,' one of the diplomats was speaking now, 'there are alarming parallels between tonight's actions, and similar uprisings in Latin America during the nineteen eighties...'

Troy began to tap his foot. "Maybe there's better coverage on another station?"

Alice started changing channels, shards of colour and dialogue flashing into the darkness of the room: celebrity faces, mansions, a police chase, a jumbo jet, breath freshener, cat food, stain remover...

Adam turned to Troy. "When did this start?"

He shrugged. "Someone was in here watching MTV – they've been showing the Nirvana video all day – and I guess they stumbled on the news."

"Keep searching," Emil grumbled.

Alice chewed at a fingernail. "I bet my parents are watching this right now."

Ford opened another beer. "What happened to all the foreign shows?"

"You're in another country," shouted Emil. "These are the foreign shows!"

"Shut up," Alice hissed, and she stepped away from the television. The screen switched again to the night vision camera: dark shapes moved about with abrupt, unstable gestures. Figures crouched behind walls and trees, faces distilled to pixelated silhouettes of green and black.

"This is bad," Adam said, before he could stop himself.

Alice looked at him, face red. "I said, shut up."

There were more images of tanks forming around the milky background of the parliament building, each new camera angle narrated by a different voice. People shifted in their chairs. Alice started to pace.

The next morning all of the expat teachers congregated in the cafeteria to meet a guy from the American consulate. Around them the kitchen staff gathered stray cutlery and wiped down tables. Steam had formed on the windows along the opposite wall, clouding the view of the street. The consulate worker looked tired and impatient. "It was a long night," he explained.

Troy sat on one of the tables, unshaven and smoking. "You're telling us."

"You've seen the coverage. The consulate is taking this seriously. No one knows how big this is going to get, so all foreigners are being advised to leave."

Candace bit at her lip. "This has never happened to people I know."

"Is it certain?" Alice murmured. "I mean, is there actually a coup happening?"

He shrugged. "They have a habit over here of this sort of thing."

The others sat on tables or stood about in the doorway, unsure of what to say.

"What about our jobs?" Alice said. "We can't leave our students."

The guy from the consulate nodded as though he had thought of this. "The university is being closed and, like I said, everyone who can leave is being advised to get out. There are flights tonight. I'd be on one if I were you." His voice was flat. "If things do start to blow up, the airlines will stop flying and you don't want to be stuck here if that happens."

Troy looked at the others, gauging the meaning behind their expressions before speaking. "I guess it's settled then."

People stood, put on coats and began moving toward the door.

"Wait," Adam interjected, speaking for the first time. "What about Andrew?"

When Petya came home he paused in the kitchen. The lights were off though it was early evening, and the objects in the room now seemed undecided, as though on the verge of vanishing. The city he had grown up in had almost disappeared in the fog drifting through the streets. Even the lights from other buildings were clouded and intermittent against the wash of shadow pressing on them. He held his breath. Everywhere there was a hush of expectation, a fraying pause of concentration, like that of someone about to lose his balance.

He turned back to the hallway, then stopped. "Katya?"

His sister sat at the table.

She smiled at him in the dark. "You're home late."

"What are you doing?"

"I am thinking."

"Is everything all right?"

"Of course not."

"What I meant – "

"I know what you meant."

He hesitated, searching her face in the shadow. "All right then."

"You're not going to sit?"

"Sorry," he stopped and looked around uncomfortably. Even in the shadow, she could see him colour. "There's still a lot of packing..."

Though he did not begin his new position until January, the artefacts of her brother's life were already melting away, his books and clothes leaving in a series of FedEx boxes for the other side of the world.

Katya stood and turned on the light. "Did you get your visa today?"

"Yes. The clerk told me it was processed very quickly," Petya said. "He said they must really want me," and in his face it was clear how happy this made him.

She put her hand on his arm. "You don't want to leave the packing until the last."

"That's how I see it, too," and he smiled with relief. Then, as he was about to go, he frowned and suddenly squinted at her. "Are you sure you're fine?"

She nodded. "I'm just worried."

Petya stiffened, drawing in breath and holding it. "He didn't have to go. He chose his fate, though he knew it jeopardized everyone."

"Do you know why he went?"

Her brother turned into the hallway, not speaking until his back was to her. "If it was to spite me, then he is a fool."

"It was not for that," she interjected, following him into his room. "You remember the stories Grandma used to tell? The Party and the War and all of it. We never took those things seriously, either of us. But I can see now that they meant more to him. He lost his arm when he was a child. Have you and I ever really *thought* about this?"

They were standing among the boxes and suitcases in Petya's room. He began folding clothes in an effort to ignore her, but Katya kept talking. She wanted to explain things as she understood them, feeling suddenly that it was important for Petya to understand them too. Before it was too late.

"I can't blame him for leaving. We don't understand what it all meant to him. Those things were just there in the background for us, like something on a radio you're not listening to. But to him they were real, and when they ended so did the life he had always known." She paused, aware of the struggle on her brother's face. "There are experiences for which we do not have words, for which a person cannot find language to express what is inside him. It's the translator's foil. Such a person is uniquely alone. No one can speak for him."

Then, because Petya did not reply, she caught at his shirt, pulling on it until he met her gaze. "Can you tell me that you don't wish things had not changed, that life was still what we thought it would be when we were children?"

Though he did not reply, she saw by Petya's gaze that he felt at least a part of this. She kept holding his arm as she spoke, hanging on while she could.

"If we feel this, then imagine how badly he longs for the old way? If we lost the future, then he surely has lost the past."

Petya's eyes narrowed.

"Whatever he is doing in Moscow is about what he has lost. And if I did not see it before, then at least I do now. We can't just leave him, without trying to help."

Petya stepped back. "You are not going there."

She straightened. "Someone has to."

"It must be you?"

"You will be on a plane."

"He has chosen to lose himself, Katya. You don't have to. You can still come with me. You could finish your degree in California."

"That's not going to happen now."

He looked about them, his face suddenly defeated. "What will you do when there is nothing left?"

Katya let go of him, her hand coming to her mouth. "You're really going, aren't you?"

The colour left her brother's face. His arms hung limply at his side. He stared at his hands, as if willing them to move, to fix what was broken. "I have to save myself. I would take you too if you would come."

"I can't leave them."

"If you did not leave with that American professor, then I don't suppose you will leave with me."

She started at the mention of Andrew, and for a moment her face cleared. "He did not want to leave," she muttered, her voice suddenly distant. "He turned down a job. He wants to stay."

"Where is he now?"

"I don't know. Maybe he has gone back now, with everything that's happened."

Sister and brother stood there in the silent flat, looking at one another across the great distance of that moment.

"I can't stay here. I can't. Not even for you. I know what that makes me, and I'm sorry for it. I don't want to hurt Father, or you, or Mother. But there it is. I have to save myself."

"It is the right thing. I am choosing to stay, just as you are choosing to go. Neither of us is wrong." Her face brightened. "And who knows – maybe I can talk Mother into visiting you?"

He laughed suddenly. "Can you imagine Mama there?"

"I can't imagine you there. But you will be. So why shouldn't she go one day, too?"

"That's true. Think about it. I can go now. I am free to come and go as I choose. But the possibilities – Katya they're horrifying. Standing here just now it occurs to me that I might never again talk to you in this room. Think about that – to never talk to my sister in my home. In the flat where we grew up! Where will we be the next time we talk? When I call you from Los Angeles, bring the phone into my room and stand exactly where you are now and that's how I'll see you..." Petya sat on his bed. "It's both exhilarating and terrible. To say you will never again set foot in a place that has been the frame to the canvas of your life, to know that you will never again see a place that is as familiar to you as your own hand. What changes! What will life be like next week? Next month? A year from now? Everything has changed."

"Yes," Katya said. Her voice was low again and far, far away.

Katya went back to the church to talk with Spacinov, whom she had not seen since her father left for the capital. She was wearing a wool blouse of her mother's and a heavy coat.

Spacinov was at work in his chamber.

"Good news," he said, she entered. "Our priest has found another purse!"

"Yes, I saw the workmen are back."

"It's a deep purse this time. Émigrés in America and Europe looking to help reconstruct the Motherland."

Katya raised her eyebrows. "Sounds promising."

"For you, too, perhaps," and he raised his thick eyebrows meaningfully.

"What do you mean?"

"I have money now for an assistant."

"Me?"

"I could teach you to restore the murals and icons. Even to paint them." He waited for Katya to reply, but she was very quiet and he paused what he was doing to look at her. "What's wrong?"

She wanted to weep but held herself back, resisting the fear which welled inside her.

Instead she told him how things were with her, though at first he did not understand.

"It can't be so bad. What do you need? Only enough to feed yourself..."

"Not just myself," she said, glancing at him. And then, for the first time, she passed one hand over her stomach in a hushed, pensive reflex. Her fingers quivered with the quiet rush of warmth.

He stared at her, unable for a moment to speak. "Oh, I see. I see."

"Yes," Katya nodded. "It will not be long before they all do. I must go to Moscow. I need to find my father."

"You don't think he will come back anyway, after things have blown over?"

"I don't know what he might do, what might happen. Perhaps, if he knew how badly we need him, he might come back and we would be together again."

"Ah, Yekaterina..." the old man stroked his beard, his face thoughtful as he watched her. "Why not wait? Grief is a poison that becomes its own antidote in time."

Katya smiled distantly. "My father has suffered a long time."

"I was speaking of you," he said, his voice softening.

For a moment she stared at the old man, not wanting to speak. "Thank you for your offer," she said at last.

He waved at her. "Don't say no just yet. You may still come back to it."

She drew closer to him, glad with his answer. "What is it you're working on?"

He moved so that she could see his progress.

Katya looked at him. "The figure is very fine."

"You recognize her?"

"I do."

She felt his hand come to rest on her arm.

He smiled at her, a little sadly. "Now I will give her your eyes."

ADAM STOOD alone in the accordion-like berth between the train cars, watching the country pass. Crows leapt from the undergrowth next to the tracks, their wings hanging in the long shadows of dusk. Soon the trees gave way to farmland, fingers of frozen earth stretching black and exposed into the horizon. To his right was the first-class compartment he had just come from: foreigners and businessmen, students from the West with little flags sewn into Gortex coats. Everyone was trying to get to an airport.

His bunk was in a cabin shared with a group of foreign students. There were three of them eating a chicken on the foldout table by their window. Bottles of beer balanced between their knees, wax paper spread out as plates.

Adam stood at the door in his new *shapka* and wool coat. Their eyes narrowed. He checked his ticket.

A man in a college sweatshirt finally spoke. "Are you lost?" he said in English, annunciating slowly.

A backpack lay open on the bunk closest to the door, the word GRACE stitched with pink yarn into the tags of the clothes.

One of the women smiled, a hand resting on her purse.

Adam looked again at the number on his ticket, and shook his head apologetically. "*Izvenitia.*"

As he turned into the corridor their voices came hushed and furtive at his back. "I hate it when they stare like that," one of the women whispered.

"Did you see him looking at your things?"

Adam decided to stand in the berth between the cars, unsure of what to do. Beneath him the floor shifted with the rhythmic convulsions of the train. He fingered his ticket. Through the door on his left he watched the crowded groups in the second-class car. People stood in the corridor, their voices alive with a language he would never understand. From the window he watched as the train passed one of the old collective farms. A derelict sprawl of grey buildings, machinery, mud tracks, a loitering cow, sagging fences. Then for a long time there was only the vast expanse of ploughed earth, dotted here and there with trees or distant buildings. He opened the window and instantly the corridor flooded with the rush of cold air. Adam closed his eyes, for a moment feeling only the wind on his face and the rhythmic shudder of the train. He felt calm when he opened his eyes, and he smiled to himself as he looked about at the other passengers. Then he saw her.

Katya stood among the others on the train, staring as Adam had at the passing country. The train shuddered and he squinted as her face appeared and disappeared between the arms and heads of other passengers. Finally, he caught her eye through all of the confusion and Katya started as she recognized him.

She coloured but did not turn away. For a moment they stared at each other through the crowded corridor. At last she moved to where he stood.

"Why are you here?"

He watched her, feeling strangely calm as though he were seeing her again at the university.

"Hello, Katya."

Her mouth became thin, and her stare hardened. "Why are you here?"

"Andrew is in Moscow."

She paled. "What is he doing?"

"He wanted to be there. He thought he should support the protestors."

"Of course he did."

Adam glanced out the window. "No one has heard from him since he left. I thought someone should make sure he is okay."

"You do not even speak Russian."

He shrugged and bit at his lip. "Then I will speak English."

They swayed to the rhythmic shaking of the train. Adam gripped the handrail to steady himself.

"Where will you look for him?"

"He wanted to be part of the protest. That's the place he will be." He squinted into the wind that rushed through the open window, a smell of earth and frost folding around them. "Why are you going?"

She was quiet before replying. "My father is also there."

"He's gone to see the fighting?"

"He has gone to fight."

Adam saw the way her face changed when she spoke of him. "He's old for fighting, isn't he?"

"I am bringing him home."

"I see."

The train passed through a village, and his gaze took in the whole place at once: a woman in a red sweater, smoke rising above houses, dogs rushing from their yards to bark at the train, a boy fishing in the river. On the horizon was a tractor, yellow and distant as a star.

Katya was looking at him. "When you find Andrew," she began, "will you tell him something for me?"

"Of course, if I can find him. What is it?"

Her expression stiffened with sadness but also pride, he thought.

"I need him to know something. It is very important…"

He listened, at first surprised, then becoming calm, as he grasped what she was saying. When she was done, he felt her grip his arm. "You will tell him for me?"

"He has no idea?"

She shook her head. "Will you tell him?"

"Of course." He searched her face, trying to find her thoughts. "It is going to be okay, you know."

She turned to look out the window. "Will it?"

"Yes."

Katya paused, watching her hand on his arm and wondering what there was still to say. She glanced at his clothes, smiling suddenly in spite of herself. "I did not recognize you at first."

He grinned. "I know."

"Whose coat is it?"

"It's mine."

"It is not a tourist's coat."

"I'm not a tourist."

Their eyes met, and for a moment Adam held on to her stare, not wanting her to go.

"No, you're not."

The berth shook with a jolt and she turned to leave, but then stopped herself and faced him. "I finished translating the final poem."

"What's that?"

"The last poem. I finished it."

"Did you? That's good."

For a moment she stared again out the window, and Adam stood with her, neither of them knowing what to say. From the window came the damp smell of coming dark and the open land. Two old men pushed between Adam and Katya, returning to their bunks. A woman sang quietly in one of the compartments to a crying child.

Katya smiled, sadly it seemed now. She held out her hand formally, and it felt stiff and awkward in his own.

"I will find him."

Katya held his gaze for a final instant, and then blinked and let him go. "Thank you." Then she turned into the corridor crowded with passengers, and in a moment she was gone.

Adam searched until he found an empty bunk in one of the second-class cars. For a long time he lay watching shadows and lights pass across the ceiling. The others in his compartment ate or read in their beds. One of the men opened a bundle wrapped in newspaper, setting out an over-ripe pear, bread, two cans of sardines, a jar of milk, biscuits.

Adam watched the man pick out a fish, fingers slick with grease, which he offered to him. He thanked the man, who nodded and went on to offer a fish to each person in the compartment.

Propping himself on his elbow, Adam unwrapped the bandage on his hand. The palm was a mass of scabs, cracked and brittle like thin ice, and beneath it he could feel the pain of healing.

His thoughts wandered back to Katya, who slept somewhere on that train. "Why am I here?" he muttered, and one or two of the passengers looked curiously at him.

What would he tell Andrew? What could he say to him?

Through the window he watched the passing fields, the expanse of open land and shadow. Andrew had come all the way to that country to find a father only to discover he was long dead. For this Adam could not leave his friend, could not leave the child who would never know his father.

The countryside faded entirely into darkness. A man sang quietly to himself in the bunk below him. Voices in the hall grew silent. The rhythmic sound of the train filled the shadows, lulling people toward sleep. From down the corridor came the low insistence of a child's keening, followed by the mother's lullaby. Adam listened to the child, and knew that somewhere on the train Katya was listening as well. Long after the child had fallen silent, Adam thought of Katya and what he would say to Andrew. But how do you tell a man what it is to be a father if you have never held your own child, if it has never heard your voice speak its name? What made him a father? How is it possible that the thing which has defined you most, is also something you never experienced? Would he try to articulate to Andrew that he had only known the pain of his son's absence, which, though terrible and punishing, still made his child real? How could he explain to Andrew that what he feared now was that his grief would fade? He was terrified if he stopped feeling the loss, then even that would be lost, too. The final trace he had of his child was the pain of its absence. Would he say all this to Andrew? Would it help him to decide what would happen next?

At some point in the night Adam decided he did not know what words he would say when he found Andrew, but he understood with equal certainty that the words, whatever they happened to be, would be enough.

"There is a child," he whispered. "This is all I will need to say."

Drawing his coat over himself, Adam lay back in the bunk, the scarred hand opened on his chest. His thoughts slowed, settling finally on the icon he had seen in the church. His fingers fumbled inside his coat until he found the photograph of Clare and their child. Cracks had formed in the celluloid where it had been folded and bent, but they were both there still, as they had been that day. In the tired light from the corridor he could just make out Clare's face, and he began to weep, silently but with his complete self.

The train pulled into Moscow's Belorussy Station at dawn, the sun cold and white as a cataract. Overnight the temperature had dropped and as he brushed at the condensation on the window, Adam saw that the city lay damp and chilled. In the streets people walked bundled in coats, hats drawn down over faces, breath trailing like scarves behind them.

Around him there was great commotion as the other passengers collected their belongings, checking luggage and buttoning their coats. The quiet fraternity of the previous night had been swept away with a restless self-absorption, and people pushed their way along the corridor clogged with people and baggage. Adam hesitated at first, feeling a wave of panic at the reality of finding Andrew. Leaning into the corridor, he craned his neck to see Katya among the other passengers. Through the window he scanned the crowds milling about with impatience and purpose.

"What am I doing here?" he muttered. "How will I find him in all this?"

A voice of inarticulate importance boomed over speakers in the great station, and Adam was met with a rush of frigid air and the smell of diesel exhaust and creosote which flooded the teeming corridor. The line of passengers began to move, and Adam found himself caught up among them, being pushed toward the exit at the end of the car.

He looked back, wishing he had not left his bunk. He felt unprepared for this, barely awake really, and if he had thought it possible Adam would have gone back to his compartment to compose himself, to double check that this was really happening, to reconsider why he had come here. But there was no chance to pause, and he found himself on the stairs, one hand clinging to the railing and his left foot perched awkwardly on the final step. And in the next instant the press of bodies thrust him onto the platform.

Here he was flanked by the blue passenger cars of different trains which formed a channel for the current of human movement that immediately caught Adam and carried him along like a leaf. The quiet confidence he'd felt the previous night abandoned him now, and Adam felt a surge of panic as he was swept up in the voices, the trundle of luggage trolleys, bits of harried conversation, cigarette smoke, the hissing of the engines. He instinctively squinted as if trying to hold back the commotion from his thoughts. People became impatient, muttering as they pushed at him in their hurry. But Adam still held back, afraid to accept the crowd's trajectory. What he yearned for was the anchor of familiarity, and in each rushing face he hoped to find Katya.

At the far end of the station stood the exit beneath a massive stained glass window, and it was there that he saw Katya making her way from the station. Adam lurched forward at the sight of her, and he pushed his way through the countering eddies of people that congested the station. He was breathless and sweating as he passed the kiosk where Andrew had bought coffee a few weeks before, and then Adam had passed through the black iron doors and was standing in the morning rush and glare of Moscow.

The commotion of the city met him in the street like an angry dog. People greeted loved ones emerging from the station. Taxis pulled up and jettisoned passengers onto the sidewalk. Cars sped past the station. Two panhandlers played clarinets at the round message board where Andrew had stopped to get directions. Across the street, workmen used pneumatic hammers to break up the road, while others shovelled the fragments into a waiting truck. And there, on the busy sidewalk beneath a sign for a new restaurant, was Katya. Even from that distance Adam could see the determination which propelled her forward into the crowd. The next moment she began to fade among the people on the street.

Feeling desperate, he called Katya's name, trying to reach her through the commotion and ferment. She kept walking, unaware of him, and almost immediately she disappeared again in the crowd.

"What the hell am I doing?" Adam called out, his voice carried away by the rush of people where it drowned in the anonymous noise of the city.

There was, Katya found, a manic sort of fatigue among those inside the parliament building, an exhausted restlessness that caused friction between the young men fingering Kalashnikovs, and the older, out-of-shape volunteers. It was early afternoon when she arrived there from the train station. She had used her English to tag along with a group of journalists who talked their way past soldiers at the barricade and then again to get past a group of men in balaclavas and Adidas track suits stationed at the parliament's marble stairway. Inside the building, the noise and sunlight vanished and she found the parliament's halls and rooms claustrophobic with accumulated odours and refuse. People pushed about in the half-light, others sat against the walls holding weapons, their voices hostile and exhausted. Some called out to her, asking about what was happening outside beyond the barricade. There was an uninspired attempt to search her and the journalists for weapons, after which she was left to look for her father.

After a little asking a tall man outfitted with a rifle and a large military coat offered to take her to Ivan. "Sure I know who he is. There aren't many one-armed fellows in this place."

The man guided her through the stairwell, using a rolled-up newspaper dipped in kerosene as a torch to see in the dark. Trash and filth had accumulated on the stairs. Katya tried not to examine the ground as they went, but it was impossible to ignore the stench and in the end she had to press one hand over her mouth as they went.

They came to a landing and followed a passageway leading to the corridor on that floor. "I saw him here last night," explained the man. There were dozens of people in the hallways or loitering in ransacked offices, and Katya stopped to ask them about her father. Some knew at least who he was, others vaguely recalled seeing a one-armed man. Each time she came to someone asleep on the floor, the tall man helped her pull back blankets or scarves to see the face. In one office, the floor was entirely covered with sleeping bags. Out of this surface protruded a dozen faces, their bodies otherwise buried in the confusion of the floor.

Her guide waved his torch to get their attention, but no one stood. In frustration he yelled and kicked at the mess. "Hey there, wake up! We're looking for someone!"

One of the heads stirred and the eyes opened languidly. "Don't come in here."

The guide looked at Katya and shook his head. At the end of the corridor, they stopped by one of the windows and the man set down his rifle on the ledge to light a cigarette.

"He's not here," she said. Her voice was strained and despairing.

The tall man thought for a moment as he smoked. "He could be higher up. I used to see him on one of the floors towards the top."

Katya looked out the window at the crowds on street. "He could be anywhere. We'll have to search each floor."

"I don't think so. Most people here find a place and stay in it."

Her breathing was heavy and sweat ran down her back. The sensation made her shiver. "I could not do this without your help."

He smiled, and here by the open window Katya could see that he was not much older than her. "You're not the first child to come looking in this place for a father."

"Do people always find who they're looking for?"

"They're usually here somewhere."

"Well, thank you."

He shrugged. "What else am I going to do?"

After this they returned to the stairwell and climbed to another floor and continued searching for her father.

Finally a young man directed them to an office on the south side of the building overlooking the barricade.

Katya and her guide made their way in the half-light, stepping over sleeping bodies, and ammunition boxes and garbage. In an office at the end of the corridor they found a man sitting alone by the window.

"There he is," said the guide. "That's him."

Katya thought there had been a mistake. She did not recognize the person who stared at her. The first thing she noticed was that his boots were untied, and a sock had been pulled carelessly over the bottom of his pant leg. Hair sprawled in different directions from under a rough woven hat. He sat bowed and twisted, like a branch before it breaks. The man's face was creased and marked with dirt which seemed to deepen the vacancy of his expression.

'This man is not my father,' Katya thought. But as she turned back to the hall she heard her name come from the stranger.

"Yekaterina?"

She stared at the limp sleeve of the man's coat, and her heart sank. "Papa?"

Ivan looked at her distractedly. It was a moment before he seemed able to focus on her presence. "Katya, how did you get in here?" he muttered.

She shrugged. "I told them who I was."

Ivan sighed and gestured with an exhausted frustration. "There is no discipline here," he shouted. "All we have is coming and going indiscriminately!"

Katya drew closer but halted when she saw the pistol in his hand.

"We could be infiltrated by their agents – we could be infiltrated by someone delivering pizza!" He moved to the window and began yelling at the crowd far below. But within a few seconds the

547

outburst exhausted him, and when he faced Katya he was panting. "You can't mount a defence this way. What do they think we're doing here?"

Her face flushed and she clenched her hands. "What are you doing here?" she asked, trying to keep her voice down.

He looked at her. His voice dropped to a whisper. "I am waiting for the end," he said, carefully pronouncing each word.

Katya shook her head. "Come home with me, Papa. It's not too late, we can leave."

"Leave?" he retorted, his voice growing shrill again. "With the tanks here?"

She stepped forward, half watching the gun in his hand. "Papa, how do you think this is going to turn out?"

As she spoke he seemed to calm again, and he sat down on a chair next to the window. It was growing late, and the grey light settled on him now like dust.

She rested a finger on his arm.

Feeling her touch he turned to her, pivoting his other shoulder towards her. And then suddenly the colour ran from his face and he shut his eyes.

Katya leaned closer. "Are you in pain?"

"Just now I tried to touch your face with my old arm. My child arm. But when I touched you, you weren't there. For a moment I thought – I hoped – this was a dream." He looked down at the sleeve of his missing arm. "It is a difficult thing, to carry the past with you like a ghost. To have it always with you, and for a part of you to be always there...I used to think sometimes that it would drive me out of my mind." He drew away from her and covered his face. "I don't think I can go back. But I don't know how to end this. I thought everything could be saved here."

He straightened a little to peer out the window at the barricades. "Look at them. They invite chaos. But they don't see how it will be. And, as for them –" and he gestured at the hallway behind him. "All of my enemies are here – the monarchists, the fascists, the democrats – all here fighting the same lost battle with us. How am I to be their ally? We have nothing in common except that we hate the same thing. Many have already left on one pretext or another...."

As he spoke his shoulders sank. "It wasn't supposed to be like this," he said, looking at his daughter. "Our enemies have always brought war to us. And we could always win those wars.

Our enemies have never understood what it meant to fight us, what we were willing to endure. But where is our war now? Here? This pathetic gathering in which you find me? I thought I was fighting a real war...."

He showed her the gun as if for proof. "But that's not what is here. Look out the window! This is a battle in which only the losers have shown up to fight. The war is over. You can see it everywhere." His voice became suddenly brittle and shrill, then just as suddenly it lowered again to a whisper. "I'm not afraid to suffer. I can endure. You and your brother cannot imagine what I can endure. But this – " he gestured at the window. "I came to fight a war that has already happened. When was the war, Katya? When was it? When did we lose? Subov would know..."

"Who is Subov?"

A thought passed across his face, and for a moment the filth and age seemed to lighten. "I never told you of Subov? What about Larissa? No? How can you not know about them? These people saved my life. They saved your life. You are here with me now, in this place, because of them."

Katya cried silently. She touched her father's hand. "Come home."

The tall man was still waiting in the hall. He helped Katya and Ivan through the stairwells and corridors. The group of men in balaclavas stood about watching through the glass doors of the building's lobby. They didn't bother to speak as the father and daughter passed.

"I'm going home!" Ivan shouted. But no one bothered to reply.

Outside the cold brought Ivan back to himself, and for a moment he blinked against the chill of the air. There beyond the broad lawn of the parliament building were the barricades and military vehicles and crowds he had seen from the window, now arrayed before him in the half-light like shadows.

"There are so many people..." he muttered.

"Oh yes," Katya replied. "Just wait until you see them all. The whole world has come to see how this will turn out."

Ivan nodded at the soldiers and police who milled about at the edge of the barricade. "They will let us through?"

"Why wouldn't they?" Her mouth felt dry. She had not thought about this. "We are not threatening anyone…"

She moved forward holding her arms in the air to show her intention. The air was cold, but she could feel sweat forming on her face. Her hands shook and she had to concentrate. She could see tanks and armoured vehicles on the road that ran in front of the building. In the distance, there were crowds on the overpasses and pressed against the barriers. She felt a thousand eyes upon her, sensing their detached interest in her fate. 'They are waiting to see if we live,' she thought. 'That is why they look…' She stopped, suddenly unsure about going on.

"It will be alright," her father said, his voice strangely confident. He stepped in front of her and moved forward. "Come along…"

They could see other people moving in different directions across the lawn or crouching in the mangled gardens. Katya and her father walked slowly, keeping close to trees and bushes whenever they could. Katya searched the barriers and clotted groups of soldiers and police in riot gear, looking for an opening among them. But as they approached one of the barricades shots were fired, and they both fell as the threads of tracer bullets appeared over their heads.

Katya heard her father's voice. "Keep still. Don't move!"

More shots were traded, followed by cries from somewhere close. A swath of bullets passed over them, and they cringed. Ivan groped about until he found his daughter's hand, and pressed it to him.

"Lie still," she heard her father say. "We could be shot by either side now."

He was standing along the perimeter, staring at the crowds. The cold had lingered into the afternoon, and people moved with a stiff and almost pained restlessness. The crowd glared at the cordon of military personnel with agitation and boredom. Smoke from oil drums drifted among the onlookers like wraiths. Most people Adam passed did not make eye contact, but the stares of those who did were at once both untrusting and curious. As he searched for Andrew, he kept noticing three boys wandering through the crowds wearing backpacks filled with bottles, each with a piece of cloth sticking from its neck. In the centre of a small group a woman held up a photograph of a soldier, while onlookers watched her curiously. Adam stared as the woman cradled the portrait against her chest, as though nursing at her tired breast. By one of the orange water trucks stood soldiers, talking together in loud voices to remind people that they were there. At a spot near the barrier an icon had been set on a cardboard box, and as Adam went by three women were kneeling before the image, their lips twitching with prayer. Walls on nearby buildings had become a smear of graffiti and poetry and old song lyrics. In one place he stopped where someone had written *See the Radiant Future*! in veins of red paint that ran down the wall.

Farther on there was a commotion starting between soldiers and a young woman in a blue coat who shouted at them and gestured at the parliament. "Why are you here?" she demanded in Russian. "I voted for those people. Do you understand me? I voted for them! Why are you here?"

The soldiers stared back impassively at the woman, while an officer yelled and tried to wave her back. More yelling followed, and a crowd began to form around the woman. "Who do you serve? Who gave your orders? Look around – do any of you know why you are here?"

Another officer appeared and the first one stepped away. Behind them, the soldiers looked on through holes in their riot shields. The new officer spoke in a low voice to the woman and she stopped yelling. More people appeared, among them a group of old men carrying homemade flags on broomsticks. For a moment Adam was so intent on watching what was happening he did not hear his own name being called.

But when he turned around there was Andrew watching him. Adam caught his breath and then called out in return, a sense of relief flooding over him at he stared at his friend.

"What are you doing here?"

There was a long scratch at Andrew's temple which he kept touching, and his eyes looked back at Adam with a distracted intensity. He had not shaved in days and creases of dirt stretched like cracks about his mouth and eyes. He was wearing the same clothes as when Adam had seen him off, except for a *shapka* which was new. Behind him loomed the whiteness of the parliament against the blue sky.

They stood for a moment staring at one another.

"Do you know where you are?"

Adam grinned. "Do you mean exactly?"

"You know what I mean."

"I'm glad I found you."

"It was me who found you, actually."

"You know what I mean."

Andrew put his hands on his hips. "So what are you doing here?"

Adam stepped back from Andrew, feeling suddenly defensive. "All this shit started," he pointed around at the soldiers and hostile crowds, "and no one had heard from you."

Andrew opened his arms wide, but his voice was caustic. "I'm just fine."

"Okay, then. The others will be relieved."

"They should be here, too."

"They've gone home."

Andrew dropped his arms. "Really?"

"It's been all over the news..." he gestured around them. "Do you know how all of this looks on a television? Everyone is pretty worried."

"And you're the one who stayed. How ironic." He glanced over his shoulder at the parliament. "They should be celebrating. Look at everyone here. All these people have come out because the politicians they voted for have locked themselves into the democratic centre of the country. Think about that. Would anyone have guessed this could happen here?"

Adam shook his head. "Even your mother wouldn't have guessed it."

"You're right," Andrew blinked, and for an instant his expression softened. "But she always hoped it would."

Adam followed his gaze to the white parliament building behind them.

"What would you have done if you hadn't found me?"

"Honestly," he shrugged, "I don't know."

"But what would you have done?"

Adam looked around at the people that pressed on them. "I found you."

Andrew's face stiffened again. "That was a long trip you took getting here."

He stepped forward now, sensing Andrew was slipping away. "Has it been dangerous here?"

"Not yet," Andrew looked mournfully over his shoulder. "But it has potential."

"And you want to be here for it? For whatever happens?"

"Of course, I do. You should too. Everyone should. All the others sitting at home or wherever they are watching the future on television – they should be here. Katya – everyone should be here. Where it's happening."

The three boys with their backpacks of Molotov cocktails pushed past Adam. "There's something I need to tell you."

"Tell me what?"

The crowd pressed on Adam, pushing them uncomfortably close. He felt the other people distracting Andrew. "I have a message for you."

He crossed his arms. "What's going on?"

"Not here."

"That's precious. Do you understand how small you seem, coming here with your important message while all of this is going on? Doesn't that strike you as particularly ridiculous?"

"Is there a coffee shop, at least? A restaurant? It's not something we can talk about with all this going on."

Andrew spat. "This should be good."

He started at the anger in his friend's voice. "Yes. It should be."

Andrew glanced over his shoulder at the crowd and then swore. "I better not miss anything..."

When they entered the flat, Adam had to pause as his eyes adjusted to the darkness. Andrew disappeared through the other end of the hall, and after a moment voices and sounds of moving about came from somewhere in the apartment. Adam followed the noise, passing through the hallway into a living room. Clothes and sleeping bags lay about on the floor, where two or three people were asleep. In the kitchen a woman was talking with a short bearded guy about the standoff. On the far wall was a pair of glass doors that opened onto a balcony overlooking the courtyard.

"Here," Andrew said, appearing with a glass. "I found bread and something to drink."

His fingers felt cold as he took the glass, but the wine ran warm to the bottom of him. "Who are these people?"

Andrew shrugged. "People."

"Whose place is it?"

"I don't know," he said defensively. "Whoever it is, they won't mind if you stay here, if that's what you mean."

"That's not what I meant."

"I didn't think so."

Adam tore off a piece of bread.

Andrew looked restless and pissed off. "How's your hand?"

"Sore."

Digging a cigarette from his pocket, he unlatched the glass doors and stepped onto the balcony. The cold swept in. One of the people in sleeping bags moaned and rolled closer to the wall.

Adam stared at Andrew's back, watching the smoke coil around his neck.

"You've changed," he said at last, his voice betraying more than he had intended.

"You haven't," replied Andrew with equal regret. "I need to get back to the protest." He hesitated. "You could come...?"

"I saw Katya."

His cigarette made a small popping sound as it hit the ground.

"She's here?"

"She was on the train."

Andrew straightened and something flickered across his face. "To find me?"

"Her father, I think," and then, because there was no real segue for these things, he told Andrew matter-of-factly what Katya had said.

He turned toward the window, pale sun resting on his cheek. Birds called from the naked tree in the courtyard. Adam watched his face change as the news settled in him, like a stone falling in water.

"I don't have to do anything right away," he said finally. "I have months."

In the kitchen the fridge cut on.

"Eight, actually."

"There's time."

Adam flinched. "You should go to her now."

"Do you know where she is?"

"Her father will be at the demonstration. We can find her. You need to talk to her."

"How will I find her in all of that? You saw how many people are there."

"I found you."

"What would I do then?"

Adam shrugged. "Just find her. You'll figure out the rest."

"Can't she find me?" Andrew sat heavily on the couch.

"Don't be stupid. She wants to find her father. You of all people should understand why."

He ran both hands over his face.

"A child can change everything. It's probably something your father realized too late. Don't make that mistake."

Andrew put his hands on his knees. "Let's not talk about my father."

"Why not? That's why you came over here in the first place."

Andrew considered him for a moment. "Why are you here Adam?"

"You should see her."

Andrew stared at him for a long time. "I probably should. But we're in Moscow now, and there's a coup in progress. The army is here for the President, and the people have come out for the deputies in the parliament. This country had a free election and now the President wants to silence the elected representatives. There are tanks and guns. No one thinks this is going to end well. And you think I should talk to Katya at this moment."

He shoved his hands in his pockets, and stared. "Yes."

"And that's why you're here?"

"Talk to her. It could change everything."

Andrew stood and put on his coat. "Look around us," he said, grinning at Adam in that way he had for hiding grief. "Everything has already changed."

After Andrew had gone Adam stood for a long time in the silence of the flat. There was trash on the floor and on tables. Sleeping bags and bedding lay tangled in corners. The place smelled of other people. He found some books on one of the shelves and flipped through them restlessly. He tried to lie down, but people kept entering or leaving the flat, most of them to sleep or look for someone. No one paid attention to Adam, except to grunt or ask if he had cigarettes. When he couldn't stand it any longer, Adam took his coat and left. Outside the afternoon was waning. A few blocks up he found an American fast food chain, and he joined the queue in front of the restaurant. There were a lot of foreigners waiting, groups of friends speaking English and German. It reminded him of all the restaurants he had gone to in Galinsk with the other expats, and he wondered where they were now. Probably they were home, he realized. Back to where they came from.

There was a noise down the road then, and those standing about watched in amazement as a truck and then an armoured car sped by with hangers-on who waved flags and stolen riot shields. Behind them came an assortment of vehicles, each overflowing with passengers. There were calls and excited expressions, hands gesturing. From a passing taxi, one man leaned into the street holding a megaphone and shrieking at pedestrians in a garble of breathless umbrage: "...rrrrs and sisters, unite with us at the television station. Let the people crush the oppp-p-p-p..." his voice disappearing as it had emerged, a stuttering smudge of unintelligibility. One of the last vehicles was a blue military truck with a broken tailgate, and in the back seven or eight men cheered at those they passed. Among them was Andrew.

Adam tried calling to him, but his voice was lost in the commotion, and he stood mechanically rubbing his burnt hand, feeling helpless as the truck disappeared from sight.

He turned to a woman standing next to him in line. "English?"

She nodded, as though used to the question. "A little."

"Those people – one of them said something about a television station? Do you know where that is?"

Before the woman could reply, Adam was distracted by the deep clatter of heavy metal rumbling up the road, like thunder. Adam forgot what he was doing, and stepped into the street for a better look. Vehicles darted out of the way, pulling over or turning off the road, making way for a column of green personnel carriers which moved up the street.

People began to laugh, someone calling out, "You'll never catch them at that speed!" But the soldiers continued unhurried, as though they had measured the route already.

From the turrets and windows leaned men in blue and green uniforms, Kalashnikovs resting on their arms. No one spoke or gestured to those on the street.

As Adam watched the column a vague foreboding came over him. The vehicles turned at the top of the street, and those watching grew bored and returned to the queue.

Adam started to run.

Someone yelled but he did not look back, and people in the street parted at the sight of him. People pulled each other out of his way. A woman blocked her child from his path. An old man gestured rudely from a bench. For Adam none of this existed though. All of his concentration focused on the column of soldiers.

After he had gone several blocks a cab came up beside him, and a guy wearing a blue Press jacket leaned out the window to yell something.

Adam shook his head, slowing just enough to speak. "What?"

"Where are you going?" the man said in English.

"I have to warn a friend," he panted, only half aware that he wasn't making any sense.

The cab stopped several meters ahead of him. The door opened and the guy appeared again. "Want a ride?"

There were two others in the backseat, a woman with the same press jacket as the first guy and a thin man holding a large camera. Adam squeezed next to them while the one who had yelled got in front with the driver.

"Do you know where he's headed?"

"Who?"

"Whoever it is you were running after."

Adam wiped the sweat from his face. "Something about a television station."

The guy up front spoke in Russian to the driver, and the car immediately picked up speed.

"You should be able to pass the military group," Adam added. "They didn't seem to be in a hurry."

The woman stared, "How do you know that?"

"They weren't breaking any speed limits."

The cameraman was looking at him strangely. "Did you know you're bleeding?"

"It's nothing," he pushed his hand into the pocket of his coat. "Thanks for picking me up."

The guy smiled carelessly at him over the seat. "You seemed to know where you were going."

Adam started to laugh.

The woman frowned at him. "Are you okay?"

"Definitely not," he said. "I have a friend up there."

"With the protesters?"

"They don't know what's behind them."

After a moment they could see the back of the military column, and the cab made a sudden turn at the next street. The little car roared along the narrow lanes, only returning to the main road when they were ahead of the column.

The driver glanced in the mirror and began talking in Russian.

"What's he saying?"

"You were right." The guy in the front was biting his lip. "They're not going fast at all."

The cameraman whistled. "I don't like it when the Army seems in control."

"So then," the woman glanced at him ironically. "How are you enjoying Russia?"

Adam wiped the sweat from his face again and looked about, trying to take everything in. "Time of my life."

"Don't be too harsh." This from the front seat. "Where else can you go to a museum of the last revolution in the morning, and after lunch cab it to the next one?"

From where he sat, Adam could see a block or two ahead where the street was clotted with vehicles and people. The cab stopped as it approached, and as they got out Adam was caught up in the press and noise of the crowd. He did not see the journalists again.

It was impossible to tell how many people there were, and in a moment he lost all sight of the cab. He was enveloped by the crowd, so that all he had to direct himself was the shrill metallic voice from a megaphone. Toward this he instinctively moved, pushing his way through the forest of people – elbows and knees, fists, slack-jawed fear, stares of mute camaraderie, a fight; cigarette smoke, sweat, nameless offence, alcohol, diesel exhaust and piss; yells, chanting, someone with a guitar, car horns. All these things became a single organism which swallowed him, took him on as one of a thousand appendages, so that he was at the same time himself and part of something unrecognizable.

In the crowd time ceased to exist, and at one point Adam noticed with surprise that it had begun to grow dark. Coming to a truck, he climbed over a group of people to stand on its roof. Surveying the canopy of heads and placards and banners, he saw that the greater portion of the crowd lay behind him, that he had pushed to a cluster of vehicles which he supposed had been the ones he'd seen carrying the first protestors. Not far from him was a circle of armed men, and in the centre of them stood the man with the megaphone who continued yelling into the crowd.

Adam spotted Andrew on the hood of another car, and he got down and made his way toward it. But when he found the vehicle Andrew had moved on and it was another moment before he saw him, this time waving a riot shield from atop a police car.

When he came to the car, Adam was stopped by the sight of Andrew, who seemed now a gross caricature of himself. His hat was gone and one sleeve had completely come away from his leather jacket. His face was streaked with sweat and dirt, a bruise protruded over his right eye. The rest of his features were compressed and distorted as he called out slogans and obscenities in hoarse yells.

Adam hesitated, then got onto the hood, only to be struck by the shield Andrew was waving. At first his friend did not know him, but as recognition spread over his face he reached out and embraced Adam. "You're here – I can't believe you're here…!"

Adam didn't try to respond, but instead let his friend slap him on the back. "Can you believe it?" he kept saying, yelling to be heard above the crowd. "It's happening – it's happening!"

"What's happening?" he shouted, but Andrew had turned back to the crowd and didn't answer. Andrew gave him a police truncheon that hung from his belt, and together the two of them stood on the car and joined the incoherent howl. Adam gave himself up to Andrew's excitement, feeling for the first time the thrill and disembodiment of that moment. A number of others climbed on the car, and Andrew put his arm around one of them.

A dark haired girl wanted to wave Adam's truncheon, but as she went to grab it she drew back and made a face at him. He looked at the stick to see what offended her, noticing then a tuft of hair at the end of it.

A group of soldiers had formed in front of the station, and on them the protesters now hurled threats and stones. Something was thrown through a window, and smoke could be seen coming from the main floor. The man with the megaphone joined in the abuse of the soldiers, and Andrew explained to Adam that they were demanding the military give up the station. The crowd's anger mounted and it seemed as though they would get their way. But just as more people surged forward, a green truck lurched from among them and drove into the front of the building. People scattered, diving out of the way was windows along the main floor burst from the impact. And then there was a sudden gasp and the air broke open with gunfire.

Red and blue sparks streaked into the crowd, and everything seemed to implode upon itself. At the edge of his vision Adam saw the dark haired girl stumble, and then he was falling with her. The air was knocked from him. All sound disappeared and he could only stare at the asphalt next his face. He was vaguely aware of sounds, horrible noises, coming from very far away. The sounds mean fear, he knew, pain and danger. But those things were not there in the asphalt, and for what could have been a long time or an instant Adam could only stare at the ground, his attention locked on individual bits of sand and grit next to his face.

And then all at once his breath returned in a convulsive gasp. He choked, his lungs clawing through dust and smoke for enough air. He pulled himself up, still choking. He looked around, taking in images and sounds and smells he could not hold on to, which he would not find again until months later in his sleep. The shrieking for help. Blood. The expressions of shock and disbelief on faces of the injured. Vehement hiss of tear-gas grenades. The odd popping sound windows make in a burning car. Stench of vomit. The spreading stain of urine on a dead man's jeans. Someone clutching at his foot. Whine of bullets and shrapnel. Behind it all the wild panting of his own breathing. These things surrounded Adam, washed over him, and released him, then swallowed him again. He felt them, smelled and saw them, but could no more hang on to them than he could clutch water. Years later he would still be trying to describe them, to use words to understand what had happened that night, the way a drowning survivor tries to describe the currents that almost took him.

As he emerged from one of these waves of terror, he gathered himself enough to call out Andrew's name. He strained to listen through the havoc for his friend's voice, but then a shell tore off the hat of the man in front of him and Adam was knocked down again by the sheer shock of what had happened. He gagged, stumbled up, spitting bile, and then called Andrew's name again, begging his name into the crowd of sprawling, running shadows.

He found a low wall where he hid with some of the protestors. Wounded people crawled to them. Others lay crying, sometimes calling out names. Several vehicles had caught fire during the fighting, as well as the corner of the television station, and together the flames filled the area with wild, hysterical light. Spotlights were shone into the street, turning the growing haze of smoke into clouds of yellow and pink.

There was the hollow tapping of guns, while from a hundred directions red and blue tracer bullets carved at the surrounding darkness. Adam peered above the wall, occasionally calling Andrew's name. At last someone yelled a reply, and in the half-light of the fires he saw his friend crawling out from the shadows. In a moment he was kneeling behind the wall, the others slapping him on the back while he grinned triumphantly.

The next morning, Adam lay for a long time with his eyes closed, feeling nothing. Gradually sleep began to relinquish his senses, and he became aware of things around him. When he opened his eyes he remembered what had happened, the events of the previous night staring back at him like an empty well. There was a sick feeling in his mouth, like fruit gone bad. He looked around and saw there were nearly a dozen other people in the flat, some with makeshift slings and bandages, others bruised or cut, their clothes ragged. These people slept on whatever furniture was available, while a few lay on the floor or propped in corners.

He hid in the washroom to think. In the mirror his skin looked white as an egg. Adam held his head under the tap. When this did not work he stood in the shower, letting the frigid water wake him. His skin began to pebble, thoughts passing over him at a distance. What was he doing? Why had he come here?

"Fuck you, Andrew," he whispered.

A tremor ran through him as he stepped out of the shower. A pounding of distant shells rattled the room.

"Hurry up in there," the hammering again. Andrew's voice.

Adam found a towel on the floor. "What do you want?" he said, opening the door.

Andrew stood in an old bathrobe.

Water dripped from Adam's hair, running down his back. He shivered.

"You alright?"

Adam pushed past him and went into the kitchen. He found a bottle with something still in it, and he drank it.

Andrew sat on the counter and lighted a cigarette, watching him. Adam's hands shook, and he had to press them against the table to make them stop.

"It's not as though you shot anyone."

He stared at Andrew. His pulse raced, and he felt sweat on his back. A bug lay on the counter, feet grabbing at the air. Sun lay on the counter between Adam and Andrew.

He searched Adam's face. "Was last night a bad scene? Of course it was. People died. But you have to remember, history – and I mean history with a capital H – was made last night, and you were there." He shook his head in disbelief. "You should be thankful for last night."

"I'm thankful I'm alive."

Andrew frowned. "It's like you don't want anything to happen to you," and he found another cigarette.

"Enough has happened already."

"I know. Actually, I don't know because you won't talk about it, though I can probably guess a fair bit. It's clear that you have lost something. But you insist on ignoring the fact that loss is always part of a larger purchase. You've lost something, that's true. But you have gained something else, something difficult, perhaps. Something you never wanted. But still you have it and before you didn't. The only question that remains is what will you do with what you've gained."

Adam started, his voice bitter. "And what about you? First you lost your mother, then you gave up your career to find your father, who it turns out is long dead. Then you lost Katya. That's a hell of a lot to lose in a year. What the hell have you gained?"

Andrew glanced around the grim little kitchen by way of answering him. "This moment in this place," he said. "That's what I've gained. I'd never have come to this place if my mother hadn't died. I'd be back home trying to be for her whatever it was that my father had been."

"And the child."

"What?"

"You're going to be a father. What you gained is the child."

His voice grew very quiet. Smoke trailed from the cigarette, a seething finger of ash. "You're right."

They sat for a while not saying anything. A group of pigeons huddled next to the window. Adam was gazing at Andrew, unable to look away.

Eventually Andrew's face lightened and when he spoke again his voice had regained some of its confidence. "It was a good thing, you coming here. If you let yourself, you may even learn to like it."

"People were shooting at me. It's hard for me to let go of that."

Andrew stared at the end of his cigarette. "Then let me tell you," he began. "What you overlook was the significance of that moment. They won't show that stuff on TV – how could they? But you were there. You need to hold on to that," and his voice faded on his lips in a ghost of blue smoke.

"Did I not mention people were shooting at me?"

"Where do you think I was? I was lying beside a dead guy, okay? His face was right there," he gestured, holding the cigarette to his nose. "I felt his last breath. After he died there was just me hiding behind his body with tracer bullets like mosquitoes looking in the dark for my blood. And when the smoke began to lift I looked around, and there were all those bodies. It was like a nightmare and a ballet together," and Andrew sighed. "Terrible? You betcha. But it's the most important thing that's ever happened to me."

"Was it worth it?" Adam asked incredulously. "I mean almost getting shot."

"I've never been so free from myself." Andrew rested his head against one of the empty cupboards. "The professors back home would never recognize me..."

"You talk like you're sorry it's over."

"Over?" He looked up. "We're not stopping. The old totems of power and terror are still around us. The police, the old leaders, the secrets people – their world was blown open last night. People have seen what they are." He was blowing smoke rings now, big hoops like halos.

Adam's brow quilted. "I thought you would support the President, not the coup leaders."

"The President has shown himself to be no better than the rebels. Hell, three years ago he was a communist. You should listen to the people standing around at the barricade. They want a total change. They want a new kind of country, without the same old guys running things. They want the freedom everyone keeps talking about. It's all going to change now. Did you see the cameras? The rest of the world is here. Russia will never be the same. Ever. There's no going back."

He set down the empty bottle. "Are you going to look for Katya?"

Andrew ran both hands through his hair, looking unsteady. He squinted for a moment, as if trying to focus on his friend's face. "What happens if I find her? Tell me that, Adam. What happens then?"

A morning fog had come up from the river during the night and crept along the lawns and streets about the Parliament. It drifted in rags, rising atop the river's embankment and skimmed over the deserted freeway where it passed between the barriers and trucks, caressing the barrels of tanks. By the time it reached the grounds, the fog had thickened into an unbroken mass that stretched across the freeway, snaking like a thief's finger among the doorways and side streets. The parliament sat on a hill, and the swaths of fog stole up the lawn, rising silently up the broad marble stairs. Katya watched as the fog approached from beneath tanks and military trucks, enveloping soldiers, coiling about the base of trees, drifting over the bodies on the lawn around her. She felt the first chill as it reached her. She did not breathe while it passed over her, but crossed her arms to draw her coat tight and keep the cold from finding the child inside her. Above her the parliament stood white and silent. The windows looked down on her like black eyes, and behind them she knew men stared down at them with guns. In the sky Katya saw no stars, but at one point in the night she noticed the distant light of a plane far above her, and for a moment she forgot about the danger and the cold, and wondered about the people in that plane and their lives and where they were going.

Sometime before dawn her father whispered to her about moving toward the barricades, but then there were sounds of shooting from the east end of the building and they had to stop.

When she woke again, Katya saw that frost had settled about them. Behind her the sun had begun to appear, burning away the fog which still drifted in tatters among them. Farther on she saw the milky outline of soldiers and crowds down by the barricades, and over their heads the turrets of stirring tanks. She heard the urgent murmur of voices, and a number of figures dispersed in twos and threes among the trees and shrubbery of the surrounding grounds. Engines started, growling like woken dogs. Diesel plumes hung in the air like flags.

A few feet away from Katya, Ivan stood squinting into the thinning fog.

"Papa! What are you doing?" she whispered, gesturing. Katya looked around at the soldiers and vehicles in the distance. "Someone's going to see you. Get down!"

"Always remember this moment," he said in a voice that made her stare. "Remember it. Remember what happens today. Remember..." and for a moment Ivan's voice trailed off.

"It was like this at Leningrad..." he said at last, and his words came from far away. "There was an instant every morning just as I awoke, when there was no war and no hunger, no cold. It was wonderful. The joy of not knowing. And then all at once I would remember where I was, and the feeling of innocence would be gone. I think that moment each morning was what helped me survive. It was like a secret ration card. I would go all day surrounded by the dead, by pain, but always there at the back of my mind was the anticipation of waking the next morning and being, for that briefest of times, happy again."

Katya trembled.

"Remember this moment, Yekaterina." Ivan looked down at his daughter, the glint of sunlight occluding his face. "We are hanging in this instant between the old and the new. In this moment nothing is decided," and he sighed as the sun finally broke through the fog to rest on them.

A figure approached them through the remnants of fog, and Ivan seemed to come to himself. He bared his pistol and the man quickly moved off, camera still clicking at the other bodies on the lawn.

Further down the hill there was a stirring in the crowd. Voices came now through the haze. All around them was a bridling of energy, the sound of equipment, a sharp intake of breath.

Katya started up, sensing instinctively that something was happening. With a glance she took in everything about her. The hoarse call of soldiers, the bristle of weapons. In the middle of everything it seemed, stood her father, very still.

Then a deep thud rang out, and one of the tanks recoiled. The next instant a window in the parliament exploded, and Katya gasped at the gash of black and red that tore open the stillness. Then the air itself seemed to burst open.

When Andrew and Adam got there it was still early, though the grounds around the building as well as the surrounding streets and bridges were thick with tanks and soldiers, protestors, journalists, onlookers. They reached the front of the crowd just as the report of the first shell resonated over the area. Then both sides began firing all at once.

Adam watched figures pitch backwards as though struck at once by the same shell, gaps unexpectedly appearing on bodies, pieces coming away. People toppled from the barriers, crowds collapsing upon themselves, everyone crushing one another in the panic. The air around Adam was torn by a succession of rapid breaths. Holes materialized in the car next to him. Glass shattered and then the ground was hurrying at his face.

All along the street tanks and other units began firing on the building while the grainy images of those in doorways and windows were swallowed by the flash of the shells' impact. Scabs of smoke and fire scorched the exterior of the building, while from inside snipers targeted the crowd. Still taping, journalists peered behind vehicles, cameras gorging on the confusion. Teenagers, rather than flee the bullets, ran headlong into the fighting, pausing just long enough to wave at the cameras. After watching others do this, a boy no more than twelve came out from beneath a truck, gesturing to a group of reporters with his arms. An instant later he lurched backward, fell spitting blood.

Adam cringed at the heavy smack of bullets that struck the vehicle behind him, all the time watching in disbelief at the confusion around him: a woman looking at the hole in her shoulder; two men struck in chorus by the same shell; others torn and staggering, a man fleeing on a single leg, his hands clutching at those around him. The crowd broke apart, falling back into the surrounding streets and buildings, leaving the wounded behind them. Individuals rushed around in this vacuum of noise and shock, gored, broken, spun about.

The crowd faded, and the wide lawn before the building opened and Adam glimpsed Katya standing alone with an old man. Over the noise he yelled at Andrew, pointing her out among the disorder. They called to her, but she stood motionless, and together they crawled to another car to get closer.

Katya had been so focused on her fear of what might happen that she was stunned when it did. All at once everything came apart: a car exploded, the man with the camera fell, behind her fire spilled from the parliament, her overloading senses trying to locate order in the succession of images and sounds. For a moment she remained unmoving, holding onto her father's sleeve, trying to pull him back toward the barricade.

When the shooting started Ivan froze, the fevered realness of the fighting coming to him like a remembered nightmare. He watched the cameraman clutching at his stomach, mouth wrenched open with shock. Along the barricade the former density of the crowd imploded, giving way. People ran, hands held up against the sky.

He watched as the last remnant of hope to which he had tied his life seemed to perish in a moment of sudden certainties. Beside him someone was pulling at his arm. His child arm.

Katya screamed.

Ivan squinted at his daughter as though seeing her from a great distance. For a moment he closed his eyes and his face relaxed. When he looked up his thoughts were far away, and for a moment he was a boy again.

Katya watched her father, the calm of his face, seeing the flicker of decision cross his features. And then the next moment he seemed to come apart, two or three rounds striking his body simultaneously so that parts of him spun in different directions at once.

Adam saw Katya, saw the old man shatter. He willed her to duck, get down, run from the bullets which kicked up the ground about her. Still she did not move.

Adam's voice faltered. The child.

He crawled a bit farther, then ran for her. The air was smeared now with smoke and tracer bullets. Adam shrunk at the clatter and whine of shells, squinting to make her out in all of the confusion.

Reaching Katya, he caught at her hand and for an instant they stared at each other, trying to grasp their presence together in the unravelling moment. And then they were running back through the shooting toward the car where Andrew knelt.

Adam watched as he rose and sprinted toward them, at the same time seeing the strobes of rifle fire from the building behind him. Seeing, too, the sudden shock in Andrew's eyes and in the same instant something come away from his face. He fell headlong into the mud, taking Adam down, too. As he got up Katya was beside him and together they dragged Andrew back to the car.

They sank next to him, shock hollowing them both so that for what could have been a brief or a protracted time neither was aware of the fighting around them but instead only looked upon the broken face between them, and the reflection of a morning sky in the empty eyes.

As he returned to himself Adam tried to catch Katya's attention, though it was a moment before she could look up. Even then neither spoke nor gestured, except to stand together and run back through the pageantry of bodies and smoking cars, the stray arms left behind with watches still keeping time.

When they reached the bridge, they were met by a cluster of reporters. One of them grabbed Katya. "Do you speak English?"

People pushed around them, yelling. She gazed at the reporter, stunned. "Of course."

Instantly his voice became self-conscious and deep. "Tell us, what do you think this means for everyone who hopes for freedom in Russia?"

Katya started, her eyes becoming flat and disdaining. Her mouth tightened and she gazed at the reporter. "You should be more careful with words."

Then, looking back over her shoulder, Katya stared at the fire rising from the parliament, the sky behind it now darkening with smoke. At that moment, surrounded by the rushing and the noise and the lengthening fingers of flame, it occurred to her – such a *naïve*, such a very obvious thought. 'That is the face of history. It is how this moment will be known.'

The reporter let go of Katya and turned toward a sudden, approaching noise. From the confusion an old man appeared among them like a horse from a burning barn. His scream was that of a child in pain – a primal sound that resonated under the skin of those who heard it, down to the bones, into the teeth. His hands were held against his face, but between his fingers they saw the wildness in his eyes. People stopped what they were doing as he appeared, something about his pitched cry seeming more terrible than their own fear.

A moment later the old man was gone like a ghost into the crowd. And then just as suddenly people returned to themselves. Only Adam continued to stare after the old man.

Katya grabbed him and pushed past the cameras. When they were through the crowd, she turned without stopping and with a backward glance Katya glimpsed the pillar of smoke scarring the parliament building, the black plumes rising into the morning sky until it darkened, like a false dawn.

It was only then that she realized she was still holding the empty sleeve of her father's coat.

AT THE STATION they found the trains still running, and Adam stood at the gate while Katya bought tickets. Half an hour later, as the train pulled away, the shock of what had happened began to wear off, and for some time neither of them spoke, choosing instead to be with their own thoughts.

At last Adam spoke. "Where are we going?" The idea having only just occurred to him.

"A safe place. Away from here."

Adam watched the way she touched herself, at once recognizing the gesture and its fearful expectation, its significance. "Are you going to be – what I mean is," nodding at her hand, "how are you?"

She smiled defiantly, though with sadness. "You told him?"

He nodded. "He wanted things to be different."

"Do you think it would have changed anything?"

"It would have changed everything. It has changed everything."

She covered her face. "I do not know what to say."

Adam's own fingers were trembling as he held her hand.

The sky was beginning to darken when they got off at the empty station in the woods. They stood together on the platform, watching as the train faded back into the night. Adam looked about. "It has changed since we were last here."

Katya stepped off the platform and onto the path. "As you said, everything has changed."

Above them, wind whispered in the branches, while on the ground everything was still. It had snowed earlier in the day, and the path leading to the cluster of cottages lay smooth and unspoiled before them.

They walked silently through the woods and into the open field, leaving a trail in the thin layer of snow that had fallen, marking their solitary way. The sky was heavy and grey as wet ash, and beside them fence posts pushed like bones through the ground.

In the field two people hunched with picks, chipping potatoes from the soil.

"Have you any money?" Katya asked.

He found some bills, and she called to the woman who came over with her basket. Katya bought as many as would fit in their pockets, and they continued along the road.

The settlement of cottages sat undisturbed as they passed among the lane that led to Yasna Danielovna's *dacha*. Inside they were met with the now distant odours of fall. Adam looked curiously into each room, finding Katya standing outside in the yard next to one of the benches.

"You need to eat," he said at last.

Adam filled a pot with water while she started the stove. After this he brought in wood for the small fireplace, and by the time the potatoes were boiled the cottage had begun to warm. On the sill above the sink Katya found Petya's radio, and while they ate she searched it for a clear signal, finding none.

"I've heard that people in the Arctic have many words for different kinds of snow," she said, looking out the window. "I wish I knew what they called this."

He stared with her into the darkness at the window. A tree groaned in the cold. The rattle of branches could be heard in the wind. "You said you had finished your translation."

Katya looked up. "What?"

"That poem, the one you could not finish. You said you had found the difficult word."

A quiet, indefinable expression passed over her face. "Yes, but not in the way you think."

"How so?"

"I could not translate the poem as it was. So I changed the writer's meaning. I had to. It was the only way. I made the poem speak to Russians."

He moved from the window and sat next to her.

"My brother reminded me that I must sometimes choose between honoring the work I am translating, and those who will read it."

"How did you do this?"

"I could not translate your word, so I had to find one of our own."

"What was the word?"

"*Volja.*" Her face became distant. "It is a convict's word," her voice lowering as her thoughts wandered beyond the small cottage and into the surrounding forest. "It is not equivalent to 'freedom' as you know it in English. It is the freedom seen by one who may never have it. The word is infused with a prisoner's desire to escape, to travel, to release oneself, even for a short time."

He thought about what she had said. "You did not translate the poem, then. You wrote a new one."

She looked at him, and when she spoke her voice had softened. "I have made it a Russian poem."

Adam held the word in himself. "*Volja.*"

She smiled sadly at him. "You pronounce it well."

That night they sat in the small kitchen, listening to the stillness around them. The fire died down, and the cold crept back into the cottage. Katya stirred the coals and woke the slumbering heat. Flame started, and the room began to tremble with light. Moving to the window, she looked into the yard. It was snowing again.

Adam thought of the word she had chosen, whispering it to himself. He sat in the fire's wavering light, weighing the word, seeking its balance on his tongue.

The wind began to rise. Next to them the fire stirred.

Outside, wind moved among the trees and their branches clattered against each other. At the sound Adam looked up and in the window glimpsed his silhouette and, through it, the falling snow. He watched for a long time as each flake passed through him, settling into a picture that was almost whole.

EPILOGUE

"FIRST, THERE must be light." Spacinov spoke to Katya with that voice she knew so well by then, deep and sluggish with thought. "Good light. Preferably the sort found at dawn on a fine day, or by a clean burning candle such as ours. Bad light is always part shadow, a deception.

"Also, you may wish to have a preliminary sketch at hand – on paper or perhaps a board. Trace out each figure in composite, though do not waste time with details. These will come later.

"Never forget the traditions," and as he said this she watched his finger flutter in the candlelight. "They are the ancient grammar of icons. Without them your vision will be incomprehensible. Only a picture.

"Finally, remember when you are painting to save the eyes until last. The eyes of an icon have no tradition governing them. They are yours alone to create. Through them you will speak to those who would see. By them your work will fail or succeed, vanish for all time or be remembered.

"Now, relax your hand. Look into that blankness where one may see everything." Saying this, the old man pressed his hand over her eyes.

"This is how it begins."

ACKNOWLEDGEMENTS

THIS BOOK was inspired by the people I was privileged to know and experiences I had while living in the former Soviet bloc. I have never forgotten the students and professors I worked with there. I will always be humbled by your generosity, intelligence and passionate engagement with literature and ideas. Thank you, especially, to Olga and her family, to Yuri, Dmitry, and to Charles for getting us there in the first place. To my friends from Canada who were there with me – Colleen, Tom, Peter, Andy, Lisa, Melanie, Nicole and Elizabeth – my gratitude for your friendship and humour at such an important time in our lives.

Along the way, I have received tremendous support from many people. My sincere thanks to Matt, Isabel, Dana, Jim, Kaley, Mel, Reverend Ron, Father Dimitrios, Sheila, Scott, Jeanette, Joy, Carolyn, Glen and Jobyna, Graham and Sophie, Jen and Sachin, John and Kate, Todd and Sarah, Andrew and Michela, CL and Rob, Karen and Bryan, Jen and Noel, Jill and Adam, and to Mike for the straight talk.

I am indebted, in particular, to my colleagues at the Writers' Group – Amy,

Manfred, Peter, Helen, Will, Steve, Kristin, Stephanie, Brad, Bill, Donna and in particular John, who has read (and reread) more of my writing than anyone. I am also deeply grateful for Max – I will always be thankful that he found me first. And to DLG, who knows why.

I am very thankful for my wife, Sara, for her love, humor, intelligence and patience – all of which helped me through the writing of this book.

I have dedicated this novel to my parents, who have provided not only a lifetime of love and support, but also instilled an invaluable work ethic and love of learning in their children. Thank you, Mom and Dad.

AUTHOR'S NOTES

THROUGHOUT THE writing of this book, I have relied heavily on a number of texts. I am indebted to Anna Wierzbicka's *Understanding Cultures Through Their Key Words*, and particularly the third chapter on the fascinating difficulties of translating the English word 'freedom.' Any mistakes stemming from my reading of her remarkable book are entirely mine, any insights and revelations are entirely hers. Similarly, David Remnick's *Resurrection: The Struggle for a New Russia*, and Harrsion Salisbury's *The 900 Days: The Siege of Leningrad* provided detailed information of the sieges of Moscow's White House and the city of Leningrad, respectively. I have relied heavily on their accounts and observations.

I have tried, though I fear unsuccessfully, to keep a record of the books and articles which helped me as I wrote this book; the record of these sources are found in the Bibliography, below. Where I have deviated from historical timelines or events, I have done so for the purposes of fiction; all such embellishments or errors, intended or otherwise, are my own.

As I have noted above, though the historical setting of this novel is real, the characters are fictional and any parallel they may have to real people is accidental. Likewise, Galinsk, where much of this novel is set, is not an actual city, but rather an amalgam of many places where I worked and visited.

On page 181, I have quoted from the third book of Milton's *Paradise Lost* (lines 18-24). I have used John Bradshaw's 1878 edition of the poem, with the minor exception that I have modernized Bradshaw's spelling of "sovran" in line 22, to sovereign.

BIBLIOGRAPHY

Ascherson, Neal. "Law v. Order." *London Review of Books.* 20 May 2004. Web.

Barker, Adele. "The Culture Factory: Theorizing the Popular in the Old and New Russia." *Consuming Russia: Popular Culture, Sex, and Society Since Gorbachev.* ed. Adele Baker. Durham: Duke UP, 1999. 12-48.

Berlin, Isaiah. "Two Concepts of Liberty." *Four Essays on Liberty.* Oxford: Oxford UP, 1969.

Billington, James H. *Russia In Search of Itself.* Baltimore: Johns Hopkins UP, 2004.

Bushnell, John. *Moscow Graffiti, Language and Subculture.* Boston: Unwin Hyman, 1990.

_____. "Paranoid Graffiti at Execution Wall: Nationalist Interpretations of Russia's Travail." *Consuming Russia: Popular Culture, Sex, and Society Since Gorbachev.* ed. Adele Baker. Durham: Duke UP, 1999. 397-413.

Cavarnos, Constantine. *Orthodox Iconography*. Belmont: Institute for Byzantine and Modern Greek Studies, 1977.

Chamberlain, Lesley. "New Eurasians: How Russians have long reacted to revolution." *The Times Literary Supplement*. (15 May 2015). 14-15.

Dostoevsky, Fyodor. *Devils* (1871). trans. Michael R. Katz. Oxford: Oxford UP, 1992.

The Economist. 18-24 November 1989.

_____. 16-22 December 1989.

Florensky, Pavel. *Iconostasis*. trans. Donald Sheenan & Olga Andrejev. Crestwood: St. Vladimir's, 1996.

Ferguson, Niall. "Look back at Weimar – and start to worry about Russia." *The Telegraph*. 1 January 2005. Web.

Gessen, Masha. *Dead Again: The Russian Intelligentsia After Communism*. New York: Verso, 1997.

Goldgeier, James M. & McFaul, Michael. "What to Do About Russia." *Policy Review*. October & November 2005. Web.

Goscilo, Helena. "Introduction: Centrifuge and Fragmentation." *Studies in 20th-Century Literature*. 24.1 (Winter 2000).

Hoffman, Eva. *Lost in Translation: A Life in a New Language*. New York: Penguin, 1989.

Ignatieff, Michael. *Isaiah Berlin: A Life*. Toronto: Viking, 1998.

Kagan, Robert. "History's Back: Ambitious autocracies, hesitant democracies." *The Weekly Standard*. 25 August 2008. Web.

Krasner, James. "Doubtful Arms and Phantom Limbs: Literary Portrayals of Embodied Grief." *PMLA*. March 2004. 218-232.

Manev, Oleg. "The Influence of Western Radio on the Democratization of Soviet Youth." *Journal of Communication*. 41.2 (Spring 1991). 72-89.

McGregor, Caroline. "The Maverick: Outspoken writer Viktor Yerofeyev has a theory about why Russians place their trust in strongman regimes." *The Moscow Times*. 9-15 July 2004. Web. 9 July 2004.

Milton, John. *Paradise Lost. The Poetical Works of John Milton*. ed. John Bradshaw. vol. 2. London: W.H. Allen, 1878. 1-348.

Montaigne, Fen. "Russia's Iron Road." *The National Geographic*. June 1998. 2-33.

_____."Russia Rising." *The National Geographic*. November 2001. 2-31.

Nes, Solrunn. *The Mystical Language of Icons*. London: St. Pauls, 2000.

Nepomnyashchy, Catherine Theimer. "Markets, Mirrors, and Mayhem: Aleksandra Marinina and the Rise of the New Russian *Detektiv*." *Consuming Russia: Popular Culture, Sex, and Society Since Gorbachev*. ed. Adele Baker. Durham: Duke UP, 1999. 161-91.

Ouspensky, Leonid, & Lossky, Vladimir. *The Meaning of Icons*. trans. Crestwood: St. Vladimir, 1982.

Pipes, Richard. "Flight From Freedom: What Russians Think and Want." excerpt. *Foreign Affairs*. May/June 2004. Web. 13 May, 2004.

Putman, John J. "Moscow: The City Around Red Square." *National Geographic*. January 1978. 2-45.

Ramos-Poqui, Guillem. *The Technique of Icon Painting*. Tunbridge Wells: Search Press, 1990.

Ready, Oliver. "Lost in Thought." *The Moscow Times*. 3 September 2004. Web. 9 February 2015.

Remnick, David. *Resurrection: The Struggle for a New Russia*. New York: Random House, 1997.

Ries, Nancy. *Russian Talk: Culture and Conversation During Perestroika*. Ithaca: Cornell UP, 1997.

Ryback, Timothy W. *Rock Around the Bloc: A History of Rock Music in Eastern Europe and the Soviet Union*. New York: Oxford UP, 1990.

Sakharov, Andrei. *Memoirs*. trans. Richard Lourie. New York: Knopf, 1990.

Salisbury, Harrison. *The 900 Days: The Siege of Leningrad*. New York: Da Capo, 1969.

Satter, David. *Darkness at Dawn: The Rise of the Russian Criminal State*. New Haven: Yale UP, 2004.

———. "Not So Quick: Is Russia Really Becoming Part of the West?" *National Review Online*. Web. 19 November 2004.

———. "A Small Town Affair." *The Wall Street Journal*. 7 September 2004. Web.

Saunders, Paul J. "Why 'Globalization' Didn't Rescue Russia." *Policy Review*. February & March 2001. Web.

Schmid, Ulrich. "The First Corporate Revolution: Social uprising in the Ukraine." *Sign and Sight*. 1 March 2005.

Shishkin, Mikhail. "Poets and Czars, From Pushkin to Putin: The sad tale of democracy in Russia." *The New Republic*. 1 July 2013.

Simmons, Ann M. "Scraping By." *Time*. 7 December 1992. 74.

Solzhenitsyn, Alexander. *Nobel Prize Lecture*. trans. N. Bethell. London: Stenvalley, 1972.

Specter, Michael. "The Devastation." *The New Yorker*. 11 October 2004. 57-69.

Starr, S. Frederick. *Red and Hot: The Fate of Jazz in the Soviet Union 1917-1991*. New York: Limelight, 1994.

"Still Calling for Help." *The Economist*. 15 January 2005. 49.

Tartakovsky, Joey. "Strange Creatures: A review of *Russia in Search of Itself* by James H. Billington." *The Claremont Institute*. 25 April 2005. Web.

"The Blood Red Revolution." *The Economist*. 21 May 2005. 43.

Time, 7 December 1992.

Urban, Michael. "The Politics of Identity in Russia's Postcommunist Transition: The Nation Against Itself." *Slavic Review*. 53.3 (Fall 1994). 733-65.

Uspensky, Boris. *The Semiotics of the Russian Icon*. ed. Stephen Rudy. Lisse: The Peter de Ridder Press, 1976.

Vesilind, Priit J. "Berlin's Ode to Joy." *National Geographic*. April 1990. 104-132.

Wagnleitner, Reinhold. "The Empire of Fun, or Talkin' Soviet Union Blues: The Sound of Freedom and U.S. Cultural Hegemony in Europe." *Diplomatic History*. 23. 3 (Summer 1999). 499-524.

Wheeler, Gordon. "Translator's Introduction." In Barbara Heimannsberg and Christoph J. Schmidt, *The Collective Silence*. trans. C. Harris and G. Wheeler. San Francisco: Jossey-Bass, 1993.

Wood, Tony. "First Person." *London Review of Books*. 5 February 2015. 13-16.

Wierzbicka, Anna. *Understanding Cultures Through Their Key Words: English, Russian, Polish, German, and Japanese*. New York: Oxford UP, 1997.

Zamyatin, Yevgeny. *A Soviet Heretic*. ed. & trans. Mirra Ginsburg. Chicago: Chicago UP, 1970.

Zizek, Slavoj. *Tarrying With the Negative: Kant, Hegel, and the Critique of Ideology*. Durham: Duke UP, 1993.